T0320037

The Structural Foundations of International Finance

NEW HORIZONS IN INTERNATIONAL BUSINESS

Series Editor: Peter J. Buckley
Centre for International Business,
University of Leeds (CIBUL), UK

The New Horizons in International Business series has established itself as the world's leading forum for the presentation of new ideas in international business research. It offers pre-eminent contributions in the areas of multinational enterprise - including foreign direct investment, business strategy and corporate alliances, global competitive strategies, and entrepreneurship. In short, this series constitutes essential reading for academics, business strategists and policy makers alike.

The Structural Foundations of International Finance

Problems of Growth and Stability

Edited by

Pier Carlo Padoan

Executive Director, International Monetary Fund, USA

Paul A. Brenton

Senior Economist, International Trade Department, The World Bank, USA

Gavin Boyd

Honorary Professor, Political Science Department, Rutgers University, USA and Adjunct Professor, Management Faculty, Saint Mary's University, Canada

NEW HORIZONS IN INTERNATIONAL BUSINESS

Edward Elgar
Cheltenham, UK • Northampton, MA, USA

Published by
Edward Elgar Publishing Limited
Glensanda House
Montpellier Parade
Cheltenham
Glos GL50 1UA
UK

Edward Elgar Publishing, Inc.
136 West Street
Suite 202
Northampton
Massachusetts 01060
USA

A catalogue record for this book
is available from the British Library

Library of Congress Cataloguing in Publication Data

The structural foundations of international finance : problems of growth and stability / edited by Pier Carlo Padoan, Paul A. Brenton, Gavin Boyd.
    p. cm.—(New horizons in international business)
Based on a conference sponsored by Saint Mary's University, Halifax, in May 2000.
Includes index.
1. International finance—Congresses. 2. Banks and banking, International—Congresses. I. Padoan, Pier Carlo, 1950– II. Brenton, Paul. III. Boyd, Gavin. IV. Series.

HG3881.S786 2003
332′.042—dc21

2003048536

ISBN 1 84376 386 9

Printed and bound in Great Britain by MPG Books Ltd, Bodmin, Cornwall

Contents

Figures

Tables

Contributors

Gavin Boyd is an Honorary Professor in the Political Science Department, Rutgers University, Newark, New Jersey, and Adjunct Professor in Management, Saint Mary's University, Halifax, Canada.

Paul A. Brenton is Senior Economist at the World Bank, Washington, DC, USA, in the International Trade Department.

Jordi Canals is Dean, IESE, University of Navarra, Barcelona, Spain.

Thomas F. Cargill is Professor of Economics, University of Nevada, Reno, Nevada, USA.

William R. Emmons is in the Division of Bank Supervision and Regulation, Federal Reserve Bank of St Louis, St Louis, Missouri, USA.

Maximilian J.B. Hall is Reader in Economics, Loughborough University, Loughborough, UK.

George G. Kaufman is John F. Smith Jr Professor of Finance and Economics, Loyola University, Chicago, USA.

Sarianna M. Lundan is Associate Professor of International Business, Strategy, University of Maastricht, The Netherlands.

Pier Carlo Padoan is Executive Director, International Monetary Fund, Washington, DC, USA.

Elliott Parker is in the Economics Department, University of Nevada, Reno, Nevada, USA.

Frank A. Schmid is in the Research Division of the Federal Reserve Bank of St Louis, St Louis, Missouri, USA.

Alain Verbeke is McCaig Chair in Management, University of Calgary, Calgary, Alberta, Canada.

List of abbreviations

AMF	Asian Monetary Fund
APEC	Asia–Pacific Economic Cooperation forum
ASEAN	Association of Southeast Asian Nations
BIS	Bank for International Settlements
BOJ	Bank of Japan
CAC	Collective Action Clauses
EAD	exposure at default
EFA	European Economic Area
ECAIs	external credit assessment institutes
EMS	European Monetary System
EMU	European Monetary Union
FDI	foreign direct investment
FDIC	Federal Deposit Insurance Corporation
FDICIA	Federal Deposit Insurance Corporation Improvement Act
FILP	Fiscal Investment and Loan Program (Japan)
FSLIC	Federal Savings and Loan Insurance Corporation
FTAA	Free Trade Area of the Americas
IFC	International Finance Corporation
IFI	independent financial institution
IMF	International Monetary Fund
IPO	initial public offering
IRB	internal ratings-based
LCR	least cost resolution
LDP	Liberal Democratic Party (Japan)
LGD	loss given default
M&A	mergers and acquisitions
MITI	Ministry of International Trade and Industry
MNE	multinational enterprise
MOF	Ministry of Finance (Japan)
NAFTA	North American Free Trade Area
OECD	Organisation for Economic Co-operation and Development
P/E	price/earnings
PSI	private sector involvement
R&D	research and development
RAR	risk asset ratio

S&L	savings and loans
SBC	state-controlled bank
SDRM	Special Drawing Rights Mechanism
SOB	state-owned bank
SRE	systemic risk exemption
TBTF	too big to fail
TIIS	Treasury inflation-indexed securities
VaR	value at risk

Foreword

This volume has come out of a conference sponsored by Saint Mary's University, Halifax in May 2002. When the conference was planned the speculation-led boom in the USA that had developed during the 1990s had ended, with sharp reductions in investor confidence, and severe effects on the real economy. These effects were made more serious by several large fraud-related bankruptcies, starting with the Enron affair, which added a new dimension to our deliberations.

Our interest in the ways in which the bidding up of stock prices during the boom was affecting growth was aroused by numerous contributions to the research literature which questioned the sustainability of the stock appreciation. This occurred especially with reference to claims that the wealth effects were making possible increases in productivity, through uses of new technology, that would sustain the boom. Then, as the boom was ending, it was argued by several experts on monetary policy that the speculation should have been dampened by reducing the availability of credit. The destructive effects of the boom's collapse, it was suggested, would have been less serious if prudent monetary tightening had ended the destabilizing 'irrational exuberance'. The latter phrase was coined by the Chairman of the US Federal Reserve.

The persistence of the post-boom recession, despite monetary loosening intended to facilitate recovery, has raised questions about the dangers of further booms and declines. There has been a long sequence of these, going back to the 1920s, and the issues to consider have become more urgent because of the internationalization of financial markets that has been facilitated by the general elimination of controls on capital flows and by advances in information and communications technology. Massive flows of international investment, particularly portfolio flows, can now feed into a speculative boom in a major industrialized state, and the countries from which this investment has been drawn can experience acute vulnerabilities after an economic decline in that state. Efforts by that country to revive its economy by expanding exports can be difficult because of distress in the countries from which it has attracted investment. Destabilizing flows of capital have also at times moved into emerging markets and their cessation and withdrawal, as in the case of Asia in the latter part of the 1990s, can lead to a financial crises with the potential for contagion.

Our conference and the preparation of the conference volume have benefited from continuities in research with our 2001 conference on *Alliance Capitalism*, which resulted in a volume with that title edited by John H. Dunning and Gavin Boyd (Edward Elgar, 2003). A cumulative development of policy-relevant insights has been intended, with expectations that these will also be relevant for corporate management and leaders of industry associations.

Sustained collegial interactions during and after the conferences help to generate a sense of community, for further collaborative engagement with issues confronting policy-makers and corporate management. Opportunities can be discovered for deeper examination of fundamentals that demand attention, as structural interdependencies between countries become larger and more complex. This is the basic challenge of globalization.

The most valuable insights, it is commonly recognized, develop in friendly discussions. We have been fortunate in this regard, and I wish to express my appreciation of the quality of the exchanges between the scholars represented in this project. With the completion of this conference volume, several of the participants have been engaged in research on proposals for a Free Trade Area of the Americas' (FTAAs), following a conference on this subject sponsored by Saint Mary's University in September 2002, as an event associated with the Annual General Assembly of World Trade Centres, hosted by the Atlantic World Trade Centre, Halifax.

I look forward to the publication of the volume which is to come out of that conference, and to further occasions of this kind which make it possible to relate university research to the deliberations of government and corporate leaders. Planning for our next conference is focusing on issues of structural and policy interdependence between the NAFTA members and the European Union.

J. Colin Dodds, Ph.D.
President and Professor of Finance
Saint Mary's University

Preface

Industrialized countries are becoming more and more knowledge based, with the use of advanced technologies in production and marketing, the operation of their financial sectors, and the functioning of their systems of governance. The highly complex systems which are being formed are said to be 'new economies', in several senses, referring to their degrees of integration, their productivity levels, and the scale and diversity of their allocations of investment, but also to their interdependencies. Their structural linkages with each other are becoming larger, through transnational production and arm's-length trade, with high-volume financial flows. In this vast process the evolution of their economic structures is being shaped more and more by multinational corporations, and those corporations, as competitors or alliance partners, are also becoming more interdependent with each other.

In the emerging global pattern, efficiencies result from large-scale coordinations of operations within corporations; market efficiencies and failures result from collaboration and rivalries between the corporations; and government efficiencies and failures interact with the market efficiencies and failures as policy levels engage with macromanagement tasks through fiscal, monetary and microeconomic measures. Altogether there is deepening integration in the world economy, and its evolution depends very much on scales and methods of coordination, in all the complexities of intercorporate relations and of policy interdependencies.

Coordination in the financing of productive activity is especially important for all the interdependent growth, and the main purpose of this volume is to assist understanding of this very demanding requirement for stable development in the world economy, including Third World areas where industrialization has been very difficult. Financial sectors, while operating with understandable home-country bias, are funding international production, more and more, in search of high returns, under pressures from investors with generally short-term expectations. Firms attaining higher profits and higher-growth countries thus tend to be advantaged, while market discipline challenges less efficient enterprises and lower-growth national economies. All the productive funding, however, is linked with high-volume speculation, which can involve excessive risk-taking.

The speculation, when successful, causes asset appreciations which tend to generate irrational investor optimism, and can encourage collusive market manipulation. Several attributes of a country's economy can facilitate or hinder the speculative asset appreciation, and, when this begins, it draws more investment from other countries where speculation is less active and growth is lower. Investor optimism, however, can give way to a sharp decline, triggering herd-like quests for safer investments. A financial crisis, then, can cause a recession, with severe effects on the real economy and on others with which it is linked through investment, cross-border production and trade.

The vicious sequence has been evident in the USA since the ending of its speculative boom in the 1990s, and has been apparent, with more serious results, in Japan since the early 1990s. Financial sector problems in each case have been issues in larger contexts of failures in meeting coordination requirements. A key failure has been a divergence of financial enterprises away from the funding of production in real economies. This has become an extremely urgent macromanagement challenge.

We are very grateful to Saint Mary's University, Halifax, for sponsoring our conference on the ways in which real economies are affected by the operations of international financial markets, and we are especially grateful to the university president, Dr J. Colin Dodds, for his participation and hospitality. We see wide scope for new forms of advice to corporations and governments in the new economies of the industrialized countries, and in the emerging economies of the Third World, for which challenges of dependent growth have become more demanding, indicating needs for collegial cooperation by Western and Japanese firms and administrations.

Pier Carlo Padoan
Paul A. Brenton
Gavin Boyd

1. Economic structures and finance

Gavin Boyd

The real economies of the industrialized and industrializing countries are the structural foundations of international finance. Savings resulting from their productive activities and exchanges flow into financial systems which fund further production, with investments in new technology that increase efficiencies and thus make available further savings for use by financial enterprises. The productive dynamic, however, has been changing, with large increases in speculative operations by the financial firms, and with extensions of their operations across borders to form an *international* financial system. Within this system a strong concentration trend has developed, through mergers and acquisitions, and financial corporations assuming prominence in this trend have become more active in global speculative operations. These involve massive financial flows, driven by quests for rapid large-scale gains with reduced tax exposure, and far exceed the funding of productive activities in the real economies. That has to be regarded as a problem of market failure, and it is all the more serious because the speculation tends to become destabilizing, because of information problems, high risks and irrational investor optimism.

The USA, because of the size of its economy, its extensive structural links with the rest of the world, and the global reach of its financial corporations, is at the centre of the international pattern, and its multidimensional involvement is expanding, especially because of a strong speculative propensity in its financial sector. This is increasingly significant because that sector is very prominent in an international oligopolistic trend, which is linked with a similar trend in the external growth of the US real economy. The two trends have tended to become more active because of a prolonged financial crisis in Japan, dating from the early 1990s, and because of the continuation of decades of slow growth in Europe, despite a new dynamic imparted by monetary union, and despite greater stability due to much lower levels of speculative activity by financial sectors. The US real economy, however, has been severely affected by a recession following the collapse of a boom during the 1990s in which speculation drove stock prices to unsustainable levels: there were unwarranted hopes that these could be maintained through productivity increases made possible by investments in new technology, but the wealth effects of the boom went more into consumption, rather than productive investment.

The internationalization of financial markets has developed since the 1970s, when the US and European governments abolished controls on the movement of funds across their borders. Maintenance of such controls, for exchange rate stability, restraint on inflation and the funding of national enterprises, had become difficult because of large increases in the numbers and sizes of transnational enterprises: they had become more and more capable of moving funds across borders, within their own structures. Large financial corporations, competing for speculative and productive opportunities in foreign markets, were sources of pressure and advice for the lifting of capital controls.

An internationalization of market efficiencies and failures has followed, with far-reaching effects on real economies, which have been linked structurally by the expanding operations of transnational enterprises building international production systems. The prominence of US firms in the related concentration trends, and in a restructuring of real economies, has been a major factor in the internationalization of market efficiencies and failures. Meanwhile, with those concentration trends, European and to a lesser extent Japanese financial sectors have been drawn into closer association with US financial corporations and producer enterprises.

Complex patterns of reciprocal causality have emerged, with problems of international governance. In national market economies coordinated through relational cooperation between firms, and between firms and governments, productive dynamics have been sustained through substantial financial sector funding of producer enterprises, with limited diversions of funds into the pursuit of speculative opportunities in world financial markets. Germany has been the most significant example of a coordinated market economy, but its productive dynamics have been weakened by difficulties in management–labour relations, a conservative bias in the funding of industry, the attractions of international speculative operations for its financial sector, and the burdens of heavy welfare state spending. In the USA, as a liberal market economy, causal relations between the financial sector and the real economy have become less functional, as noted, in vicious.circles in which the financial sector has been a source of severe destabilization. This, it must be stressed, is a serious problem for the world economy. In prospect is the danger of greater exposure to the disruptive effects of speculation-led instability in the USA, weakening the nation's entrepreneurial dynamism and its contributions to global growth.

REGIONAL AND CENTRAL INSTABILITY

During the US boom of the 1990s the world economy was subjected to stresses by financial crises in East Asia and Latin America. Those in East Asia had special significance because they disrupted economies that had achieved high rates of export-led growth: external revenues had been financing outward-oriented industrialization at rising technological levels, thus attracting much foreign direct investment and portfolio flows. The Latin American crises affected lower growth and less outward-oriented countries that had been over-coming the negative effects of ventures in import-substituting industrializa-tion, under technocratically less competent administrations.

Links between real economies and financial sectors in the industrializing East Asian states were vulnerable because of weak development and regula-tion in the latter. Vicious circles of reciprocal causality were activated by investment inflows after financial liberalization. These inflows were attracted by high growth, but contributed to currency appreciations that slowed export expansion while increasing imports. A competitive Chinese devaluation, moreover, also reduced the export earnings of these states. Increasing current account deficits then caused currency depreciations, which were made more serious by large capital outflows. Financial crises thus hindered further imple-mentation of the established growth strategies, while disrupting an extensive Japanese regional production system linked with a production system estab-lished by Japanese firms manufacturing in North America. Meanwhile it became evident that weak financial sectors under deficient regulatory systems had been responsible for drastic falls in investor confidence, ending high-growth periods during which excessive risk-taking had led to large accumula-tions of external debt.[1] The costs of premature financial liberalization were thus very clear, but assistance from the International Monetary Fund was pred-icated on continued financial openness, with acceptance of entries by US and other foreign financial enterprises. The disrupted political economies were thus challenged to find ways of building more integrated and more coordi-nated production systems, with greater reliance on domestic funds, so as to enhance structural competitiveness with increased economic sovereignty, while accepting increased foreign direct investment, notably from US firms that had previously been less active in East Asia than their Japanese rivals.

The crises in Latin America disrupted economies that had made much less progress in the implementation of outward-oriented industrialization strate-gies but that had also liberalized underdeveloped and inadequately regulated financial sectors, and that had attracted excessive capital inflows, which had caused currency appreciations, in conjunction with foreign borrowing for fiscal expansion. Export-led growth thus became difficult, while declines in investor confidence had severely disruptive effects, motivating capital flight. Recoveries, especially in Brazil and Argentina, the two largest problem coun-tries, became very uncertain. The attitudes of international investors were influenced by awareness that Latin America, unlike East Asia, had a long history of financial crises, in which the incompetence of successive unstable administrations had been repeatedly demonstrated.[2] By 2002, however, the entire region was being challenged by US initiatives to establish a hemispheric free trade area, in which barriers to commerce and investment would be reduced. In return for greater access to the US market, Latin American countries would become more open to US exports and direct as well as portfolio investment, while increased financial liberalization would facilitate capital flows to the USA.

For Latin American and East Asian states the central role of the USA in the world economy now has to be viewed with anxiety because of its recession and because a recovery could be followed by further destabilizing booms, with more extensive international effects. The gravity of the US recession was increased during 2002 by numerous large-scale fraud-related bankruptcies. These indicated that managements of major producer enterprises had been attracted by opportunities for high risk speculation, with criminal trading practices, which prominent financial corporations had been assisting. Measures to tighten regulation of the financial sector were adopted by the US administration, but regulatory capabilities were being strained by the wide use of highly sophisticated financial instruments and trading methods, and it was clear that beyond the area of national jurisdiction the regulatory endeavours would have weaker effects.[3]

The vicious cycle of causality involving the financial sector and the real economy was intended to be altered by monetary loosening to facilitate recovery, but this objective was to a considerable extent frustrated by investor caution about funding new productive ventures, and by the continued effects of the speculative propensity in the financial sector, which were evident in predatory domestic lending. Increased instability, moreover, was threatened because of the persistence of very large deficits in the current account, thus exerting downward pressures on the exchange rate; the offsetting influence of large investment inflows that had been drawn by the speculative boom, meanwhile, was diminishing, as these flows were decreasing. An important factor in this causal pattern was further expansion of the international production operations by US manufacturing firms, particularly in Europe, motivated in part by concerns that the dollar, despite the collapse of the boom, was still overvalued.[4]

Export expansion can assist recovery from the recession, but neither the European Union nor Japan can be urged to adopt inflationary policies that could draw more imports, and the incentives for US firms to produce abroad are increasing, because of the widening opportunities to expand existing international market strengths through the development of stronger presences in host countries. Reduction of the dangerous external imbalance has to be made possible by increased domestic output, that is, to close the gap between it and domestic demand. Stimulus has been provided by fiscal expansion, to complement the monetary loosening, but the main effect has been that stronger domestic demand has drawn in higher-volume imports.

FUNDAMENTAL CHALLENGES

The logical thought to be active in financial systems has been that banks and securities firms can channel individual and group savings into the funding of productive ventures by the most efficient firms, in anticipation of shares in their profits. To the extent that the most profitable enterprises are funded, and less productive ones are challenged to improve performance, a financial sector is said to be efficient. The funding, however, tends to reward short-term profitability, which may be achieved through mergers and acquisitions, followed by asset stripping, or through neglect of investment in new technology, or through high-risk speculation, or undetected fraud. Further, the financing may be based on flawed information, in markets in which commercial intelligence can be spread strategically. In the routine portfolio switching by large financial enterprises there is speculative and distant monitoring rather than active monitoring.[5]

In the highly developed US financial system a perverse logic operates. Securities firms strive to bid up stock prices through speculative trading at volumes much higher than those possible in the less developed European markets, while trading also at exceptionally high volumes in world markets for financial assets. Resources thus attracted are very much larger than those funding producer enterprises in the home economy. Meanwhile these producer corporations often seek to reduce dependence on equity financing by using retained earnings for expansion, while achieving profitability that can enhance the value of their shares and thus enhance prospects for switches to increased equity financing when opportune during boom periods. The principal risks to be avoided are falls in share prices, due to declines in investor confidence, that can adversely affect capacities to seek future equity financing.

Falls in investor confidence tend to result from awareness that stocks have risen well above levels that would be justified by prospective earnings, and these falls can be sharp because of panics attributable to information failures. In these contexts producer enterprises are also affected by information failures, and have to contend with reductions in the availability of bank financing as well as equity financing. The choices for producer enterprises, moreover, become more complex and more difficult because of exchange rate uncertainties in a recession that affect decisions about imported inputs and foreign sales, as well as estimates of changes in import penetration. The exchange rate uncertainties, affected especially by the persistence of massive US trade deficits, provide opportunities for speculative attacks on the currency, and can motivate foreign switches from dollar to euro reserves.[6]

A recession brought on by destabilizing speculation becomes a difficult challenge for macroeconomic policy, in the absence of controls over cross-border financial flows. Expectations of monetary loosening in the event of a crisis contributed to the irrational speculation that increased US stock appreciations during the 1990s, but the loosening which did occur did not sufficiently revive productive activities: financial enterprises sought higher returns from distressed lending at home and from more active speculation in world financial markets, while producer enterprises tended to respond to stronger incentives to expand foreign production. Fiscal expansion was attempted by the US administration but at the cost of large increases in government debt and later rises in taxation: political competition, long driving fiscal expansion, had been contributing to the large trade deficits, through increases in domestic demand in excess of domestic output.[7]

A recession also complicates competition policy issues. Firms with strong market positions at home and abroad can cope with an economic downturn more effectively than smaller enterprises, and can be advantaged when implementing merger and acquisition strategies, especially because of preferential funding that may be available from financial corporations. The principal issue, for competition policy in a recession, is that prospective inequalities in market strength become more significant with concerns about efficiency and equity, while the acquisition of funding and the management of operations become more difficult for small firms and new entrants: in a recession, that is, a market becomes less contestable for such enterprises.

A further problem relating to structural policy options after the collapse of a speculative boom is that potentials for entrepreneurial collaboration in the development of complementary production ventures are adversely affected by general losses of confidence, reduced investment in new technology, and reductions of funding for innovative endeavours, because of uncertainties about their returns. In a recession, moreover, there is likely to be increased distrust between firms, and alliances that may be contracted can be expected to lead more readily to mergers and acquisitions.

A final consideration, for policymakers, is that boom and decline sequences caused by financial sector speculation entail additional losses of economic sovereignty. The internationalization of financial markets continues through the sequences, and the expansion of transnational production systems also continues. Meanwhile, as noted with reference to the USA, policy-level cooperation by other major states becomes less feasible because of their losses of economic sovereignty on account of the degrees of cross-border integration in financial markets and the more active roles of producer enterprises shaping structural interdependencies.

MARKET EFFICIENCIES AND FAILURES

In the US and other real economies, efficiencies and failures in the productive operations of markets interact with efficiencies and failures in financial markets and with government efficiencies and failures, in combination with cross-border effects. In the overall pattern the USA has special significance not only because of its size and level of industrialization but also because its liberal market economy provides wide scope for independent operations by producer enterprises and financial corporations.[8] The US real economy thus becomes linked, advantageously, in asymmetric structural interdependencies with other less competitive industrialized states. At the same time US financial enterprises tend to become more dominant in world financial markets, but with disruptive effects on the real economy, through booms and declines. Of the other states structurally linked with the USA, those which are coordinated market economies tend to be better able to manage their unequal structural interdependencies, but lack bargaining strength; smaller liberal market economies are disadvantaged because of weaker capacities for collaborative management of their external structural linkages, and also lack bargaining strength.

Production efficiencies are achieved to the extent that the performance of producer enterprises is enhanced through technological innovations, organizational improvements and the development of human capital, and through intercorporate coordination, with more and more extensive complementarities. The quality of this coordination depends on balances between competition and cooperation in an intercorporate system. These balances also determine efficiencies in the exchange processes which sustain the complex production functions. When markets are seen mainly as exchange processes the commonly recognized failures are monopolistic or oligopolistic exploitation, negative externalities, informational deficiencies and the underproduction of public goods. Concentrations of market power operate against the public interest by extracting revenue well in excess of costs and by restricting competition that could increase production efficiencies. Of the negative externalities, those which are often most evident are disruptions of sectoral and intrasectoral interdependencies resulting from production relocations undertaken without attempts at adaptive coordination. Informational deficiencies, typically reflecting intense competition and low levels of trust, hinder the development of productive complementarities. Finally, the most significant public good – a dynamic pattern of coordinated complementarities – is not provided if emphasis on competition rather than cooperation results in destructive rivalries. When markets are viewed as exchange processes stimulating production improvements, with recognition of the imperatives for coordinating production specializations that become more complex with advances in frontier technology, failures to identify, develop and organize complementarities become increasingly significant.[9]

The performance of *financial markets* has to be assessed in terms of service of the real economies. As noted, the virtually preferential funding of firms achieving market dominance through mergers and acquisitions is often a misallocation of resources drawn from the savings of large numbers of passive investors. The most serious deficiency in financial systems, however, is the manipulation of stock prices through portfolio switching, to push them to high levels, which become a basis for further speculation, while generating unrealistic optimism about prospects for continued speculation-led growth. This has to be reiterated because of the severe disruption of a real economy that tends to follow a major decline in investor confidence. The problem of destabilization after a boom is all the more serious if the asset appreciations have been at high levels because of the bidding up of stocks. Moreover, this inflation of stock prices tends to be linked with instability in an intercorporate system because of speculative impetus given to the market for corporate control, which in turn affects prospects for entrepreneurial coordination in the development of production complementarities in line with technological progress.[10]

The public interest function that can be served by a financial sector can be defined in terms of the interests of a country's passive investors who, while a majority, are unable to monitor the sector's operation or the performance of producer enterprises. Outward flows of investment from financial corporations can be at the expense of domestically based growth, without the knowledge of the passive investors, and these outward flows can finance international speculation as well as the growth of productive capacity in other states that contributes to the development of concentration trends in the world economy. Outflows of passive investment from Europe to the USA, while open to assessment as movements of funds to the most profitable producers, have illustrated the significance of this public interest issue in international finance.[11]

With the linking of real economies through trade and investment, the efficiencies and failures of their markets, extending across borders, is most visible in the expansion of international production systems, especially through mergers and acquisitions. The dominant trend is oligopolistic domination of an increasingly integrated world market, with disruptive competitive restructuring in the building of the international production systems, and uses of market power to restrict new entrants. Information problems, in this setting, become internationalized, and overcoming these problems through acquisitions of commercial intelligence is difficult for emerging firms. Such firms have incentives to seek viability as subordinate partners in alliances with large transnational enterprises. The international production systems of those major firms operate with great efficiencies, under pressures of competition that tend to increase with global concentration trends, and the efficiencies facilitate discriminatory pricing to markets. Revenues are large enough to support very substantial investments in new technology for increases in productivity generally ahead of those possible for smaller firms. The scale of the international operations, however, can incline managements toward high-risk ventures, sophisticated methods of personal enrichment, and collusive trading practices that inflate earnings.[12]

The prominence of US corporations in the internationalization of market efficiencies and failures shaping linkages between real economies is exceptional because of its scale and because of the involvement of US financial enterprises in the externalization of national booms and declines. This complex and far-reaching transnational activity, it must be stressed, is expanding without coordination, thus contributing to the evolution of a liberal international market economy, in which questions about US macromanagement and issues of international economic policy cooperation are demanding attention.

GOVERNMENT EFFICIENCIES AND FAILURES

Market failures, if they are not being overcome through corporate competition and cooperation, can be considered to demand governmental responses, in the public interest. This is well understood with respect to the danger of monopolistic or oligopolistic market exploitation, but there is less shared comprehension about the range of negative externalities that can be remedied by governmental action, and about the large area of issues concerning under-provided public goods there is a lack of consensus. In the USA the established liberal policy tradition is a source of expectations that corporate competition will increasingly provide necessary public goods, and that governmental attempts to fulfil this function will fail, because of incompetence and abuses of office for private gain.[13] Potentials for government action to enhance market efficiencies are not recognized, except with respect to the maintenance of law and order, the development of infrastructure, and the regulation of the financial sector, as well as the system of corporate governance. Broader understandings of administrative responsibilities guide macromanagement in Europe, and are related to general acceptance of the functional logic of cooperation between the policy and corporate levels, but such collaboration tends to be viewed in the USA as a factor contributing to weak growth in the European Union.

In the USA the basic policy challenge is to achieve a final solution for the long-standing irrational speculative propensity in the financial sector. This has been awaiting correction since the 1920s, and the multiplication of US structural and investment links with the rest of the world has made it an urgent issue for the world economy.[14] As such, it is related to the international effects of prolonged US fiscal expansion and the dangers associated with the persistence of massive US trade deficits. Protracted fiscal expansion has become a serious problem in Europe, but with weaker international effects, and, although European growth is slow, it is relatively more stable because of lower levels of speculation; the external balance, however, has to be improved through substantial reductions of the large flows of passive investment to the USA, and this has to be stressed because of its significance as a consequence of macromanagement failure.[15]

The prolonged US failure to curb destabilizing financial sector speculation has been a consequence of problems of governance, in which intense political competition has hindered institutional development, consensus formation and functional aggregations of interests. These problems have been made more serious by the expansion and diversification of US corporate international production activities, through increases in rivalries and conflicts of interest at home, and by the political influence of the financial sector, exerted with the aid of large resources acquired through global operations. A solution has to be found through the development of strong peak producer associations capable of providing sound and influential advice to policymakers, promoting cooperation between US transnational enterprises, and working for functional reform of the financial sector. The gravity of these requirements has to be stressed because of the severity of the latest recession and because accountability to strong peak producer associations is clearly needed to supplement the discipline which US regulators are endeavouring to impose on managements extracting private gain from their control of company finances, without regard for shareholder interests.[16]

Problems of governance, and the established liberal policy orientation – sustained to a significant degree by corporate awareness of those governance problems – have hindered recognition that extensive entrepreneurial coordination for the development of production complementarities is a public good to be striven for, and that technocratic sponsorship of collaborative corporate activity for this purpose is becoming increasingly necessary. This has to be affirmed because of the significance of new technologies, especially generic technologies, for the development of advanced production capabilities, and because of the importance of general increases in security for managerial focus on the enhancement of those capabilities. Neglect of the task of promoting consultative interactions for extensive entrepreneurial coordination has to be regarded as a policy failure. It must be reiterated, moreover, that the costs of this deficiency rise as technological advances are made without sufficiently broad collaborative applications, and as firms independently expand their foreign production activities, without cooperative management of their home operations.[17]

Understanding of the policy imperatives to sponsor collaborative managerial learning, for entrepreneurial complementarities, can be aided by studies of the dynamics of advances in frontier technology, in which the public interest can be served by technocratic participation in the generation of knowledge, and technocratic advising to align corporate decisionmaking with the common good. The rationale to be grasped, although drawn from complex research findings, is simply that progress in the widening areas of frontier technology benefits most from collegial research, that potentials for commercial application have to be explored and sought through collegial entrepreneurial consultations, and that collegial sharing of the risks and costs of research is in the public interest, but that this interest must be served by governmental expertise to assist concerted entrepreneurial planning and the development of a collegial corporate culture, as well as to ensure the provision of related infrastructure expansion.[18] Intensely competitive intercorporate relations, managed with low levels of trust and averse to cooperation with the administration, produce a fragmented pattern of research endeavours, and exploration of their potential applications tends to be limited by individual corporate emphasis on self-reliance. A non-cooperative corporate culture, moreover, influences the public funding of research, directly, and through the trading of favours with legislators. This can be considered a reason for the avoidance of public funding, so that research will become entirely a private sector responsibility; the interests of all producer enterprises in the development and diffusion of advanced technologies, however, clearly have to be served through the collegial entrepreneurial learning that can be encouraged and assisted by a technocratic authority.[19]

The centrality of the US role in the world economy, which warrants concentration on the cross-border effects of US macromanagement efficiencies and failures, necessitates focus on the dynamics of this liberal political economy, but with the understanding that its growth is becoming more and more dependent on the management of structural and policy interdependencies, under conditions of declining economic sovereignty. The cross-border effects of government efficiencies and failures in Europe are weaker, as noted, but large structural and investment links with the USA entail vulnerabilities, and accordingly there are vital interests in contributing to US policy learning, although this is difficult, and in working for stronger regionally based European growth, although this is also difficult. The prospect, however, is very substantial expansion of the scope for regionally based growth with the entry of East and Central European states into the European Union. Yet in the longer term the spread of market-based corporate governance in the enlarged union, with the development of large-scale trading in shares, will involve increased vulnerabilities in the interdependence with the USA.[20]

INTERNATIONAL INSTITUTIONAL ISSUES

In conjunction, market efficiencies and failures and government efficiencies and failures, extending internationally, raise questions about governance in the world economy. Declining economic sovereignty in the USA, and to a lesser extent in Europe, must raise doubts about what may be achieved through international policy-level cooperation, and makes it necessary to consider how constructive collaboration may be promoted between producer enterprises and between financial corporations, in alignment with endeavours by policymakers. Existing institutions for consultation and cooperation are not adequate for governance of the intensely competitive and often predatory operations in world financial markets and the equally competitive but potentially much less destabilizing activities in global product markets. In both types of markets, especially the former, concentration trends are insufficiently restrained by competition policies, and the continuation of the trends entails further reductions of economic sovereignty.

Associations of financial groups, often inappropriately termed 'communities', assert their interests in limiting increases in domestic and international regulation, and typically represent to policymakers that minimal controls are necessary to attract investors into financial centres, and that business can be lost if rival centres allow less supervised trading. In the USA popular and high-level pressures for stronger regulatory discipline have been increased because of the prominent cases of fraud during 2002, but the speculative propensity in the financial sector has not been weakened, and the stronger pressures for effective regulation have had a domestic focus. Imperatives for reorientation of the financial sector toward more funding of productive rather than speculative operations have received little recognition.

Attempts by financial authorities and representatives of financial groups to reduce dangers of destabilization in world markets have sought to moderate risk-taking by setting capital adequacy requirements at prudent levels. These have been resisted by financial sector managements, in protracted discussions, because of the prospective limitations on freedom for risk management in the pursuit of speculative opportunities. Policy-level zeal, in this context, has been weak, but has been somewhat disguised by displays of approval for autonomous methods of risk calculation by financial institutions, despite the dangers for the large numbers of passive investors. Governmental concerns with levels of risk management have reflected understanding that financial sectors tend to be strongly oriented towards speculative trading that can promise substantial rapid returns with much tax avoidance, and with sophisticated risk-spreading.[21]

In the USA very high-volume trading in financial assets has developed mainly because of the heavy reliance of producer enterprises on equity financing. Vast numbers of shares have been on offer, investor quests for high returns have tended to push up stock values, and this effect has been reinforced by financial enterprises switching large portfolios for profitable trading. The availability of vast quantities of shares for trading, with prospects of appreciation because of the pressures of portfolio switching that bids up prices, has made possible strong financial sector expansion. Banks have been drawn into this process, because of its profitability, and it has expanded externally, becoming the principal driving force in the internationalization of financial markets, that is, with speculation in other financial assets, including forms of government debt, domestic and foreign.[22]

The scope for US trading in financial assets has contrasted with the effects of stable orientations toward productive funding in systemically more integrated political economies, notably Germany. This comparison makes it necessary to consider whether changes in the US system of corporate governance may be needed for reform of the financial sector and for necessary change in the international financial markets which it is tending to dominate. A key issue is whether US manufacturing and non-financial service firms can be induced to rely substantially on bank financing, with acceptance of the consequent monitoring and the security of further entitlement. If relational financing is to be encouraged, anticipation of greater overall stability may have to be offset by the recognition that entrepreneurial dynamism may be reduced by the conservative orientations of the lending institutions.[23]

The policy-level responsibility, clearly, is to serve the interests of the large numbers of passive investors seeking higher returns than those offered by banks, while serving the interests of producer enterprises in the stability and growth of the real economy as its structural interdependencies increase and as its vulnerabilities to destabilizing speculation in world financial markets also increase. This complex governmental responsibility has to demand recognition in a culture that accords very high value to independent entrepreneurial initiative, with scope for shareholder financing. Agency-type government, however, has the practical effect of demanding responsiveness to financial sector interests by high-level decisionmakers dependent on expertise in that sector as well as on popular approval of overall administrative performance.

Changes to systems of stakeholder governance would reduce the trading of shares, and through efficiency effects would increase the availability of retained earnings for the financing of corporate expansion, thus reducing dependence on equity financing. In the public interest, then, such changes could be encouraged by government measures, including legal protection against hostile takeovers, and tax concessions, which could be justified as innovations conducive to stability and orderly growth. It could be argued that the increases in worker security could be at the expense of overall efficiency and managerial performance, and that corporate emphasis on foreign rather than domestic production would become stronger, but more active worker contributions to the development of applied technology could be expected, under enlightened managerial direction, and this would be of increasing significance as frontier research enhanced potentials for such advances.[24] The greater corporate stability could contribute to the development of intercorporate cooperation, and the formation of stronger corporate associations. Further, public confidence in the new forms of capitalism could increase.

All the financial sector problems have consequences for monetary and fiscal policies, in the USA, Europe, and other industrialized states. Surveillance of the world economy by the International Monetary Fund and the Organization for Economic Cooperation and Development thus gives much attention to trends in growth and employment affected by changes in financial markets, and to macroeconomic policy responses and options. International Monetary Fund deliberations and assessments are conducted with special concern to detect signs of impending financial crises, but make projections with caution, and stop short of prescriptions that could be based on observed trends. The contributions to policymaking in the USA appear to be less significant than those coming from the domestically focused Federal Reserve System, while in Europe there are more influential inputs into Union-level and national decisionmaking from the European Central Bank, the European Commission, and the numerous research institutes advising member governments.[25] The Organization for Economic Cooperation and Development, as a consultative institution without active advisory and financing responsibilities, could develop a capacity for sponsorship of high-level critical reviews of the policies of major members, for collaborative policy learning, but such a function has not developed. The short annual meetings of the Group of 8 could be expanded for substantial consultations, but political will for this purpose has been lacking.

Potentials for intensive policy-level interactions are significant in Atlantic relations, on the basis of mutual recognitions of expertise and asymmetric interdependencies, but, as noted, US perceptions of Europe's inferior status limit the scope for productive dialogue, that is, in conjunction with the strength of domestic pressures on US decisionmaking. A very serious danger, then, is that earnest quests for cooperation may not be initiated unless there is a crisis. Hence initiatives for intensive policy learning in the USA can be especially significant, because of the severity of the US recession.

The critical problem for US macromanagement – the complex relationship between financial sector administration and monetary policy – is tending to become more intractable, because the speculative propensity of the financial enterprises is becoming stronger, and is operating with increasing effect in the world economy, as concentration trends in this sector continue and assume larger international dimensions. Moreover, as monetary sovereignty is weakening, it is thus becoming less effective for the promotion of recovery from post-boom declines, while these declines contribute to greater corporate emphasis on the development of foreign production. Increases in the massive trade deficits, which are major factors in this context, add to the dangers of speculative destabilization, through downward pressures on the exchange rate.[26]

POLICY LEARNING AND PLANNING

Research-intensive economic advice to governments about efficiencies and stability in world financial markets has concentrated on problems in industrializing states that have become vulnerable to reverses in portfolio flows because of weak development in their financial sectors and regulatory failings, but also because of risky industrial policies. A dominant concern has been to offer suggestions for more constructive involvement by the International Monetary Fund in the resolution of Third World financial crises. The problem of destabilizing speculation in the USA, viewed as an issue for its domestic management, has not been sufficiently recognized as a challenge for collective management of the world economy.

All the dysfunctional processes have been studied more as difficulties in complex interdependence between firms, groups and domestic as well as international structures (operating as maximizers of perceived utilities) than as indicators of developmental imperatives. System-building requirements resulting from the logic of multiplying interdependencies within and between real economies have been somewhat obscured. The domestic and international structural linkages are being shaped by enterprises seeking their own market opportunities, but there is a lack of overall coordination – an absence of system-building logic above the corporate level, especially in the USA, at the centre of the global pattern of real economies, and at the centre of the international financial system.

Public choice perspectives guiding understanding of political processes offer little encouragement that overall coordination at the national and international levels can be promoted: political leaders, bureaucrats and corporate management are expected to seek only their own advantage. Yet there is a political tradition which recognizes that well-functioning markets depend on general observance of moral principles and that representative government in the public interest necessitates extensive cultivation of civic virtues.[27] This tradition has to be revitalized so that the speculation which disrupts real economies will be seen to require resolute, high-principled engagement.

Deepening corporate-led integration in the world economy is increasing linkages between financial sectors and real economies in three major configurations, with increases in market failures that are not evoking adequate responses from firms and governments. The challenges for collective management are becoming more serious.

The most destructive pattern of interactions is in Japan. The speculation which has caused a severe and prolonged financial crisis has aggravated a destructive dualism in the real economy. Domestically based growth has contracted while outward-oriented manufacturing firms have devoted more of their internal resources to the expansion of their international production systems, yet contributing to large increases in trade surpluses which, through currency appreciation, have facilitated further extensions of foreign production activity. Macroeconomic policy failures have allowed the financial crisis to worsen, thus increasing the incentives for the outward-oriented enterprises to build more ambitious international production systems. Export earnings assist growth in the domestic economy, but not enough to counter the negative effects of the continuing financial crisis. Export dependence on the USA is very substantial, and has entailed vulnerabilities because of the US recession.[28]

Reciprocal causality between the financial sector and the real economy in the USA has also given impetus to a dualist dynamic. Decline and insecurity at home have increased the incentives of US transnational enterprises to expand their international production systems, thus limiting their contributions to domestic recovery, while the speculative propensity of the financial sector has hampered such a recovery, despite monetary loosening and fiscal expansion on a moderate scale. This relatively greater macroeconomic prudence has, however, nevertheless worsened the acute problem of external imbalance – the unsustainable trade deficit – as domestic demand has been sustained by the fiscal expansion, in conjunction with investment inflows, and by the monetary loosening. Risks of a substantial and possibly sudden depreciation of the currency have thus been increasing. A further contrast with Japan has been that the international effects of the decline of the real economy and of the financial sector deficiencies have been more extensive, particularly because of the high level of interdependence with Europe.[29]

The European Union has been relatively protected from contagion because of the weaker development of continental financial sectors. As these are deepening and becoming more internationalized, the degree of exposure to contagion is increasing but smaller-scale involvement in transnational production has limited the danger of a dualist dynamic, while exchange rate stability has been aided by stability in a rough external balance, with fiscal restraint under the Union's stability pact, despite pressures of political competition and the costs of welfare burdens that have been tending to breach its limits. The welfare costs have been higher than in the USA, and have been tending to increase because of the negative growth effects of taxation levels higher than those in the USA, and lower levels of public confidence in the Union economy, reflected in strong outflows of passive as well as direct investment.[30]

Industrializing countries, because of the weaknesses of their financial sectors, their regulatory deficiencies and their vulnerabilities resulting from financial liberalization, are exposed to destabilizing speculative capital flows, and it must be stressed that a perverse logic will tend to operate if they achieve economic growth that attracts such flows. Reversals of the flows may indeed occur while economic fundamentals remain sound because of investor reactions to financial crises elsewhere. But economic fundamentals may be unsound because of the effects of policy failures that develop after considerable growth has been achieved, due to corruption and mismanagement of funds attracted by the growth.

Potentials for the constructive management of structural interdependencies and financial linkages are significant mainly in Atlantic relations, because of the dimensions and symmetries of the interconnections between the real economies, the degrees of balance in bargaining strengths between the USA and the European Union, and the density of interactions between each side's corporate groups and policy communities. Political and corporate will for comprehensive cooperation, however, has been lacking, mainly because of problems of advanced political development and failures to build well-institutionalized economic associations. The deficiencies in Atlantic interactions have in effect prevented constructive engagement with Japan for resolution of its financial crisis, and have left the way open for further uncoordinated involvement by US and European financial enterprises in developing countries, with dangers of opportunism that may increase when significant levels of growth are attained.

Altogether, the requirements for knowledge-intensive and highly dedicated statecraft and corporate leadership are very great. A more stable, more coordinated, more efficient and more equitable international political economy has to be constituted, through broadly concerted entrepreneurship, in a spirit of solidarity, under structural statecraft. This requirement has to be added to liberal proposals for new forms of global governance.[31]

NOTES

1. See Arvid John Lukauskas and Francisco L. Rivera-Batiz (eds) (2001), *The Political Economy of the East Asian Crisis and its Aftermath*, Cheltenham, UK and Northampton, USA: Edward Elgar.
2. On the recent history of these crises see Jeffrey J. Schott (2001), *Prospects for Free Trade in the Americas*, Washington, DC: Institute for International Economics, Appendix 2.1.
3. European objections to the international reach of new US regulatory measures (*Financial Times*, 12 August 2002) led to exemptions reported in various issues of the *Financial Times* during October 2002.
4. On the factors that have sustained the dollar, see Catherine L. Mann (2002), 'Perspectives on the US current account deficit and sustainability', *The Journal of Economic Perspectives*, **16**(3), summer, 131–52. European attraction of US direct investment increased with the formation of the European Monetary Union and is being further increased by the prospective entry of new Central and East European members. US fund managers are also expanding operations in Europe – *Financial Times*, 20 August 2002.

5. On the contrasts between the two types of monitoring see Jean Tirole (2002), *International Crises, Liquidity, and the International Monetary System*, Princeton, NJ: Princeton University Press.
6. On the international role of the euro see Pier Carlo Padoan (ed.) (2001), *Monetary Union, Employment and Growth*, Cheltenham, UK and Northampton, USA: Edward Elgar.
7. See references to fiscal policy in Mann, 'Perspectives', cited in note 4.
8. See discussion of the dynamics of a liberal market economy in Peter A. Hall and David Soskice (eds) (2001), *Varieties of Capitalism*, Oxford: Oxford University Press, chapter 1.
9. See discussion of coordination processes in Hall and Soskice, *Varieties of Capitalism*, cited in note 8 and in John L. Campbell, J. Rogers Hollingsworth and Leon N. Lindberg (eds) (1991), *Governance of the American Economy*, Cambridge: Cambridge University Press.
10. On the dynamics of the market for corporate control see Mary O'Sullivan (2000), *Contests for Corporate Control*, Oxford: Oxford University Press.
11. For figures on the outflows see *Survey of Current Business*, **82**(7), July 2002, 10–17.
12. The well-publicized Enron case in the USA is an example.
13. See Hall and Soskice, *Varieties of Capitalism*, cited in note 8.
14. On the history of US financial crises see Robert J. Shiller (2000), *Irrational Exuberance*, Princeton, NJ: Princeton University Press. On risks for the world economy see Martin Wolf, 'Down time', *Financial Times*, 17 July 2002.
15. See Thomas L. Brewer, Paul A. Brenton and Gavin Boyd (eds) (2002), *Globalizing Europe*, Cheltenham, UK and Northampton, USA: Edward Elgar, chapter 11.
16. See Eric Orts, 'Law is never enough to guarantee fair practice', *Financial Times*, 23 August 2002.
17. For a discussion of government roles in industrial development see David C. Mowery and Richard R. Nelson (eds) (1999), *Sources of Industrial Leadership*, Cambridge: Cambridge University Press, chapter 9.
18. These points, based on observations on the development of production interdependencies between firms in Nicolai Foss and Volker Mahnke (eds) (2000), *Competence, Governance, and Entrepreneurship*, Oxford: Oxford University Press, are further developed in John H. Dunning and Gavin Boyd (eds) (2003), *Alliance Capitalism*, Cheltenham, UK and Northampton, USA: Edward Elgar.
19. A vital governmental responsibility is to serve the interests of the large numbers of passive investors: this is well recognized as a regulatory function, but it also has to be recognized as an advisory function based on the significance of new technology as a public good requiring exploration in the light of common interests.
20. See Brewer, Brenton and Boyd, *Globalizing Europe*, cited in note 15, especially chapter 7.
21. On the risk management issues see Bank for International Settlements, 72nd Annual Report, 8 July 2002, Basel, chapter VII.
22. Ibid., chapters V, VI and VIII.
23. For extensive discussions of this issue see Xavier Vives (ed.) (2000), *Corporate Governance*, Cambridge: Cambridge University Press; 'Symposium on finance, law and economic growth', *Oxford Review of Economic Policy*, **17**(4), Winter 2001; and Stephen S. Cohen and Gavin Boyd (eds) (2000), *Corporate Governance and Globalization*, Cheltenham, UK and Northampton, USA: Edward Elgar, 2000.
24. See Foss and Mahnke, *Competence, Governance, and Entrepreneurship*, cited in note 18, especially chapters 2 and 3.
25. See Brewer, Brenton and Boyd, *Globalizing Europe*, cited in note 15, chapter 9.
26. See Mann, 'Perspectives', cited in note 4.
27. See Jenny Stewart (1993), 'Rational choice theory, public policy, and the liberal state', *Policy Sciences*, **26**(4), 317–30, and discussion of social capital in Peter A. Hall, 'Social capital in Britain', *British Journal of Political Science*, **29**(3), July, 417–61.
28. Magnus Blomstrom, Byron Gangnes and Sumner La Croix (eds) (2001), *Japan's New Economy*, Oxford: Oxford University Press, chapter 12.
29. See Brewer, Brenton and Boyd, *Globalizing Europe*, cited in note 15.
30. Ibid.

31. See Robert O. Keohane (2001), "Governance in a partially globalized world', *American Political Science Review*, **95**(1), March, 1–14 for a liberal perspective on issues of global governance. In this perspective strong tendencies to seek hard and precise agreements for economic cooperation tend to be ignored, but they have potent effects on the outlooks of policymakers, and for the benefit of the international community they have to be supplanted by understandings of imperatives for structural policy cooperation. See'Symposium on legalization and world politics', *International Organization*, **54**(3), Summer 2000, and Alexander Wendt (2001), 'Driving with the rearview mirror: on the rational science of institutional design', *International Organization*, **55**(4), autumn, 1019–50. For further comments on the liberal perspective see Ha-Joon Chang (2002), 'Breaking the mould: an institutionalist political economy alternative to the neo-liberal theory of the market and the state', *Cambridge Journal of Economics*, **26**(5), September, 539–59.

2. From overlending to crisis, to a new international financial regime? Lessons from the 1990s*

Pier Carlo Padoan

The 1990s have witnessed a dramatic increase in financial liberalization and integration, in terms of deepening financial activity and of the number of countries gaining access to market lending. Indeed, financial liberalization represents one of the most important structural transformations of the past few decades in the international system, with deep implications for the way international economic relations develop as well as for the way economic policies are carried out. While peculiar in many respects, the developments of the past decade follow a familiar pattern in international financial relations. After the recovery from the debt crisis of the 1980s that led to a decrease in international lending to emerging economies, financial markets, supported by a wave of liberalization and deregulation, returned to a phase of lending euphoria that eventually produced fragilities and crises that, in the second half of the past decade, have hit Asia, Latin America and Russia. As after every major crisis, the policy debate that followed has led to reassessments of how to deal with international financial integration. Such reassessments center on macroeconomic policies; the role of international financial institutions; the need to support markets with more effective regulation and institutions; and the so-called 'new international financial architecture'.

This chapter offers a quick overview of the major transformations in international financial relations during the 1990s and of the policy lessons that can be drawn from the sequence of euphoria, overlending and crises. It then discusses the prospects of establishing, in forms consistent with the current state of international financial relations, two regimes: a macroeconomic regime, to provide sustainable growth, and a regulatory regime, to overcome market failures and solve collective action problems associated with the operation of financial markets. These are the two regimes that, as the history of financial relations shows, are needed for financial markets to operate effectively, while minimizing the risks of instability.

THE 1990s FINANCIAL LIBERALIZATION AND FINANCIAL CRISES

Financial liberalization offers opportunities but carries risks. Over the past decade emerging market economies have enjoyed increasing financial market access. Financial flows have flooded those emerging markets that, according to general judgment, were promising growth and profit opportunities. Up until the Asian crisis the key issue in international financial policy discussions was that of 'excessive capital inflows', as emerging market policymakers were encountering difficulties in controlling liquidity inflows that were leading to rising inflation, real exchange rate appreciation and, eventually, financial instability and constraints on growth.[1]

The 1990s were also the years of widespread financial crises. At the beginning of the decade monetary and financial instability had produced a major monetary crisis in Europe, where the exchange rate mechanism of the European Monetary System collapsed in the fall of 1992, and a major financial crisis occurred in Mexico in 1994. These events were followed by other major crises, with exchange and banking collapses hitting Asia, Russia and Latin America.

At the beginning of the current decade the picture is somewhat different. Europe has acquired substantial monetary and financial stability through the successful launching of the euro. Russia and most Asian countries (with the exception of Indonesia) have recovered from the crisis. Latin America remains a troubled region where, after the collapse of Argentina, neighboring countries, with the exception of Chile and Mexico, have entered a phase of market instability, associated with political uncertainty and plagued by contagion.

Financial instability has surfaced in developed countries as well. In the USA, the Enron and Worldcom cases have disclosed fragilities and, more importantly, lack of transparency and regulatory failures in the corporate and financial sectors that have led to substantial losses in financial markets. Partially related to these events, in mid-2002, the dollar entered a depreciation phase that subsequently lost momentum in the face of a widening US current account deficit pointing to payment imbalances.[2]

These events remind us that, while financial instability has always been a feature of capitalism, the ways financial instability manifests itself reflect the specific features of each phase of international financial relations. These specific features are worth considering in more detail.

In industrial countries (especially, but not only, in the USA) private demand, both consumption and investment, has been increasingly leveraged. This has been accompanied by, and partly related to, dramatic productivity increases following the development of information and communication technologies. Indeed, what makes the past decade particularly relevant in this respect is the interaction of substantial productivity growth, thanks to the adoption and diffusion of 'general purpose innovation', and the increasing reliance on finance to support both investment and consumption. These factors created a self-reinforcing mechanism of increasing productivity, higher investment, rising profit expectations, wealth-induced consumption, sustained output and employment growth.[3]

It is tempting to depict such an interaction, which has developed especially in the USA, as a dynamic process, leading to an explosive (unstable) path, typical of many episodes in financial history. We cannot explore this issue here, but we note that this episode highlights the complex relationship and, on occasions, the mismatch, between economic fundamentals and market expectations, as reflected in financial variables. Again, in its general features, this is not a new phenomenon, but its characteristics are specific.[4]

A first point worth noting is that, as the Enron, Xerox and WorldCom cases suggest, sources of financial fragility in advanced economies may be related to lack of transparency, inadequate accounting standards, and ineffective regulation and supervision. These aspects may remain blurred during phases of expansion, especially when they are prolonged, but act as powerful amplifiers in the slowdown and when instability increases. In addition, the diffusion of 'balance sheet fragility' makes it more difficult for the leveraged demand mechanism to resume strength in the upswing of the cycle, when it materializes.

A second point is that international transmission mechanisms have become more complex and more closely related to the formation of expectations. Over the 1990s there has been a dramatic increase in interdependence. Market integration has proved to be a powerful channel of transmission of the benefits of growth and technological innovation during the upswing of the cycle. However, it has also proved to be a channel of transmission of disturbances well beyond traditional trade linkages. The direction of causality in the international transmission mechanism still largely goes from the USA to the rest of the world, including Europe. However, while the direction of transmission has remained unchanged for decades, the traditional trade channels cannot account for its intensity. Closer scrutiny of the transmission mechanism from the USA to the EU highlights the following aspects:[5] (1) the correlation between economic cycles in the two regions is stronger than the correlation between trade variables; (2) the correlation between financial variables has significantly increased, and (3) increased correlation has been affecting domestic demand in the EU through wealth effects, which have become increasingly relevant both in Europe and in the USA, and through the correlation between expectations and confidence measures in the two areas, so that, for example, when confidence declines in the USA, demand declines in the EU.

Finally, relationships between large advanced regions remain imbalanced and exchange rates are slow to adjust to them, as indicated by the fact that, up until the first quarter of 2002, the dollar was overvalued with respect to the euro by approximately 20–25 percent.[6] Lacking orderly exchange rate changes, financial markets are subject to increasing strains in financing payments imbalances, raising the question of the overall sustainability of those imbalances. Again, this is not new. Historical experience shows that the dollar has gone through large cycles and that reversals in its nominal and real value can take place in relatively short periods.

A widely held view is that the sustained overvaluation of the dollar over the second part of the 1990s has been the consequence of large capital inflows, attracted by profit expectations, as opposed to low profit and growth expectations in other industrial areas and in the euro area in particular. As the latter persist over time, a weaker dollar would reflect weaker profit and growth expectations in the USA rather than improved prospects in the euro area.

Increasing financial interdependence has been accompanied by changes in the demand and supply of financial resources. On the demand side, an increasing number of emerging market economies have used market financing. The supply side has seen changes in terms of actors and instruments. Syndicated lending by banks prevailed in the 1970s and 1980s. Bond and equity financing prevailed in the 1990s, for both private and sovereign borrowers. The lending boom of the 1970s saw syndicated banks lending, often aggressively, to emerging markets concentrated, then as now, in Asia and in Latin America. The lending boom led in the early 1980s to a debt crisis, sparked by debt default in Mexico and Brazil, the recovery from which took most of the decade. The borrowing boom of the 1990s, instead, replicated, to some extent, the characteristics observed between the two world wars, with a prevailing role of bond and equity financing as opposed to bank lending.

One important implication of the return to bond and equity financing is that, with respect to syndicated bank lending, collective action is more difficult as creditors are more dispersed and often lack effective leadership, a feature that is crucial in crisis management and debt restructuring (and to which we shall return when discussing the new financial architecture issues).

On the debtors' side, emerging market economies have, often aggressively, pursued capital account liberalization with the purpose of improving access to private lending. Experience has shown, in many cases too late, that capital account liberalization, in order to deliver the benefits of increased access to financial markets, must be carried out according to appropriate timing and sequencing, especially when other sectors of the economy, particularly those related to trade and manufacturing, are still to be liberalized.

In some cases (for example Korea) 'wrong sequencing', while initially generating substantial capital inflows, added to fragility as short-term capital liberalization was implemented before structural adjustment in the corporate and financial sectors was completed, thus paving the way for quick capital reversals once structural imbalances in fundamentals, including governance problems, became clear to investors. In other cases (e.g. Latin America) capital account liberalization, accompanied by only limited trade liberalization, generated serious debt servicing problems.[7] All in all, the recent experience suggests that the effects of capital account liberalization on growth are mixed if flows other than foreign direct investment are considered.[8]

One negative aspect of increased interdependence is contagion. Financial contagion has played a key role in aggravating the capital account crises of the late 1990s. The crisis in Argentina, at the end of 2001, had initially led many observers to hail the disappearance of contagion, justified by the increased ability of markets to discriminate between 'bad' and 'good' countries ('policies') that had allowed investors to pull out of the Latin American country in advance of the final collapse. Months after the breakout of the crisis in Argentina several Latin American countries were undergoing severe stress, including Uruguay, Paraguay, Venezuela, Peru and Brazil, pointing to more, not less, contagion, although in some 'delayed form'. Growing financial interdependence has also multiplied the channels of contagion. While pure 'financial contagion', as incorporated in the correlation between spreads of emerging market debt, may have settled down thanks to the increased ability of investors to diversify, more traditional contagion, through depressed activity levels, is still at work, feeding a vicious circle of widespread decreasing debt service capacity, which leads back to financial contagion.[9]

The crisis in Argentina also sparked off forms of 'political contagion', that is, the option, for policymakers in indebted countries, to step back from market-oriented policies, seen as the ultimate cause of the crisis, or more simply, the resumption of administrative controls to check deposit withdrawals. The introduction of such measures has undermined confidence in the solvency of the banking system of many Latin American countries, as the liquidity crisis in Uruguay in June 2002 shows.

Last but not least, contagion can take the form of what could be called 'election contagion' as the anticipation of the electoral victory of market-unfriendly candidates (or believed to be such) casts doubt on the ability of the future government to implement policies needed to service debt (such as the case of Brazil in the summer of 2002). Contagion, in such a case, is transmitted through the expectation that the success of market-unfriendly candidates in one country can benefit similar candidates in neighboring countries.

POLICY IMPLICATIONS OF DEEPER FINANCIAL INTEGRATION

The major change that national economic policies face as global financial interdependence develops is that the focus of external equilibrium shifts from a current account to a capital account perspective. This shift in emphasis also highlights that external equilibrium has to be addressed as an intertemporal problem where financing and adjustment interact. As external financing is largely market provided, policymakers have to pay increasing attention to the way their actions influence market expectations and assessments of national performance. Looking at the experience of the 1990s, this very general point can be articulated as a number of more specific aspects, as follows.

Fixed exchange rates are unsustainable in a world of high capital mobility, if domestic policies are inconsistent. This is simply a restatement of the 'inconsistent triad' theory developed by Robert Mundell. Hard evidence in support of the theory was provided at the beginning of the past decade when the move to full capital liberalization in Europe led to the EMS crisis of 1992, and was reinforced by the Asian and Latin American crises later in the decade. A related point is that macroeconomic disequilibrium can (and often does) hide microeconomic (balance sheet) disequilibria. Again, the Asian crisis has demonstrated how banking crises go along with, and often anticipate, exchange rate crises.

A number of more specific policy implications follow. A first one relates to the choice of the exchange rate regime. Open economies, especially the ones where capital account liberalization has proceeded further, should adopt flexible exchange rates or, alternatively, join monetary unions (the so-called 'corner solution' approach). The second option has seen a number of variants over the 1990s, including the adoption of currency boards and dollarization.[10] Evidence of the performance of these arrangements is mixed, however, as the opposite cases of Argentina and the Baltic countries show. A necessary condition for the success of such arrangements is fiscal discipline, so as to assure debt sustainability. However, fiscal discipline may not be sufficient, as one major problem with dollarization or currency board arrangements is that they have to be set up with an 'exit strategy' in mind. This was not available for Argentina, while for the Baltic countries the exit option is EU and EMU membership. The reason to have an 'exit option' is that the benefits of extreme currency arrangements are largely associated with the credibility gains the country enjoys. The costs are associated with the loss of monetary policy autonomy, which may end up imposing strong constraints on growth if the benefits from lower interest rates vanish, thus making the arrangement unsustainable if no exit option is available.

Finally, whatever the choice of the exchange rate regime, the credibility needed to sustain capital account liberalization requires sound microeconomic management, and transparency and information at balance sheet level, so as to allow markets to better assess risk, and fiscal discipline, as an increasing supply of domestic debt generated by over-expansionary policies would hardly meet demand at a sustainable price.

This leads us to what is perhaps the most controversial and difficult challenge for policymakers in a context of financial liberalization: the interaction between domestic policy, debt and growth. The wave of capital account liberalization of the past decade has shown: (1) that financial openness and integration are beneficial for growth, to the extent that they allow countries to borrow to finance the growth process itself, but (2) risks of financial instability are always present, and (3) debt is unsustainable without growth.

Debt-based growth necessitates a virtuous circle of tight fiscal policy, high confidence, low interest rates, low debt service, high growth. Hence, the policy dilemma is to preserve confidence while not hurting growth. Growth ultimately depends on factor accumulation as well as on technology accumulation, and evidence indicates that growth is positively correlated with open trade and with capital flows as major vehicles of technology diffusion.[11] Nonetheless, in addition to supply-side considerations, demand-side considerations play a role as well. Tight demand management is beneficial to growth in that it raises private sector confidence (and hence lowers the cost of debt) by an amount that would more than offset the short-term contractionary effect. Unfortunately, while this prescription is true in a general sense, the experience of the last decade suggest that the nature of the trade-off between the confidence boost and the contraction effect of tight polices remains an unresolved issue. More importantly, country-specific aspects are very relevant in determining the institutional, political and social feasibility of such a general policy prescription. To put it differently, international financial integration has, at the same time, produced more uniformity in the exposure of countries to market behavior and highlighted the importance of national specificities in the policy response to the pressure of international markets.[12] Hence an appropriate blend of (general) rules and (country-specific) discretion is all the more needed as financial integration develops.

A NEW FINANCIAL ARCHITECTURE?

The crisis of the 1990s has led to a large wave of criticism of international financial institutions (and the IMF in particular) and to the call for a new 'financial architecture'. The criticism of the IMF has centered on its policy prescriptions for indebted countries, including the one to maintain fixed exchange rates in a situation of high capital mobility, thus imposing heavy deflationary costs. The move to floating exchange rates, critics argue, came too late and at high costs. In addition, these costs were unevenly distributed, also because Fund policies, in many cases involving very sizeable rescue packages, had largely the effect of bailing out private investors while imposing substantial hardship on populations.

More broadly, the discussion about policy prescriptions centers around the appropriate degree of involvement of national policymakers, international institutions and markets in the effort to enhance crisis prevention and crisis resolution in a highly interdependent financial system. This discussion, in turn, is articulated around two, closely interrelated, aspects: (1) the appropriate mix of policy adjustment, external official financing and private sector involvement (PSI), and (2) the norms and institutions that are needed to deal with sovereign debt restructuring.[13]

Up until, and including, the financial crises of the late 1990s a standard mix would have been tight policy adjustment followed by (generous) external financing, which could eventually prove to be insufficient, thus leading to more policy adjustment as a precondition for further external financing. The criticism of the Bretton Woods institutions has pointed to the need to revise policy prescriptions, limiting large bailouts, but also to increase private sector involvement in crisis resolution on the basis that markets should share the benefits and costs of their lending decisions. Ideally, the overall financing gap of an indebted economy should be addressed by a more appropriate mix of a smaller gap (through policy adjustment) and a more balanced distribution of financing between the private sector and multilateral institutions.

This, of course, is easier said than done, and boils down to the well-known problem of dealing with debtor and creditor moral hazard. Debtor moral hazard occurs when debtor countries would rather default than implement costly adjustment policies in the belief that they will be bailed out by international lenders. Creditor moral hazard occurs when markets lend to high-risk countries in the belief that international institutions will not allow them to fail, or that, at least, they will be able to recover most of their loans thanks to the resources devoted to bailing out the debtors.

The 'new approach' to crisis resolution, formally discussed at the Prague 2000 annual meeting of the IMF and the World Bank, calls for a new attitude from international institutions towards both governments and markets. Governments must be persuaded to adopt more effective adjustment policies in the belief that they will not be financed without limits. This implies that Fund/Bank programs will have to be better designed (also through the streamlining of conditionality attached to program financing) and better implemented (through increased ownership of programs by national authorities, which should add to the credibility of the commitments). Markets, on the other hand, should be persuaded that they cannot rely on unlimited bailouts, and creditors should be involved in providing refinancing and debt rollovers during crises.

Ideally, under the 'new approach' creditors would be convinced of the opportunity to remain involved in crisis situations by the same arguments laid out above. Programs would have a better chance to succeed and official financing would be limited; hence the alternative to involvement would be default without bailouts. In this way, the Fund and the Bank would play a 'catalytic role' in that their decisions about program design and program financing would send the appropriate signal to markets, setting the conditions for a return to normal, market-based, debtor–creditor relationships.[14]

Views differ over the efficacy of the 'new approach'. It is still too early to say whether markets and policymakers will believe that international institutions are changing their approach so as to minimize moral hazard. It is undeniable, however, that both the World Bank and the IMF are involved in a process of thorough policy revision.

The second component of the new financial architecture deals with the norms and institutions that should be set up to deal with debt restructuring. As mentioned above, one important feature of the way international financial markets operate today compared with 20 years ago is the increasing share of equity and bond financing as opposed to bank financing. This has made collective action problems more difficult to solve, given the very large number of market participants and the higher risk of free-riding. Other things being equal, a larger number of participants makes the catalytic role of the Fund and the Bank more difficult and could undermine the success of the 'new approach' to crisis resolution.

To deal with this, proposals have been advanced for a new mechanism to deal with debt restructuring of sovereign borrowers special drawing rights mechanism (SDRM).[15] The proposals call for a formal arrangement by which, in case of a severe crisis, a debtor country would enter a situation of temporary standstill during which debt service would be suspended, as well as any legal action against debtors, so as to provide a breathing space to organize an orderly debt restructuring, negotiations with creditors, and discussions about an adjustment program with the IFIs. Versions of the proposals differ with respect to issues such as the identification of the party that should call the standstill (the debtor, the IMF), but many agree that the mechanism would represent a useful complement to the 'new approach' to crisis management, and it would facilitate private sector involvement in crisis resolution.

Reactions to the proposal have been far from universally positive, however. Major opposition has been voiced by representatives of the financial community,[16] who see the SDRM proposal as a mechanism which would limit their freedom of action. Initial resistance has also come from the US administration, partly responding to private sector pressures, and from emerging markets, arguing, like the private sector, that the SDRM would increase the cost of borrowing.

Also, as a reaction to the 'statutory' SDRM approach, the US administration and financial community have pushed for a 'market-based' approach, according to which lenders would, on a voluntary base, introduce Collective Action Clauses (CAC) in contracts for bond issuance to sovereign borrowers. These clauses would provide rules for key issues – including lenders' representation during restructuring, and exit arrangements – aimed at solving the collective action problems associated with large groups of lenders such as bondholders. The introduction and diffusion of CAC is referred to as 'market based' in that they should be adopted by market participants on a voluntary basis. CAC already exist in a number of contracts issued in EU jurisdictions, but they are not used in contracts issued under US jurisdiction.

Notwithstanding their genesis, many see the statutory and market approaches as complements rather than substitutes, as the diffusion of CAC in bond contracts would facilitate debt restructuring and the practical implementation of SDRM. Some have seen the introduction of CAC as the feasible 'first step' towards the introduction of stabilization elements in international financial markets, until a full SDRM can be put in place. Closer scrutiny, however, has shown that in both cases time and effort would be needed. Widespread adoption of CAC would require substantial leadership from industrial countries to convince both markets and other sovereign borrowers that CAC would not add to the cost of borrowing – as emerging markets fear – while increasing market stability. However, the US administration has been lukewarm in agreeing to 'lead by example'. Even if such difficulties were to be overcome, the time needed for a decisive shift towards a widespread adoption of CAC would not be less than what is needed to set up a full SDRM.

In sum, a new financial architecture requires a new relationship between markets, countries and IFIs to implement new approaches to traditional policies and to design and implement new rules for financial markets. Progress so far has been slow, to say the least, reflecting disagreement between the major actors on the analysis of the causes of financial instability and on prescriptions. In conclusion, the appropriate political-economy setting for a new financial architecture in not yet available.

POLICY REGIMES FOR FINANCIAL INTERDEPENDENCE

Sound governance of global financial interdependence requires addressing two main issues: (1) maintaining macroeconomic stability and growth with high financial integration; and (2) designing and implementing institutions so as to minimize costs of financial instability while maximizing access to markets. Neither issue is new. They have been, implicitly or explicitly, at the top of the agenda during all phases of major international financial integration. However, as mentioned, each historical period carries unique features that require that the solution to be adopted takes due account of the specific institutional, economic and political environment .

Addressing governance issues in the international system requires setting up international 'policy regimes', that is, norms and institutions that regulate the interaction of markets and policy actors, including sovereign states and international organizations, in the absence of supranational governments. We explore perspectives on such regimes, which we will refer to as a 'macroeconomic regime' and a 'regulatory regime', according to five criteria: (1) *economics*, that is, the economic blueprint around which to organize the regime; (2) *best practice*, that is, the identification of a benchmark model to guide the practical implementation of the regime; (3) *control over outcomes*, that is, the capability to obtain the desired outcomes through policy action; (4) *incentives for policymakers* to take the appropriate policy action; (5) *leadership*, that is, the possibility to generate sufficient leadership to establish and support the regime and to overcome collective action problems associated with international cooperation.

The Macroeconomic Regime

There is no doubt that, over the past decade, the USA, thanks to the dramatic increase in productivity associated with the introduction and diffusion of new technologies, has provided the main, if not the only, engine of growth for the world economy. Over the same period the EU, and especially Japan, have grown at a much slower rate, if at all. Such a configuration is not sustainable in the long run, both in terms of foregone growth and because of the consequences of uneven growth, reflected in payment imbalances between the USA and the rest of the world. A sustainable configuration would require that the role of engine of growth be equally shared between the USA, the EU and Japan, and that payment imbalances be addressed by an appropriate blend of adjustment (including through exchange rate changes) and financing.

Economics

The economics for the regime is based on the idea that growth is associated with technological accumulation and trade and investment openness.[17] The latter provides market access and enhances technology diffusion from the center (where the bulk of technological accumulation takes place) to the periphery. Trade and financial openness should proceed at a balanced pace. Payments imbalances should be partly financed by capital flows and partly adjusted through exchange rate changes, avoiding excessive accumulation of external debt and persistent exchange rate misalignments.

Best practice

It is natural to look to the USA for best practice as far as growth and technology accumulation are concerned. Both the EU and Japan are lagging behind, in terms of technology accumulation, output and employment growth. The EU potential rate of growth is about one percentage point lower than the USA. Japan has been in recession for almost a decade. In both cases, although to a different extent, structural reforms are needed to allow for the benefits of the new technologies to be fully reaped in terms of higher productivity, output and employment growth. The EU has launched the Lisbon Strategy, at the EU Council meeting in March 2000, to establish, by 2010, a dynamic knowledge- based economy through a large acceleration in structural reforms and further integration.[18] Many of the features of the Lisbon Strategy are inspired by the US experience. Nonetheless, results so far have been disappointing. Japan has achieved even less. The roots of Japan's stagnation are structural and reflected in the interaction of bad bank exposure and stagnating investment. Resumption of growth would require deep structural adjustment and appropriate monetary and fiscal policy.

On trade policy, best practices are harder to find. All three major industrial areas adopt substantial impediments to market access – either in the forms of trade barriers or through subsidies – especially in sectors like agriculture and textiles, where the comparative advantages of developing countries exist. However, while the level of protection is high in all three areas, the direction of trade policy has been different in the two major trading partners, towards less protection in the EU (for instance through the 'Everything but Arms' initiative), towards more protection in the USA, through the acts passed by the Bush Administration to support domestic steel, agriculture and textiles producers.

Finally, on macroeconomic policy best practice is again to be found in the USA, at least as far as monetary policy is concerned. Alan Greenspan's management of US monetary policy has contributed significantly to the exploitation of the benefits of technological innovation and of the developments in financial markets that have supported aggregate demand. The US decade- long performance of high employment and output growth and of low inflation owes as much to skillful policy management as it does to the structural features of the US economy, including the wider room for maneuver for policy provided by higher potential output growth. The other side of the coin has been, and remains, the systematic disregard of external imbalances, the current account deficit and dollar overvaluation.

The policy stance in the EU has been different, concentrating on the process of monetary unification, on price stability and fiscal consolidation. It is fair to say that the environment in which EU policy is implemented offers more limited room for maneuver, given the lower potential output growth and the less advanced degree of financial integration and sophistication. As structural reforms, in the framework of the Lisbon Strategy, proceed, room for maneuver should increase and so should the contribution of the EU to global growth.

Control over outcomes
Control over outcomes is high for macroeconomic policies in the USA, and more limited in the EU (or, rather, in the euro area), given the hybrid nature of

the policy model, which combines supranational (monetary) and national (fiscal) policy elements, as well as the structural impediments associated with incomplete integration. Control over outcomes is very limited in Japan, given the structural impediments and the inefficacy that fiscal and monetary policies have shown so far in supporting growth.

Control over outcomes is substantial in trade policy, both for the USA and the EU (also given the role of the Commission in this area). Indeed, no major agreement in trade issues can be achieved without the support of the two major players.[19]

Incentives to policy action

While maintaining its course in macroeconomic policy the USA should pursue open trade policies more decisively, so as to increase market access for other advanced countries, but especially for developing and emerging market economies. Incentives to act in this direction are weak, as pressures to resist liberalization, dictated by the requests of special interests, are very powerful, as the decisions to protect steel, textiles and agriculture sectors show. In addition, the USA is, apparently, not very sensitive to the incentives that, historically, in the USA and in other major countries, have driven trade liberalizations at home, that is, to obtain reciprocal trade opening elsewhere and/or to obtain non-economic objectives, such as security concessions, by other countries to which market access is granted.

The EU is facing stronger incentives to pursue both more growth-oriented policies and more trade openness. EMU should provide the appropriate macroeconomic framework. The Lisbon Strategy has been launched precisely to increase the growth potential of the EU through the exploitation of the new information and communication technologies. Yet, as mentioned, the EU is still growing at a low rate, below its in any case small potential growth rate, and the pace of structural reforms remains slow. One explanation for the lack of progress is that national differences, and preferences, are still strong in resisting the impetus for reforms (which would increase the growth potential) subject to the monetary and fiscal discipline required by the Stability and Growth Pact and the independence of the ECB. So, absent a strong common view, the option to wait, and postpone politically costly transformations, continues to prevail. As for trade policy, while recent moves have been in the right direction, decisive steps that would greatly benefit both developing and emerging markets, such as a substantial reform of the Common Agricultural Policy, are still resisted by national and sectoral interests.

In short, while the EU, acting as a unified actor, would have a strong incentive to act as a global player, national incentives remain tied to specific and often conflicting special interest preferences for the *status quo*, suggesting that the impetus and the effort that have led to the single currency represent, to a large extent, a unique case of common goals prevailing over individual ones.[20]

Finally, Japan should also pursue a deep transformation of the economy to revert to high and sustained growth rates, thus contributing to global expansion. So far, however, the incentive to change does not seem to be strong enough to replace the option to wait, that is, to remain in the state of stagnation that has prevailed over the past decade, given the high costs that deep reform would necessarily entail.

Leadership

A macroeconomic regime is a global public good and, as such, requires leadership for its establishment and preservation. Successful international monetary and financial systems have, in most cases, been built around a hegemon, a leader country that has provided macroeconomic stability and open markets to itself and to others. Such was the Bretton Woods system, established around US leadership after the conclusion of World War II. Today, leadership is lacking as the USA is not willing to pursue global objectives such as widespread market access and the EU is not able to overcome the conflicting limitations of national preferences for the development of a strong role in global governance.

The Regulatory Regime

An effective regulatory regime for global financial interdependence should be based on rules that cope with market failures so as to enhance market efficiency while minimizing instability.

Economics

Such a regulatory regime is needed because asymmetric information, moral hazard and collective action problems cause persistent failures in financial markets; hence appropriate rules and institutions must cope with them. As mentioned, such a regime would see borrower–lender contracts regulated by Collective Action Clauses – to solve collective action problems during crises, prevent crisis and resolve them through appropriate official financing, policy adjustment and private sector involvement. Affirmation that official lending in crises is not unlimited, that is, there is no 'benevolent international lender of last resort', would limit moral hazard. Private sector involvement in crisis resolution would make markets (lenders) accountable for their mistakes in lending in terms of lower profits, or losses. Their losses and their mistakes would not be covered and remunerated by the public resources through international institutions. The cost of crises, given that crises will ways happen, could be limited thanks to institutional mechanisms for orderly debt restructuring. Finally, countries would have to implement adjustment polices that would be costly, but such costs could be lower than they have been so far, and could be more evenly distributed across the population.

Best practice
There is hardly any best practice for such a regime. As mentioned above, Collective Action Clauses are applied in contracts falling under European jurisdictions, but not in those falling under US jurisdictions. Official lending by the IFIs, especially in the aftermath of the Asian crisis, has been huge and by many considered excessive. The IFIs have often been criticized for the lack of transparency in their lending decisions. The involvement of the private sector in sharing the cost of crises – by for example rollover of debt to countries facing repayment problems – has so far been limited. Crises have been deep and prolonged, and their evolution has been often very disorderly, thus producing further disruption. The cost has mostly fallen on countries (debtors) and, within these, on the weaker and poor, highlighting the need for social safety nets in adjustment programs.[21]

Control over outcomes
The absence of best practices cannot be explained by the lack of control over outcomes. Quite the contrary; leading industrial countries could go a long way by moving towards a more stable and efficient international regulatory regime. The adoption of CAC in international lending contracts could be requested by national regulatory authorities on those contracts issued under their national jurisdictions. Similarly, national authorities could increase the involvement of the private sector which falls under their jurisdictions through forms of 'moral suasion' (although many question the effectiveness of such measures). They could also push forward the introduction of a debt restructuring mechanism, even if it requires the modification of international treaties. Finally, as major shareholders of the IFIs, they could significantly influence the direction of their policy action and overall strategy of such institutions.

Incentives to act
Control over outcomes, so far, has not produced significant results because incentives to act are lacking. Industrial countries hold different preferences among themselves and with respect to emerging and developing economies, and collective action problems standing in the way of the establishment of the regimes are difficult to overcome.

Additional regulation of markets, through a widespread introduction of CAC and through a statutory approach to debt restructuring would significantly change the way markets operate – increasing stability and resilience – but it cannot be excluded that it would increase the cost of lending for markets and the cost of borrowing for sovereigns.

Evidence on the impact of such regulatory changes on market performance is sparse. However, financial history has seen waves of deregulation and reregulation, the former driven by the incentive to expand market activity and the latter by the incentive to cope with market instability following market overlending.

The Asian crisis has followed a phase of dramatic expansion of international lending and it is not surprising that the current phase is one in which the move towards more regulation seems to be prevailing. The picture is mixed, however. The two major actors, the USA and the EU, have different views on the desirability of more regulation, as the former favors a 'market-based' approach to debt restructuring and the latter supports both a market-based and a statutory approach. Different preferences also reflect responses to pressure from interest groups as the US administration is highly sensitive to the requests of the banking and financial community, which does not favor either approach and would reluctantly accept the market-based approach,[22] while the EU favors a more institutional approach. At the same time, emerging market economies oppose both the introduction of CAC and the adoption of an SDRM, fearing that both would increase the cost of borrowing.

Leadership
The full implementation of either approach would require years. The introduction of CAC would mean changing most existing contracts, and the SDRM would likely require a modification of international treaties (such as the articles of agreement of the IMF). In the meantime moves towards a new financial architecture could include changes in the role the IFIs play in crisis prevention and resolution, for instance through a stricter use of official resources in crisis management (the end, or at least the limitation, of large bailouts) as well as a more active involvement of the private sector in debt restructuring, based on moral suasion.

Promoting momentum for the establishment of a new financial architecture will require strong and sustained leadership. The Prague 2000 annual meetings of the IMF and the World Bank laid out a new approach to crisis resolution in the immediate aftermath of the Asian, Russian and Latin American crises. Differences in the approaches of the USA and the EU towards regulation of international borrowing and debt restructuring do not bode well for the momentum to keep up. The leverage of the EU is weakened by the slow development of a euro-based international financial market and the diffusion of the euro as an international currency. Incentives to move in this direction are weak for the same reasons that lie behind the slow progress towards the establishment of a EU macroeconomic regime, that is, the failure to move from national to common strategies (including a common representation in IFIs). Without doubt reform and integration of financial markets in the euro area towards a fully continental system will be necessary for increases in the external influence of the EU for the establishment of an international regulatory regime. No EU position in international financial issues will be credible while differences in national regulation and policies prevent a common strategy.

CONCLUSIONS

Over the 1990s international financial relations changed dramatically under the impulse of increasing financial liberalization and integration. Expanded access to private international lending by emerging markets has favored growth but it has also proved to be a source of instability. The Asian, Russian and Latin American crises of the late 1990s have sparked off reactions against macroeconomic policy prescriptions and crisis management – as carried out by the IFIs – but also, on the positive side, pressures to develop a new financial architecture. The experience of the last and present decades confirms the view that, for an international financial system to deliver benefits in terms of sustained growth and to minimize instability, international 'regimes' – that is, norms, institutions and regulations governing international relations – are needed and, more specifically, a *macroeconomic* regime to provide a stable and sustained growth-oriented environment (based on trade openness and integration), and a *regulatory* regime to cope with market failures and minimize the costs of financial crises.

We have discussed prospects for the two regimes by looking at five issues: economics, best practice, control over outcomes, incentives to act, and leadership. It is difficult to draw any precise conclusion as to the possibility of the two regimes being established. History shows that international regimes have been set up and operated more successfully in periods associated with hegemonic leadership, that is, in the presence of a large country willing and able to solve the collective action problems facing the establishment of international governance without an international government. History also shows, however, that models of international governance without a hegemony, that is, with more dispersed leadership, are possible.[23] And dispersed leadership is what seems to characterize the current state of international relations.

The USA is pursuing what could be termed 'aggressive unilateralism', often setting international economic policy priorities by responding to special interests, both in financial and trade and industry issues. It remains, nonetheless, the major growth engine of the world economy.

The EU has, up to now, expressed a policy which could be termed 'lukewarm regionalism'. EMU is a historic achievement and it strengthens the basis for the EU to act as a major global actor. Yet EU countries find it extremely difficult to overcome national interests so as to translate the large potential EMU offers into effective common external positions.[24] In addition, slow EU growth points to structural problems that have to be solved if the EU area can join the USA in providing a major contribution to a global macroeconomic regime. The EU, therefore, seems to be caught in a 'leadership trap'. Incentives to move from national to European financial strategies and policies remain too weak as long as the benefits of the *status quo* are perceived to prevail over the benefits of change. However, change can come only to the extent that, for the purpose of obtaining a stronger international role, contrasting national priorities are set aside.

Japan and the Asian countries are pursuing a strategy of 'frustrated regionalism'. This can be seen in the attempt to define an area of regional integration, through strengthening ASEAN and, in the financial area, though the establishment of the Asian Monetary Fund. The AMF project was initially boycotted by the USA and currently Asian countries are pursuing the less ambitious 'Chang Mai initiative' to set up a regional clearing union.[25] More importantly, the contribution of Asia to a global financial and macroeconomic regime is hindered by Japan's inability to overcome its structural problems and resume sustained growth. In addition, in the longer term the relative roles of Japan and China in the region will have to be clarified.

Yet, as noted, the absence of a global hegemony does not preclude, in the case of dispersed leadership, the definition and implementation of strategies for global financial governance: regional solutions and joint leadership.[26]

Regional solutions could see leading economies, the USA, the EU and Japan, concentrate on regional integration as opposed to global integration (closed regionalism). This was very much at the center of debate in the 1990s with respect to trade agreements, following developments in Europe (the single market), North America (NAFTA) and more recently Asia (ASEAN, Asia Pacific Economic Cooperation Forum). Trade regionalism has progressed: however, it has done so along open, rather than closed, configurations, that is, with large regional blocs actively interacting and partially integrating with each other, although regional trade disputes are still very much on the agenda. Open trade regionalism could offer a solution to global trade governance if further progress towards a multilateral trade agreement lags behind. It is more problematic to see regionalism as a way to organize global financial governance. True, the establishment of EMU has indicated the feasibility of regional currency blocs and of associated regional financial markets. However, as we have discussed, financial interdependence has significantly increased, multiplying the intensity and the channels of transmission of international disturbances. Financial and macroeconomic regionalism would not insulate regional blocs from global financial interdependence.

As for a new financial architecture, a regional structure could not provide a sound basis for global financial stability, given that financial markets operate on a global scale and would need to do so according to one and not several regulatory regimes. Different regulatory regimes generate regulatory arbitrage. Regulatory authorities would therefore have to take into account regulatory evolution in other regions.

Finally, IFIs could not take separate approaches in different regional environments. Their action would have to remain global, with common principles and perspectives, lacking which their legitimacy would rapidly vanish.

In conclusion, absent one hegemon, it is unlikely that regimes for global financial governance could be set up along strictly regional lines. While large regions should, and presumably will, further strengthen their individual positions and take advantage of them, interdependence requires shared governance among the regional players. All the same, for shared governance to be effective, the USA, the EU and Asia must be on a more equal footing than in the past. This will not be entirely possible as long as the EU and Japan do not successfully complete their internal reform agenda so as to put their economies on a dynamic and sustained growth path. As history shows, strong domestic economies are a necessary, if not sufficient, condition for global leadership.

NOTES

*   The IMF is not responsible for the views expressed here.
1. See Arvid John Lukauskas and Francisco L. Rivera-Batiz (eds), *The Political Economy of the East Asian Crisis and its Aftermath*, Cheltenham, UK and Northampton, USA: Edward Elgar, 2001; Jean Tirole, *Financial Crises, Liquidity, and the International Monetary System*, Princeton, NJ: Princeton University Press, 2002; and *72nd Annual Report*, Bank for International Settlements, Basel, July 2002.
2. See Catherine L. Mann, 'Perspectives on the US current account deficit and sustainability', *The Journal of Economic Perspectives*, **16**(3), Summer 2002, 131–52.
3. See Martin Neil Bailey, 'Distinguished lecture on economics in government: the new economy: post mortem, or second wind?', *The Journal of Economic Perspectives*, **16**(2), Spring 2002, 3–22, and Jonathan Temple, 'An assessment of the new economy', CEPR, discussion paper no. 3597.
4. On the history of US financial crises see Robert J. Shiller (2000), *Irrational Exuberance*, Princeton, NJ: Princeton University Press.
5. See the analysis in International Monetary Fund, *World Economic Outlook*, October 2001.
6. See International Monetary Fund, *World Economic Outlook*, April 2002.
7. See International Monetary Fund, *World Economic Outlook*, September 2002.
8. See Lukauskas and Rivera-Batiz, *The Political Economy of the East Asian Crisis and its Aftermath*.
9. See the symposium on financial instability, *Oxford Review of Economic Policy*, **15**(3) Autumn 1999.
10. For a recent assessment, see the symposium on Exchange Rate Regimes and Capital Flows, *The Annals of the American Academy of Political and Social Science*, 579, January 2002.
11. See for instance David Dollar and Aart Kraay, 'Trade, growth, and poverty', unpublished, Washington, DC: World Bank, www.worldbank.org/ research/growth/pdfiles/Trade5.pdf,

Benn Steil, David G. Victor and Richard Nelson (eds), *Technological Innovation and Economic Growth*, Princeton, NJ: Princeton University Press.

12. See the discussion in Peter Hall and David Soskice (2001) (eds), *Varieties of Capitalism*, Oxford: Oxford University Press.

13. See the discussion by Wolfgang Flic (2000), 'Functions of economic policy in promoting efficiency of the international financial system', in Alexander Karmann (ed.), *Financial Structure and Stability*, Heidelberg: Physica-Verlag.

14. For a critique of the catalytic role played by the Fund see Carlo Cottarelli and Curzio Giannini, 'Bedfellows, hostages, or perfect strangers? Global capital markets and the catalytic effect of IMF crisis lending', presented at the conference on 'The Lender of Last Resort – Experiments, Analyses, Controversies', Paris, 23–24 September 2002.

15. See Ann Krueger (2002), A *New Approach to Sovereign Debt Restructuring*, Washington, DC: IMF.

16. For a view of the private sector on financial crisis prevention and resolution see Institute for International Finance (2002), *Action Plan of the IIF Special Committee on Crisis Prevention and Resolution in Emerging Markets*, Washington, DC: IIF.

17. See Dollar and Kraay, 'Trade, growth, and poverty' and Steil, Victor and Nelson, *Technological Innovation*.

18. On the Lisbon strategy see Pier Luigi Morelli, Pier Carlo Padoan and Lisa Rodano, 'The Lisbon strategy for the new economy. Some economic and institutional aspects', presented at the XIV Villa Mondragone International Economic Seminar on 'Institutions and Growth: The Political Economy of International Unions and the Constitution of Europe', Rome, 24–26 June 2002.

19. See Alan M. Rugman and Gavin Boyd (2002) (eds), *The World Trade Organization in the New Global Economy*, Cheltenham, UK and Northampton, USA: Edward Elgar.

20. See Thomas Brewer, Paul A. Brenton and Gavin Boyd (2002) (eds), *Globalizing Europe,* Cheltenham: Edward Elgar.

21. See Lukauskas and Rivera-Batiz, *The Political Economy of the East Asian Crisis and its Aftermath.*

22. See IIF, *Action Plan of the IIF.*

23 See Pier Carlo Padoan and Paolo Guerrieri (1988), *The Political Economy of International Cooperation*, London and Sydney: Croom Helm.

24. See Mario Telò (2001) (ed.), *European Union and New Regionalism*, Aldershot: Ashgate.

25. See C. Randall Henning, 'East Asian financial cooperation', Institute for International Economics, policy analyses in international economics, no. 68, September 2002.

26. See Pier Carlo Padoan, 'Political economy of new regionalism and global governance', in Telò, *European Union and New Regionalism.*

3. Analytical perspectives on the varieties of capitalism and structural interdependencies: implications for multinational business finance

Alain Verbeke

INTRODUCTION

This chapter briefly reviews a number of recent insights into the 'varieties of capitalism' which are allegedly found to subsist (and to prosper) in the new global economy. The modern political-economy analysis of these varieties of capitalism argues that national institutional differences will not disappear in the long run, and may even greatly contribute to the national comparative advantage of specific industries.

When applied to issues of micro-level governance, and especially the choice of financial structure, important differences can indeed be identified among firms from different countries, very much in line with the political-economy prediction that there is no single optimal governance structure or financial structure that should be prescribed to firms across countries. Each nation is characterized by a specific configuration of economic actors pursuing particular interests and characterized by historically grown relationships among them.

However, this political-economy analysis appears to miss the important point that multinational enterprises (MNEs) now play a key role in the global economy and in the creation of structural interdependencies among countries. The presence of triad-based competition in many industries, with rivals from North America, the European Union and Japan, at a superficial level seems to demonstrate that no single variety of capitalism is able to prevail in global competition, thereby confirming the above political-economy prediction. However, this observation does not imply that the presence of several varieties of capitalism is efficient or contributes to a better functioning of MNEs or national economies. Rather, the presence of such varieties poses a major challenge for most MNEs: these firms need to learn how to bridge the varieties of capitalism, and how to gain competitive advantage when faced with multiple, and to some extent contradictory, requirements imposed by national environments. The presence of historically grown national financial systems also poses important problems for governments, which need to cope with the rapid growth of international financial markets and related global best practices.

This chapter argues that multinational business finance should view varieties of capitalism, not as a inescapable given, whereby home-country practices would fundamentally determine corporate behavior, but as both a constraint and an opportunity. Varieties of capitalism constitute a constraint as they limit the potential to gain benefits of 'integration', in particular as regards the transfer of micro-level best practices (not necessarily arising from the home country) across borders. They, however, also constitute an opportunity to learn from best practices in host countries, to the extent that these practices can be 'internalized' and transferred inside the firm. From a government perspective, the 'intrusion' of foreign financial practices in the national economy may also lead to the identification of best approaches in the regulatory sphere. In other words, if it is accepted that particular institutions more effectively contribute to the development of specific types of firms or sectors (for example, the impact of advanced accounting standards or specific venture capital rules on the development of fast-growing, high-technology firms), national governments may want to emulate successes achieved elsewhere, keeping in mind that complex sets of institutional elements may need to be replicated rather than simple rules, and that national adaptation may be required in order not to disturb broader, well-functioning institutions, for example in the sphere of corporate ownership and business organization. Here, insight into the comparative effectiveness of alternative sets of financial practices may be instrumental in increasing structural interdependencies across nations.

This chapter's second section describes the value added and significance of recent work on the institutional foundations of comparative advantage, building on Hall and Soskice (eds), *Varieties of Capitalism* (2001).

In the third section, the relevance of this comparative institutional approach is discussed in the context of firm-level governance, with a focus on recent work in international financial management, especially regarding the observed differences in optimal capital structure across countries.

The fourth section then discusses the prevailing normative perspective in multinational business finance that MNEs should attempt to bridge macro-varieties of capitalism, which primarily constitute constraints on their cross-border operations. In a world dominated by a variety of institutional structures at the macro-level, the development of 'systemic', rather than 'asset-based' firm-specific advantages, implies that MNEs will attempt to exploit these national varieties of capitalism.

VARIETIES OF CAPITALISM

In the 1950s and 1960s the study of country-specific institutions received little attention in mainstream finance research, as exemplified by the work of Modigliani and Miller (1958). The rise of models as of the mid-1970s that focused on agency problems and transaction costs, including those arising from information asymmetries, was an important stimulus for investigating the role of institutions through a variety of conceptual lenses that would go far beyond the mere description of national financial systems.

The key starting-point point of recent work in political economy on the institutional foundations of comparative advantage is that important institutions, that is, key rules, both formal and informal, followed by individuals and organizations, in areas as diverse as corporate governance, labor market regulation, and education and training, greatly differ across countries. This work, inspired by North (1990), argues that institutions fundamentally affect the relationships among the key economic actors in society, including business firms, public agencies, organized labor, financial institutions and so on. The institutions themselves result from complex bargaining processes and coalition formation among various groups with specific interests. Here, a variety of regulatory and political elements largely determines what constitutes efficient micro-level decision-making, for example, in the finance area. La Porta et al. (1998 and 1999) demonstrate this importance by focusing on the impact of legal regimes. One of their conclusions is that the Anglo-Saxon common law model with substantial protection for minority investors has been greatly beneficial to the development of financial markets in those countries. However, the general legal regime is only one component of a country's institutional setting. It is undoubtedly critical to study the entire range of institutions that affect (and are affected by) the relationships among groups of economic actors with diverging interests.

In this context, a resource-based view of firm behavior is adopted. The ability of firms to develop and exploit competencies and capabilities is viewed as being largely determined by the quality of their relationships with internal and external stakeholders. More specifically, five areas of relationships are viewed as critical: corporate governance, vocational training and education, industrial relations, inter-firm relations (especially with suppliers and customers) and (intra-firm) human resources management (Hall and Soskice, 2001).

The institutions that shape the above relationships in a society are path-dependent, resulting from a particular historical trajectory of decisions and actions by the economic actors involved. In essence, as regards the governance issue, the key point is that each variety of capitalism is associated with a particular mix of coordination by markets, hierarchies and intermediate cooperative relationships. This mix will influence, for example, the choice of capital structure, that is, the relative importance of debt and equity. To a large extent, micro-level management decisions and actions are thus conditioned by collective institutions at the macro-level, which encourage particular types of firm behavior and discourage other types. Here, the well-known empirical work by Knetter (1989) is cited as an example: he found that UK and German firms exhibited different reaction patterns when faced with a similar appreciation in exchange rates. UK firms increased prices to maintain profitability, given that their access to capital in UK financial markets largely depends on sustained profitability. Their focus was on sustained access to resources available in free markets. In contrast, German firms reduced prices to maintain market share; in Germany access to capital is more independent of short-term financial performance, but maintaining market share is critical to achieve stable employment levels and good labor relations. The German firms' focus was therefore on co-specific assets, the return on which is conditioned by cooperation from relevant stakeholders operating in imperfect markets. The example above highlights the institutional complementarities both within the micro- or macro-level institutions, and between micro- and macro-level patterns in decisions and actions.

It is important to realize that individual firms have little direct control over these societal institutions and their evolution in time; rather, these institutions represent a set of opportunities and constraints, with domestic firms being well positioned to take advantage of them in terms of competence and capability development and exploitation.

An interesting premise is that no single set of institutions necessarily leads to superior economic performance (as measured by, for example, economic growth rates and unemployment levels). It is precisely the complementarity among rules prevailing in the five domains mentioned above that leads to synergies and therefore to the potential for strong economic performance.

The importance of institutional complementarities is apparent when studying the domain of corporate governance (Hall and Soskice, 2001, pp. 27–33). In the USA, arm's-length market transactions largely dominate financial markets. In the equity market, investors base their decisions to purchase or sell shares in publicly traded companies mainly on generally available information. Similar market relationships characterize the market for bond issues. Unsatisfactory performance of companies can be sanctioned through hostile bids for takeover.

This corporate governance approach is consistent with – and strengthened by – other key institutional domains:

- The education and training system focuses on the development of general skills which can be easily redeployed across firms and even sectors. Mutual credible commitments in firm-specific training are limited.

- The labor market is largely deregulated and flexible, again allowing high mobility across firms and sectors, as well as retraining.
- Competition policy fosters vigorous rivalry. Technology transfer occurs through the market (for example, labor mobility, joint ventures and so on).
- Relationships with buyers and suppliers have traditionally been dominated by arm's-length, market-contract characteristics. The corporate governance institutions discourage long-term investments in these vertical relationships. Such investments would constitute credible commitments in co-evolution.
- Human resources management uses market-driven incentives and therefore flexible reward systems. The shareholder management focus leaves no place for co-determination. Employee power results mainly from the ability to exit the company (the individual's market value). A small senior management group usually determines the firm's strategic direction.

The analysis above provides a somewhat stylized view of reality, as most established firms attempt to develop isolating mechanisms to protect against the short-term orientation of the market forces described above, namely through R&D and brand names, and thereby create the conditions required for establishing long-term relationships. But here it should be noted that such investments are usually geared toward large populations of stakeholders, not individuals or single companies. In addition, high-growth companies can build on a well-established venture capital market where personal relationships with capital providers may be critical. However, even there the ultimate goal of venture capitalists is mostly to sell the shares they received for their support, so that the long-term relationship is conditioned by the firm's trajectory of market and financial performance, with excellent performance resulting in the dilution or even elimination of the relationship with the venture capital provider.

The key conclusion of the above description is that the institutions considered appear to complement each other, thereby providing an overarching arm's-length framework within which firms need to operate.

The German case is very different. Here, dense networks with a long lifespan prevail. In the area of governance, access to capital is not determined mainly by short-run economic performance but by in-depth, insider knowledge on the firm's future potential, based on information shared by the firm with network members. Hostile takeovers are made difficult by a variety of institutional elements. Here, the firm's reputation within the network is critical, and this reputation is subject to permanent scrutiny by network members, including banks, business associations, suppliers and clients, firms with which cross-holdings exist, and even rivals that participate in joint R&D consortia, standard-setting programs and so on. It is 'reputational monitoring', not short-term profitability, that provides access to capital.

As was the case for the USA, institutions in the five other domains reinforce this functioning of corporate governance:

- The education and training system fosters credible commitments in firm-specific and sector-specific training programs, with an apprenticeship system supported by government and monitored by trade unions and employer professional associations.
- The labor market uses industry-level bargaining between employer organizations and trade unions. This leads to industry-wide salary scales for individuals with particular skill levels and therefore to weaker incentives for employees to move from one firm to the next. Cooperation between firms and workers is institutionalized, in the form of co-determination (supervisory boards with employee and shareholders' representatives), thereby limiting wage increases but also managerial power to fire.
- Standard-setting and technology transfer occur through cooperation among firms. The lower labor mobility implies that firms cannot easily secure best practices by hiring employees coming from rival companies. Cooperation with other firms is very common, and stimulated by publicly funded research programs, often set up through business associations. The creation of industry-wide standards as a result of cooperative efforts leads to industry-specific knowledge bases shared by all firms concerned. Problems arising from cooperative activities are largely governed by open-ended contracts grounded in prevailing practices condoned by the industry associations, which also intervene to settle disputes.
- Relationships with buyers and suppliers also largely follow the network approach, rather than the arm's-length model.
- Human resources management builds upon long-term employment contracts. Work councils at the firm level and consisting of employee representatives have substantial power in areas such as employment size and working conditions. Skilled workers benefit from substantial autonomy to improve production processes. The reward systems are much less market-driven than in the USA: for example, there is only a limited use of stock options to reward management. This results in more attention being devoted to goals other than simple profitability and to a stronger long-term commitment to the firm.

One of the key implications of the above perspective is that German firms would be particularly well positioned to develop competencies and capabilities in quality control, incremental innovation and product differentiation because of their network functioning, whereas the flexibility of American firms would be instrumental to radical innovation and cost-leadership, a hypothesis which appears consistent with limited empirical evidence in the field of international business (Brouthers et al., 2000).

An important question regarding the sustainability of the present varieties of capitalism relates to the influence of globalization forces. Here, Hall and Soskice (2001, p. 55) exhibit a lack of knowledge regarding modem international business research on globalization. They argue that:

> the conventional view of globalization prominent in the press and much of the literature . . . is built on three pillars. First, it sees firms as essentially similar across nations at least in terms of basis structure and strategy. Second, it associates the competitiveness of firms with their unit labour costs, from which it follows that many will move production abroad if they can find cheaper labour there. And, third, these propositions generate a particular model of the political dynamic inspired by globalization . . . In the face of threats from firms to exit the economy, governments are said to come under increasing pressure from business to alter their regulatory frameworks so as to lower domestic labour costs, reduce rates of taxation and expand international markets via deregulation.

Globalization would thus lead to convergence toward a single set of 'best-practice equivalent' institutions.

Hall and Soskice (2001) then argue that their comparative institutional perspective fundamentally differs from the view above: firms do differ across nations, other factors than low labor costs determine location, and, most importantly, existing institutions in various countries could provide opportunities for firms engaged in institutional arbitrage. Here, it is suggested that particular activities in the value chain may be located in those places where they can benefit most from specific sets of institutions (for example, R&D facilities in appropriate knowledge clusters), thereby reinforcing rather than weakening existing institutions. As a result, only limited deregulation would occur in coordinated market economies such as Germany, in contrast to liberal market economies such as the USA.

The above description of the alleged conventional view on globalization is incorrect, as demonstrated by Rugman and Verbeke's (2001a) synthesis of the recent international business literature on the location decisions of MNEs: firms are not similar across nations but have substantially different administrative heritages, much in line with the empirical work of Bartlett and Ghoshal (1989). Cost elements, although important, are not the main driver of most foreign direct investment decisions: gaining market access and obtaining strategic assets are often much more critical considerations than cost reductions on basic production factors. Finally, the global economy is not moving toward a single optimal model: on the contrary, from a firm perspective, regional strategies and efforts to become insiders in host-country clusters often require substantial isomorphic flexibility rather than an institutionalization approach (Van Den Bulcke and Verbeke, 2001; Rugman and

Verbeke, 2001b). Hall and Soskice (2001) thus bring little new insight to the research table.

Hall and Soskice (2001) recognize that the internationalization of finance does put pressure on firms, even in coordinated market economies, to become more attentive to shareholders than in the past. In their view, however, this will not lead to a weakening of prevailing institutions in those countries; on the contrary. The need to achieve risk-adjusted real rates of return required by world financial markets will push firms to rely even more strongly than in the past on prevailing home-country institutions, that is, the source of their competencies and capabilities, for example, the network relationships in coordinated market economies. In the case of substantial economic shocks, institutional complementarities will require coordinated change among the various affected economic actors.

Nations indeed use very different institutions to govern financial activities, as illustrated in Figure 3.1, borrowed from Pagano and Volpin (2001, p. 505). These differences in regulation and specific policy intervention may then fundamentally affect micro-level financial management decisions. It is also assumed that, ultimately, the historically grown, path-dependent configuration of the different interested economic actors (controlling shareholders,

| Institutional domain | Finance domains | | |
| | | | |
		Corporate finance	Banking	Security markets
Regulation	Protection of minority shareholders Co-determination Takeover restrictions	Branching restrictions Bank supervision Generalized moratoria and bailouts Bankruptcy code Deposit insurance	Insider trading code Information disclosure for public companies Opening to foreign competition
Specific interventions	Takeover prevention Privatization	Individual bank bailouts or closures Individual company bailouts	Enforcement of security markets regulation

Source: Pagano and Volpin (2001), p. 505.

Figure 3.1 Politics and finance: a road map

non-controlling shareholders, creditors, employees, managers and so on) largely drives the evolution of regulation and policy intervention.

For example, within the OECD there certainly appears an interesting trade-off between employee protection as a proxy for a *stakeholder* approach (rather strong in, for example, Germany and France), and *shareholder* protection (strong in, for example, the USA and the UK). Such differences illustrate how particular interests have influenced broad regulatory regimes and may guide specific policy interventions in specific countries. The question arises, however, whether countries can be neatly classified in boxes, given the complexity of each nation's set of relevant institutions and the sophisticated interactions among a large number of economic actors. For example, Japan has a relationship-based financial system with an important role played by banks, but also a well-developed equity capital market. The USA and the UK are both classified as liberal market economies, but agency problems in the USA in the form of managerial protection mechanisms such as poison-pills and 'corporate board entrenchment devices' are much more severe than in the UK (Mayer and Sussman, 2001).

INSTITUTIONAL IMPACTS ON FIRM-LEVEL CAPITAL STRUCTURE

Substantial empirical evidence demonstrates that firms in different countries indeed have different capital structures and that these differences are to some extent related to institutional variation across countries (see Chui et al., 2002 and Mansi and Reeb, 2002 for recent overviews). Rajan and Zingales (1998b and 2001) suggest a difference between market-based and relationship-based systems, much in line with the analysis above that made a distinction between liberal and coordinated market economies. The former are built on explicit, transparent contracts, which are enforceable in courts. In the latter, financiers who may be owners, lenders, suppliers or customers, benefit from institutionalized isolating mechanisms that allow substantial control over the firm. This control may take the form of regulation (as in the case of restrictions on hostile takeovers) or absence of transparency and lack of public disclosure of financial information. Here, long-term relationships and the associated reputation effects permit the financing system to function without extensive use of contracts or the guaranteed enforcement thereof by courts.

In terms of capital structure decisions, the differences between both systems are that the relationship-based approach permits 'intertemporal cross-subsidization', that is, a long-term rather than a short-term perspective on performance. This implies the acceptance of short-term losses if compensated by expected long-term gains.

Wald (1999), extending the work by Rajan and Zingales (1995), performed a comparative analysis of capital structures in the USA, the UK, France, Germany and Japan. Rajan and Zingales (1995) had previously conducted a comparative analysis of capital structures in the G7 countries, namely the USA, the UK, Canada, France, Germany, Italy and Japan. They found, *inter alia*, that major differences do exist among countries as regards the role of banks *vis-à-vis* financial markets. These differences, however, were found to affect primarily the type of debt used (relative importance of arm's-length financing, that is, security issues *vis-à-vis* bank loans), rather than the relative importance of debt.

Wald (1999) based his analysis on a sample of 4404 firms. He used the 1993 Worldscope database (as well as data from the ten previous years), excluding public utilities and finance companies. He used the ratio of long-term debt to book value of assets as the dependent variable. This measure of the capital structure was chosen because of its relative stability over time as compared to the total debt/assets ratio.[1] For the five countries, the ratios found were the following: 0.185 (USA); 0.098 (UK); 0.145 (France); 0.088 (Germany); 0.155 (Japan). He tried to explain this variable by several ratios measuring financial distress costs, moral hazard, tax deductions, profitability, growth and size. Each of these variables had been proven to significantly affect the debt/assets ratio in earlier, US-based empirical research.

First, financial distress costs refer to the fact that in the presence of bankruptcy costs a higher variance in earnings (measured here as the standard deviation of the first differences in the ratio of earnings before interest and taxes (EBIT) divided by total assets) will be associated with a lower debt ratio. A higher risk of bankruptcy leads to less debt.

Second, moral hazard refers to the danger faced by creditors that a firm will engage in risky investments or under-investment after issuing debt; here, the presence of tangible assets in the form of physical plants and equipment is supposed to mitigate both problems. In contrast, high expenditures on intangible assets, especially R&D, are supposed to have the opposite effect: such expenditures will decrease the long-term debt ratio.

Third, the presence of tax deductions other than those related to debt may reduce firm-level needs for tax deduction through debt.

Fourth, a higher profitability is expected to lead to a lower debt ratio, in accordance with Myers and Mailuf's (1984) pecking-order hypothesis: internal financing is preferred to avoid information asymmetry-related problems when dealing with external parties.

Fifth, firms with high sales growth are also assumed to use less debt.

Sixth, larger firms may face lower transaction costs when issuing long-term debt than smaller firms, and can therefore be expected to have a higher debt ratio.

The international comparison among five countries confirms some of the above hypotheses, but also leads to a number of results that deviate from the expectations. A few of the most interesting results are described below.

First, in the UK and Japan, a higher variance in earnings is associated with higher, not lower, debt. The most likely explanation for the Japanese case is that the firms most engaged in networks are able to take higher risks and increase debt to finance risky investments. Relational monitoring by the *keiretsu* and a limited number of creditors reduces potential control transfer problems after bankruptcy and may even reduce the probability of actual bankruptcy occurrence. This would be consistent with the varieties-of-capitalism analysis in the previous section. The same result for the UK, a liberal market economy, can unfortunately not be explained in this way.

Second, as regards moral hazard, higher investments in physical plant and equipment are indeed associated with a higher debt ratio in each country considered. Here, the varieties of capitalism do not appear to have a significant impact on this expected relation.

Third, ultimately, differences in non-debt taxation regimes (for example, depreciation allowances) appear to have little statistically significant impact on capital structure, thereby again suggesting the limited impact of varieties of capitalism on firm capital structure.

Fourth, a higher profitability indeed leads to a lower debt ratio in each of the five countries, confirming the pecking-order hypothesis. The 'institutional divergence'-based explanation provided by the author for the observed differences in magnitude of this effect among countries does not appear particularly convincing.

Fifth, only in the USA does higher growth imply a lower long-term debt ratio. In all other countries the opposite holds. For Japan this could be explained again by the functioning of many firms, in *keiretsu* networks, with effective relational monitoring. In Germany networking relationships with large banks could account for this result. But the UK outcome appears again more difficult to explain in a context of liberal versus coordinated market economies. In fact, the diverging result for the USA can likely be explained simply by the abundance of cheap capital (especially venture capital) available to high-growth companies as compared to all other nations.

Sixth, only in the German case does larger firm size imply a lower long-term debt ratio. This may be related to the German variety of capitalism where banks have historically acted as controlling shareholders, and have engaged in relational monitoring in many large companies such as Siemens and the former Daimler–Benz group. But if the concentration of power to control firms in Germany as opposed to the control dilution in the USA were instrumental to keeping debts low, why then is a similar outcome not found for Japan?

The world economy consists of more than just liberal market economies within the Anglo-Saxon tradition and coordinated market economies of the German banking type or Japanese *keiretsu* type. The question arises whether the choice of financial structure in developing countries would follow a partic-ular pattern found in particular developed economies.

Booth et al. (2001) attempted to answer this question for a sample of ten developing countries, namely India, Pakistan, Thailand, Malaysia, Turkey, Zimbabwe, Mexico, Brazil, Jordan and Korea. They studied time series data (1980–91) collected by the International Finance Corporation (IFC) on the largest publicly traded companies in each country and ended up with a mini-mum of 38 and a maximum of 99 firms for the various countries. They analyzed the determinants of different proxies for capital structure and care-fully dealt with several data-related and methodological problems in their models.

A first interesting observation in their study is that:

> there can be no simple 'matching' of countries into neat, self-contained boxes. [The] sample, of developing countries encompasses too wide a range of institutional char-acteristics. Therefore, it is not surprising [to find] no strong relation between measures of bank and stock market development, broad macro-economic factors, and aggregate capital structures for developing countries. (Booth et al., 2001, p. 96)

In contrast, their findings suggest common explanations for the choice of capital structure largely unrelated to specific institutions. For example, when comparing countries (the ten developing countries and the G7 economies), a higher equity market capitalization appears to have a positive effect on the relative use of equity, whereas a more developed debt market stimulates the relative use of private market debt. In addition, the use of debt is higher where it is given a more favorable tax status.

At the micro-level in each country, similar non-institution-related findings appear: for example, a higher profitability systematically leads to a higher rela-tive use of equity, and this conclusion holds for all countries except Zimbabwe. The underlying reasons for this are not entirely clear. High profitability may be a route to escape from poorly functioning long-term bond markets and related information asymmetries and transaction costs (pecking order hypothesis), it may reflect intangible growth opportunities against which it is difficult to borrow (agency problem), or it may simply lead to less demand for debt (poten-tially an agency problem). Another interesting observation is that firms with more tangible assets use more long-term debt (in line with conventional agency cost thinking), but have a declining overall debt ratio (in line with the conven-tional maturity-matching concept and the idea that firms should borrow less against long-term assets than short-term assets). According to the authors, such results demonstrate that 'the "normal" independent variables are significant and have similar explanatory power' (Booth et al., 2001, p. 112), although they recognize that the magnitude, and for some parameters even the sign, of the effect may be different across countries.

Finally, the authors develop a model in which the data from the various developing countries are pooled. They demonstrate that firm-specific factors help to explain capital structure: smaller firms with higher profitability, paying more taxes (measured by the average tax rate, likely another proxy for profitability) and having a more substantial share of tangible assets, also have a lower total debt ratio. As regards the long-term debt ratio, larger firms with higher profitability, paying more taxes and having a lower share of tangible assets, have a lower total debt ratio. However, country-specific factors (measured in their model by simple dummy variables) appear equally important. In fact, the relative importance of both sets of factors appears to vary in function of the dependent variable taken as a proxy for capital structure. More specifically, the long-term market debt ratio is explained better by firm-level financial variables, whereas country-level variables are more informative for the total debt and long-term book debt ratios.

To conclude, Wald's (1999) and Booth et al.'s (2001) analyses indeed demonstrate that capital structures and their determinants are not identical across countries. However, these studies also show that the varieties-of-capitalism approach, which builds on the fundamental distinction between liberal and coordinated market economies, contributes little to our understanding of what probably constitutes the single most important governance decision in business firms, namely the choice of capital structure. The Booth et al. (2001) study in particular suggests the partial 'portability' of (effective) financial management decisions on capital structure across borders, even from developed countries to developing countries. Country-specific institutional factors remain critical but do not lend themselves to simple conceptual modeling that would permit a classification of countries in rather straightforward and easily understandable categories such as liberal market economies and coordinated market economies.

Building upon the above analysis, Figure 3.2 represents four different views on the determinants of capital structure. Here, the vertical axis makes a distinction between a weak and a strong impact of country-specific factors, especially national institutions, on capital structure, whereas the horizontal axis distinguishes between weak and strong requirements imposed by the globalization of financial markets, driven by phenomena such as the growth of the eurocurrency markets, the cross listing of shares and so on.

Quadrant 2 of Figure 3.2 represents the conventional view of finance as a firm-level process, driven by micro-efficiency considerations and specific relationships between the firm and third parties in the function of variables such as the importance of tangible assets and growth opportunities. This view

Global financial market requirements

	Weak	Strong

Strong	Varieties of capitalism	'Transnationalism' (appropriate national responsiveness – integration mix)
National institutional drivers	Firm-level efficiency drivers (e.g., pecking-order approach)	Global spread of US capitalism
Weak		

Figure 3.2   Determinants of capital structure

is exemplified by concepts such as the pecking-order hypothesis (Myers and Majluf, 1984) and various strands of the agency cost approach (Jensen and Meckling, 1976; Jensen, 1986; Stultz, 1990; Berger et al., 1997).

Quadrant 1 reflects the varieties-of-capitalism approach: here, national institutions fundamentally determine the capital structure selected by firms. For example, financial systems dominated by banks are characterized by banks as large providers of both equity and debt, and firms select their capital structure in function of the banks' needs to reduce the agency problems, information asymmetries and related transaction costs they face.

In quadrant 4 we find the opposite situation: it represents the alleged global spread of US-led capitalism driven by a prime focus on shareholder market value. Substantial transparency and disclosure of all relevant financial information, and arm's-length relationships with shareholders and creditors characterize this approach. The alleged efficiency characteristics of this approach tend to eliminate historically grown, prevailing practices in individual nations, thereby leading to global convergence in financial management approaches. If this convergence occurs only slowly it is primarily because of the entrenched positions of a number of economic actors in segmented and illiquid markets that would incur substantial micro-level costs from moving toward a more efficient macro-level structure.

Finally, quadrant 3 represents the approach adopted by modern multi-national business finance (Eiteman et al., 2000). Here, firms, especially

MNEs, attempt to take advantage at the micro-level of access to financing options available outside the home country, especially those provided by integrated international capital markets. The requirement of globalization is not to emulate US-based practices, but to adopt best practices irrespective of their origin. This view is explained in more depth in the next section. It is consistent with Booth et al.'s (2001) observation that both mainstream finance theories, suggestive of economic efficiency, and country-level institutional factors, contributing to the firm's administrative heritage, are important.

This quadrant 3 perspective also prevails in the area of modern venture capital financing. Venture capital financing is almost by definition relationship-based as financing decisions are made largely on the basis of trust in an entrepreneur's ability to deliver the promises outlined in a formal business plan and debated during a number of public and more private presentations. Here, trust is assumed to compensate for the financier's relative lack of knowledge on the viability of the venture. The creation of trust may very much be influenced by local customs, the financier's prior experience with other ventures, location-bound perspectives on 'what is hot and what is not', much in line with a strong impact of local institutions. However, once the financing has occurred, the venture capitalist has an incentive to 'structure' the venture in such a way that the liquidity of his investment is enhanced, that is, that future exit is made possible. This implies structuring the venture according to global capital market requirements so as to facilitate the transition toward becoming a publicly traded company: such transition, which may involve foreign investors, must build on professionalizing management, achieving maximum transparency in the finance function and guaranteeing adequate disclosure of financial information. Quadrant 3 thus implies the simultaneous use of relationship-based elements and arm's-length elements to permit an optimal expansion pattern of new economic activities with high-growth potential.

VARIETIES OF CAPITALISM IN THE CONTEXT OF MULTINATIONAL BUSINESS FINANCE

The above analysis has suggested that the varieties-of-capitalism approach suffers from a rather superficial perspective on the potential role of international business in the development of national institutions and structural interdependencies across nations. We have established that both the heritage of national, institutional parameters and global finance requirements need to be taken into account to explain micro-level financial decisions. The question then arises what drivers can improve the international competitiveness of a national financial system and the firms that operate in it. Here, it is surprising to observe that Hall and Soskice (2001) did not include in their study any serious analysis of the functioning of MNEs. MNEs, defined as firms with value added operations in at least two countries, now dominate world trade and investment. More importantly, the share of foreign MNEs in domestic manufacturing and service provision is increasing in all OECD countries (perhaps with the exception of Germany in the recent past). The relative importance of foreign MNEs in domestic industrial production ranges from less than 2 percent in Japan to 70 percent in Ireland and Hungary, with most European countries experiencing foreign control over 25 percent to 30 percent of industrial production. In the USA, foreign participation now represents 18 percent (all data for 1998). In most countries (with the exception of the Netherlands, Norway and Poland) these investments are primarily in high-technology sectors (OECD, 2001). With such high percentages of foreign involvement in domestic economies, foreign MNEs have a substantial impact on domestic governance structures and international structural interdependencies, especially as regards finance, because of the mobility of capital and these firms' access to integrated capital markets.

A complementary approach to assess the importance of international pressures, for both firm-level behavior and the creation of structural interdependencies across countries, is to investigate the presence of large foreign rivals in the same industry. The existence of such 'global' rivals (even if they have a weak position in a particular's firm home market) imposes the need for continuous benchmarking of organizational and financial practices, at both the micro- and macro-levels. Table 3.1, from Franko (2002, p. 27) demonstrates the importance of international benchmarking in most industries. It shows, by identifying the 12 largest firms in each industry according to the Fortune 'Global 50', that most economic sectors (with the exception of computer software) are characterized by strong rivals from a number of different nations. The presence of such rivals suggests two things: first, that international benchmarking will occur at the micro-level, and second, that such benchmarking taking place in many industries simultaneously will ultimately increase structural interdependencies across nations at the macro-level, especially if the large rivals penetrate each other's markets through foreign direct investment, especially in the context of strategic asset seeking investments.

Hall and Soskice's (2001) work appears largely a reinterpretation, from an institutionalist perspective, of Porter's (1990) diamond of national competitive advantage, which has been discredited in an enormous body of conceptual and empirical research (see Rugman and Verbeke, 1998, 2001a; Davies and Ellis, 2000 for representative work in this area). Even the visual representation in 'diamond format' of their institutional framework seems to have been borrowed straight from Porter's (1990) diamond model. Porter's (1990) diamond approach argues that four elements, and the interactions among them,

Table 3.1   Changes in the world market share, major industries, 1990–2000 (Numbers of firms and % of consolidated worldwide sales of top 12 largest companies in each industry, by home country)

	Number of firms		% of sales	
	1990	2000	1990	2000
Aerospace				
USA	9	8	79	77
Europe	3	3	21	18
Canada	0	1	0	5
Autos and trucks				
USA	3	2	38	36
Europe	6	6	38	39
Japan	3	4	23	26
Banking				
USA	0	3	0	25
Europe	5	7	33	53
Japan	7	2	67	22
Building materials				
USA	3	3	13	17
Europe	6	7	61	67
Japan	1	2	17	16
Australia	2	0	9	0
Chemicals				
USA	3	2	23	23

	Number of firms		% of sales	
	1990	2000	1990	2000
Nonferrous metals				
USA	2	2	19	26
Europe	5	4	51	38
Japan	3	3	16	19
Canada	2	2	15	13
Chile	0	1	0	3
Non-electrical machinery (indus. & farm equipment)				
USA	3	4	29	36
Europe	5	3	42	24
Japan	4	5	29	40
Paper & forest products				
USA	7	6	61	65
Europe	3	4	24	23
Japan	0	2	0	12
Other	2	0	16	0
Petroleum & products				
USA	5	4	47	35
Europe	5	5	45	50
Japan	0	0	0	0
Venezuela	1	1	4	6

Europe	8	7	72	60
Japan	1	3	4	16
Computers & office equipment				
USA	7	9	73	75
Europe	2	0	7	0
Japan	3	3	18	25
Computer software				
USA	11	11	95	91
Europe	1	1	5	9
Electricals & electronics				
USA	1	3	15	29
Japan	6	6	48	50
Europe	5	2	36	16
Korea	0	1	0	6
Food, beverages & tobacco				
USA	7	6	52	50
Europe	5	5	47	43
Japan	0	1	0	6
Iron & steel				
USA	0	1	0	4
Europe	6	5	51	47
Japan	5	5	44	42
Korea	1	1	5	7

P.R. China	1	1	0	5
Mexico	0	1	0	4
Brazil	1	0	4	0
Pharmaceuticals				
USA	6	7	49	62
Europe	6	5	51	38
Printing & publishing				
USA	4	4	26	24
Europe	3	4	26	37
Japan	2	2	23	25
Canada	2	2	14	15
Australia	1	0	11	0
Textiles & apparel				
USA	3	6	21	49
Europe	2	2	16	14
Japan	5	4	42	37
Other	2	0	21	0
Tires (n = 9)				
USA	1	2	20	25
Europe	3	3	35	37
Japan	4	4	37	37
Other	1	0	7	0

Source: Franko (2002, p. 27).

fundamentally determine the international competitiveness of specific industries: these four elements are factor conditions (with a focus on specialized, created factors such as skilled labor), demand conditions (with an emphasis on market sophistication rather than size), related and supporting industries, and finally, strategy, structure and rivalry. The problem with Porter's diamond is the assumption that competitive advantage is created at home in a first stage, without involvement of foreign MNEs. Only in a second stage can firms expand internationally, but always building upon their home base where all key strategic decisions are taken. Hall and Soskice (2001) make the same mistake: they also assume that firms are fundamentally conditioned by home-country institutions, and that they can tap only selectively into host-country diamonds to take advantage of these countries' institutional strengths.

The reality is that many MNEs, especially those coming from small open economies, need to take on board from the outset the diamond determinants and firm-level practices prevailing in large trading partners (Van Den Bulcke and Verbeke, 2001). For example, most managers of large Canadian exporting firms and MNEs pay enormous attention to USA's diamond determinants, given that the USA market is ten times larger than the Canadian one. The same holds in the EU where, for example, firms from Belgium need to emulate behavior viewed as legitimate in countries such as France, Germany, the UK and the Netherlands. It could be argued that these firms still face a substantial 'liability of foreignness' as compared to insiders in these larger markets. In other words, paying attention to foreign diamond determinants does not in itself confer the same competitive advantages benefiting insiders in large nations. However, foreign direct investment precisely allows to bridge institutional differences and to become an insider in foreign nations, thereby also increasing structural interdependencies among the countries affected.

Multinational business finance builds on the observation that many national financing systems are characterized by inefficiencies. This observation does not just reflect a US-based mindset that arm's-length systems are devoid of problems and should be emulated by all other nations (for example, managerial capitalism may lead to empire-building and major agency problems, as illustrated by the Enron and WorldCom examples). Rather, it constitutes the basis of an attempt to identify the strengths and weaknesses of each national system to resolve specific financing problems. For example, there are clear disadvantages of relationship-based systems in highly developed capital markets. Irrespective of national institutions' historical trajectories, relationship-based financing is useful to firms when they face temporary difficulties that negatively affect their cash flows. It is also useful when firms invest in new, potentially highly profitable but also risky business opportunities with substantial intangible assets, poorly understood by – or even unknown to – outside financiers in underdeveloped financial markets. When markets are underdeveloped, relationship-based financing substitutes for the institutions necessary to make markets function properly (Rajan and Zingales, 1998a). However, in highly developed and competitive capital markets, relationship-based financing may lead to ignoring market performance in order not to upset relationships, even in the absence of long-term growth or profit compensation (Weinstein and Yafeh, 1998). In fact, this system may even have the perverse effect of diverting resources away from profitable opportunities abroad (from a financier's perspective) toward less attractive, but more strongly relationship-based financing requests domestically (Peek and Rosengren, 1998). In highly developed capital markets, relationship-based financing thus suffers from poor responses to price signals (thereby affecting the quality of future price signals), low financial information disclosure (which may reduce innovation and entrepreneurship) and illiquidity of financial assets and relationships (Rajan and Zingales, 2001). The point is that any expected benefits of intertemporal cross-subsidization are largely outweighed by the costs of not responding appropriately to price signals and by the lack of appropriate financial disclosure.

Hall and Soskice's (2001) analysis would suggest that obvious inefficiencies in relationship-based financing systems would lead to a co-evolution of the various affected institutions toward adapting to the new external environment. In fact, a much more effective instrument to achieve the needed adaptation may be to allow the massive entry of foreign MNEs, which can bring with them global (not necessarily home-country) best practices, thereby facilitating changes in formal regulation, in selective policy interventions and, most importantly, in the cognitive and strategic perceptions of the domestic economic actors affected. Such foreign entry may thus be instrumental to realizing the intentional strategic upgrading/reengineering of national institutions, and to directly influencing structural interdependencies across countries.

The above analysis is visualized in Figure 3.3 on the key drivers of institutional change. Here, the vertical axis on the internal drivers of national institutional change makes a distinction between the co-evolution of national institutions and the strategic upgrading/reengineering of these institutions. The horizontal axis measures the role of MNEs (both domestic and foreign) in the institutional change process; this role can be weak or strong.

The varieties-of-capitalism approach is clearly positioned in quadrant 2: strategic interactions among interested economic actors operating in domestic networks lead to the co-evolution of various relevant institutions, including governance mechanisms, when exogenous opportunities/threats demand change. The international character of MNEs, whether domestic or foreign, is not viewed as a critical driver of institutional change.

In contrast, Porter's (1990) diamond framework, which is positioned in quadrant 1, assumes the possibility of intentional strategic upgrading of diamond components, but also of the institutions that guide the interactions

Impact of MNE activities

	None/Weak	Strong
Strategic upgrading	Porter's diamond approach	Rugman and Verbeke (1990, 1998, 2001a)
Domestic institutional drivers		
Co-evolution of national institutions	Varieties of capitalism approach	institutional competition

Figure 3.3   Drivers of national institutional change

among these components, for example through business–government co-operation to advance the skill levels of specialized workers. In Porter's model, MNEs do not perform an important role in the upgrading process.

Quadrant 4 represents the opposite of Porter's (1990) approach, namely an institutional competition scenario: national or sub-national governments and related agencies try to attract foreign direct investment, which is viewed as the most efficient instrument to achieve rapid economic upgrading, and to overcome the inertia prevailing in national institutions. To some extent, this is characteristic of the situation in several Eastern European countries and developing nations, which are attempting to attract massive entries by foreign MNEs to stimulate economic growth and diversification. An interesting observation in this context is that entry of MNEs in developing countries is often followed by a substantial rise in bank loans extended by multinational banks (Weller and Scher, 2001).

Finally, quadrant 3 represents a more balanced approach. It recognizes the major role played by inward and outward investment in domestic cluster upgrading (Rugman and Verbeke, 1990; Van Den Bulcke and Verbeke, 2001), but also the need for domestic actors to design a coherent development program. Such a program should focus on attracting and developing best practices as a response to business needs rather than merely emulating a foreign system of institutions that would largely neglect the existing domestic institutional heritage and would therefore likely fail.

The above approach at the macro-level is mirrored in terms of firm-level strategy. MNEs should make use of the 'supermarket' for capital and try to overcome the market imperfections characterizing illiquid and segmented domestic markets (Baldwin, 1986). In the presence of strong international competition, firms must match their rivals' cost of capital and effective tax rates, irrespective of these rivals' nationalities (Lessard, 1986). For example, Mansi and Reeb (2002) found that US MNEs benefit from a 52 basis point reduction in the cost of debt financing as compared to US domestic companies and that substantial levels of international activity are associated with an increase in the debt ratio. This reflects the direct ability MNEs to arbitrage segmented markets (or to have easier access to integrated capital markets), and perhaps indirectly the benefit of more stable cash flows as a result of operating in multiple, imperfectly correlated markets (see Errunza and Senbet, 1981, 1984; Reeb et al., 2001).

It is important to understand the great danger of relying on national institutions for adequate financing. The case probably best known by ten thousands of business school graduates throughout the world is the 20-year-old Novo Industry A/S case, described in Eiteman et al. (2000, pp. 313–21) and based on Stonehill and Dullum (1982). It shows how a Danish company in industrial enzymes and pharmaceuticals was hindered in its expansion by the highly illiquid and segmented Danish market (in 1977) and then decided to internationalize its capital structure and sources of funds. This internationalization process became a major success but also implied that the firm had to respond to the requirements of international capital markets, for example, as regards the optimal debt ratio, rather than merely to Danish institutional demands.

A final and related question is whether MNE foreign affiliates should adopt a capital structure in line with institutional expectations in host countries or on the contrary should display the structure that most benefits the MNE's internal network. Eiteman et al.'s (2000, p. 329) answer is that the MNE benefits from important information and international networking advantages as compared to domestic firms, allowing them to exploit differences in national financial markets: 'Why should it throw away these important competitive advantages to conform to local norms that are established in response to imperfect local capital markets, historical precedent, and institutional constraints that do not apply to the MNE?'

The authors further prescribe that MNEs should attempt to conform to host-country debt norms so as to avoid penalties (whether in immediate monetary costs or in terms of more difficult networking relationships in that country). However, this conformity should only be 'cosmetic': financiers ultimately look at the MNE's overall financial performance and want to be satisfied that the firm has the best possible financial structure at the global level, not at the individual host-country level. For example, localized opportunities to lower the cost of debt (for example, through government subsidies) should be exploited to the fullest, but subsequent internal fund flows in the MNE should, obviously without violating regulatory constraints, be driven by internal network requirements, not by host-country institutional expectations.

CONCLUSIONS

This chapter on the implications of the varieties-of-capitalism approach for multinational business finance leads to five important conclusions.

First, the focus on macro-level institutions, and the interactions among them, should be welcomed. Financial management is not conducted in an institutional vacuum and dominated by universally accepted micro-level practices; for example, the choice of capital structure does vary across countries. More importantly, clear links exist between financial systems and the economic growth of particular industries (Rajan and Zingales, 1998b).

Second, there are two key difficulties associated with the varieties-of-capitalism approach. The first is the lack of clarity regarding the relevant set of institutions to consider. Hall and Soskice (2001) identify five types of key institutions, but some scholars focus on the legal system, others on the development of banking and financial markets and still others on cultural factors. If the relevant set of institutions cannot somehow be determined *ex ante*, everything can be explained *ex post* by 'institutions'. The second key difficulty relates to the use of *ad hoc* models without predictive ability and, more importantly, without a clearly articulated set of independent variables to explain phenomena such as differences in capital structures among nations and firms. Such models will do little to advance scientific knowledge in this domain.

Third, the absence of attention to MNEs and international business activities in general in the varieties-of-capitalism approach is not only surprising but shocking. How can scholars make statements on so-called 'conventional views on globalization' when they completely neglect all relevant literature that has been written in this area for at least the past 30 years, and exemplified by the research published, *inter alia*, in the key scholarly journal in this field, the *Journal of International Business Studies*?

Fourth, all firms build on a particular administrative heritage of interacting with domestic institutions in the domain of finance, but they also need to take on board global financial requirements, especially if they aim to take advantage of the opportunities provided by international financial markets. This is not a plea in favor of emulating US-based capitalism, but a prescription to adopt best global practices in financial management, irrespective of their geographic origin, as a complement to practices arising from the firm's national administrative heritage.

Fifth, national governments and related public agencies would be ill advised to rely on the natural co-evolution of domestic institutions as the key driver for adaptation to globalization requirements. If institutional change is to benefit society at large, other elements are required than interactions among self-interested economic actors that would follow game-theory prescriptions. Effective leadership to upgrade/reengineer national institutions is the key to success. Effective leadership requires clear choices by public policymakers to emulate best practices developed elsewhere, for example in the area of financial disclosure. It also implies acknowledging the major role that MNEs, both domestic and foreign, can play in this change process.

NOTES

1. Even the chosen measure is obviously associated with measurement problems. More specifically, accounting definitions of what constitutes long-term debt and assets may differ across countries. Here, it is important to note that long-term debt in Germany is restricted to periods 'over four years', leading to a lower long-term debt/assets ratio than in other countries.

REFERENCES

Baldwin, C.Y. (1986), 'The capital factor; competing for capital in a global environment', in M.E. Porter (ed.), *Competition in Global Industries*, Boston, MA: Harvard Business School Press.

Bartlett, C.A. and S. Ghoshal (1989), *Managing Across Borders: The Transnational Solution*, Boston, MA: Harvard Business School Press.

Berger, P., E. Ofek and D. Yermack (1997), 'Managerial entrenchment and capital structure decisions', *Journal of Finance*, **50**, 1411–30.

Booth, L., V. Aivazian, A. Demirguc-Kunt and V. Maksimovic (2001), 'Capital structures in developing countries', *Journal of Finance*, **56**, 87–130.

Brouthers, L.E., S. Werner and E. Matulich (2000), 'The influence of triad nations' environments on price-quality product strategies and MNC performance', *Journal of International Business Studies*, **31**(1), 39–62.

Chui, A.C.W., A.E. Lloyd and C.C.Y. Kwok (2002), 'The determination of capital structure: is national culture a missing piece to the puzzle?', *Journal of International Business Studies*, **33**(1), 99–127,

Davies, H. and P. Ellis (2000), 'Porter's competitive advantage of nations: time for the final judgement', *Journal of Management Studies*, **37**(8), 1189–213.

Eiteman, D.K., A.I. Stonehill and M.H. Moffett (2000), *Multinational Business Finance*, 9th edn, Boston, MA: Addison Wesley.

Errunza, V. and L. Senbet (1981), 'The effects of international operations on market value of the firm: theory and evidence', *Journal of Finance*, **36**, 401–17.

Errunza, V. and L. Senbet (1984), International corporate diversification, market valuation and size-adjusted evidence', *Journal of Finance*, **34**, 727–45.

Franko, L.G. (2002), 'Global competition in the 1990s: American renewal, Japanese resilience, European cross-currents', *Business Horizons*, **45**, May–June, 25–38.

Hall, P.A. and D. Soskice (2001), *Varieties of Capitalism: The Institutional Foundations of Comparative Advantage*, Oxford: Oxford University Press.

Jensen, M.C. (1986), 'Agency costs of free cash flow, corporate finance and takeovers', *American Economic Review*, **76**, 323–39.

Jensen, M. and W. Meckling (1976), 'Theory of the firm: managerial behaviour, agency costs and ownership structure', *Journal of Financial Economics*, **3**, 305–60.

Knetter, M. (1989), 'Price discrimination by US and German exporters', *American Economic Review*, **79**(1), 198–210.

Laporta, R., F. Lopez de Silanes and A. Shleifer (1999), 'Corporate ownership around the world', *Journal of Finance*, **54**(2), 471–517.

Laporta, R., F. Lopez de Silanes, A. Shleifer, and R. Vishny (1998), 'Law and finance', *The Journal of Political Economy*, **106**, 1113–55.

Lessard, D.R. (1986), 'Finance and global competition: exploiting financial scope and coping with volatile exchange rates', in M.E. Porter (ed.), *Competition in Global Industries*, Boston, MA: Harvard Business School Press.

Mansi, S.A. and D.M. Reeb (2002), 'Corporate international activity and debt financing', *Journal of International Business Studies*, **33**(1), 129–47.

Mayer, C. and O. Sussman (2001), 'The assessment: finance, law, and growth', *Oxford Review of Economic Policy*, **17**(4), 457–65.

Modigliani, F. and M. Miller (1958), 'The cost of capital, corporation finance and the theory of investment', *American Economic Review*, **48**, 261–97.

Myers, S.C. and N.S. Majluf (1984), 'Corporate financing and investment decisions when firms have information that investors do not have', *Journal of Financial Economics*, **13**, 187–221.

North, D.C. (1990), *Institutions, Institutional Change and Economic Performance*, New York: Cambridge University Press.

OECD (2001), *Measuring Globalisation: The Role of Multinationals in Economies*, Paris: Organisation for Economic Co-operation and Development.

Pagano, M. and P. Volpin (2001), 'The political economy of finance', *Oxford Review of Economic Policy*, **17**(4), 502–19.

Peek, J. and E.S. Rosengren (1998), 'The international transmission of financial shocks: the case of Japan', *American Economic Review*, **87**(4), 495–505.

Porter, M.E. (1990), *The Competitive Advantage of Nations*, New York: The Free Press.

Rajan, R.G., and L. Zingales (1995), 'Is there an optimal capital structure? Some evidence from international data', *The Journal of Finance*, **50**, 1421–60.

Rajan, R.G. and L. Zingales (1998a), 'Which capitalism? Lesson from the East Asian crisis', *The Bank of America Journal of Applied Corporate Finance*, **11**(3), 40–8.

Rajan, R.G. and L. Zingales (1998b), 'Financial dependence and growth', *American Economic Review*, **88**, 559–86.

Rajan, R.G. and L. Zingales (2001), 'Financial systems, industrial structure, and growth', *Oxford Review of Economic Policy*, **17**(4), 467–82.

Reeb, D., C. Kwok and Y. Baek (2001), 'Systematic risk in the multinational corporation', *Journal of International Business Studies*, **29**, 263–79.

Rugman, A.M. and A. Verbeke (1990), *Global Corporate Strategy and Trade Policy*, London and New York: Routledge.

Rugman, A.M. and A. Verbeke (1998), 'Multinational enterprises and public policy', *Journal of International Business Studies*, **29**(1), 115–36.

Rugman, A.M. and A. Verbeke (2001a), 'Location, competitiveness, and the multinational enterprise', in A.M. Rugman and T.L. Brewer, *The Oxford Handbook of International Business*, New York: Oxford University Press, pp. 150–80.

Rugman, A.M. and A. Verbeke (2001b), 'Subsidiary specific advantage in multinational enterprises', *Strategic Management Journal*, **22**, 237–50.

Stonehill, A. and K.B. Dullum (1982), *Internationalizing the Cost of Capital in Theory and Practice: The Novo Experience and National Policy Implications*, Copenhagen: Nyt Nordisk Forland Arnold Busck, and New York: Wiley.

Stultz, R. (1990), 'Managerial discretion and optimal financing policies', *Journal of Financial Economics*, **26**, 3–27.

Van Den Bulcke, D. and A. Verbeke (2001), *Globalisation and the Small Open Economy*, Cheltenham, UK and Northampton, USA: Edward Elgar, p. 241.

Wald, J.K. (1999), 'How firm characteristics affect capital structure: an international comparison', *Journal of Financial Research*, **22**, 161–87.

Weinstein, D. and Y. Yafleh (1998), 'On the costs of a bank-centred financial system: evidence from the changing main bank relations in Japan', *Journal of Finance*, **53**, 635–72.

Weller, C.E. and M. Scher (2001), 'Multinational bank credit in less industrialized economies', *Journal of International Business Studies*, **32**(4), 833–51.

4. Financial institutions and financial markets: the emergence of a new class of universal banks

Jordi Canals

The spread of globalization and deregulation in financial services and the increasing influence of information technologies on the management of financial institutions make up a powerful set of forces that are shaping and will define in a unique way the future of the world financial system and the national financial systems as well.

This combination of forces raises new questions about the evolution of financial systems worldwide. One of the most relevant is the role that financial institutions and, more specifically, banks will have in the financial system of the future. A few years ago, some authors (see Bryan, 1991) predicted the slow but irreversible decline of banks in industrial countries, some of them still beset by their bad economic performance in the 1980s, and all of them under the attack of new competitors from inside and outside the traditional financial system. The banks' most formidable competitor was capital markets.

The unleashing forces of deregulation, stiff competition and technological change in the main financial centers round the world in the late 1980s were appalling. Among other factors, investment banks and brokerage firms were chasing after companies and individual savers alike and propelling formidable growth in capital markets. The traditional intermediation function that banks had performed for centuries was in danger of extinction.

Are banks really losing or going to lose their role in the international financial system? Will capital markets sweep away any influence of traditional financial intermediaries? Will globalization spread the same model of financial system round the world?

These are important questions for a variety of reasons. The main one, however, is that the design of a financial system is not just a matter of interest for financial institutions. A sound financial system performs important functions in a modern society, beyond the allocation of financial resources. A good financial system is key in promoting investment and economic development, and providing stability to the economic system. On the contrary, a deficient financial system creates many problems and dampens the potential growth rate of the economy, as the recent and tragic cases of emerging markets crisis highlight.

Ten years ago, some experts predicted the decline of traditional banks and the increasing power of financial markets. Today the situation is different. As has happened in the past, many banks have reinvented their mission, placing themselves at the forefront of the changes in the financial system. In the past few years, we have seen the emergence of new large financial groups, such as HSBC, Bank America, Citigroup, ABN–AMRO or Crédit Suisse. The main feature of these financial institutions is that they are still banks that perform the traditional function of intermediaries. Nevertheless, many of them have moved beyond that role and have become major players and shapers of the destiny of financial markets.

As a result, it is accurate to say that financial markets are today more important than ever. At the same time, some financial institutions now play an increasingly important role in shaping trends in those financial markets. The interaction between financial institutions and financial markets – which is a special case of the interaction between firms and markets – has changed in the past few years and will keep changing in the new future. Its outcome will be a financial system which is different from what we have today in the western world.

In this chapter, I want to assess the emerging model of universal banks that seems to be fashionable in many industrial countries, including the USA, the UK, Germany and France, and whether this model is sustainable for banks themselves.

This chapter is structured as follows. The next section will describe in detail the strengths and weaknesses of banks-based financial systems in relation to capital-markets-based financial systems, in terms of both the efficiency of the financial system and its stability and regulatory needs. The following section will present and discuss some basic facts about the spread of the universal banking model in the Western world, as a result of diversification decisions taken by many financial institutions. Then follows a review of the main reasons behind the emergence of universal banks, focusing on their advantages and disadvantages. Next the sustainability of universal banks will be raised and discussed. This is an important challenge. If universal banks are here to stay for a long time, there are a number of regulatory challenges that financial authorities should consider. Moreover, universal banks will be sustainable if and only if senior managers learn how to manage a diversified company. In the final section some conclusions will be outlined.

BANKS-BASED FINANCIAL SYSTEMS VERSUS CAPITAL-MARKETS-BASED FINANCIAL SYSTEMS

Modern financial systems can be grouped in two basic financial models: capital-markets-based model and banks-based model. Table 4.1 presents their main features and Table 4.2 offers some quantitative information.

In the capital-markets-based financial model, financial markets have a dominant role; in part, its growth has been fostered by banks. The USA and the UK are the best examples of this model.

In the banks-based model, banks have a stronger influence. This is the case for Germany, France, Spain or Japan. These countries share some common conditions: first, the importance of long-term lending to non-financial companies, second, the slower development of capital markets, third, the significant presence of banks in capital markets as an indirect means of controlling their growth, and finally, the degree of control exercised by banks in the management of non-financial firms through their presence in those companies' boards.

The Capital Markets-based Model

The prime examples of financial systems based on capital markets are those of the USA and the UK.[1] This model basically follows the following pattern.

First, companies get the funding for their investment in capital markets. Second, there is a virtually complete separation between investors acting in capital markets and non-financial companies. The former play no part in managing non-financial companies or in setting their long-term strategy. Their only influence arises from stock prices. Markets-based financial systems provide a constant valuation of securities through price mechanisms. They propel the process of allocating financial resources efficiently between alternative projects competing for the same financing. Furthermore, capital markets provide a means of efficient risk diversification. Investors, not firms, are ultimately responsible for the decisions made in allocating the resources. Well-developed capital markets provide owners of financial assets with a high degree of liquidity.

This model has a number of disadvantages. The first is the difficulty in monitoring and supervising companies due to the fragmentation of company ownership and, hence, the fragmentation of responsibility when shareholders are not clearly involved in the company. The complete separation between capital markets and firms paves the way for the 'free-rider' problem.

Investment banks and rating agencies provide ongoing information about public companies. However, this information may be incomplete or insufficient, as these intermediaries do not always know what is really going on inside the companies concerned.

Table 4.1   Financial models

Models	Countries	Banks as financial intermediaries	Banks as lenders to companies	Banks as shareholders	Banks as strategic shareholders
I. Banks-based models					
• Specialized banks	USA UK	Yes	No	No	No
• Universal banks	Germany Spain France Italy	Yes	Yes	Yes	No
• Conglomerate groups	Germany Japan Spain	Yes	Yes	Yes	Yes
II. Capital-markets-based models	USA UK	Yes	No	No	No

Source: Canals (1997).

Table 4.2   Financial structure in the euro area, the USA and Japan (1999)

	Unit	Euro area	USA	Japan
Bank deposits	€bn	4752.2	4 742.8	4467.5
	% of GDP	77.8	55.2	111.7
Bank loans	€bn	6136.1	4 154.8	4280.8
	% of GDP	100.4	48.4	107.0
Outstanding domestic	€bn	5422.7	14 140.8	5061.1
debt securities	% of GDP	88.8	164.6	126.5
Stock market	€bn	4346.0	13 861.1	6275.8
capitalization	% of GDP	71.1	163.3	137.7

Source: Belaisch et al. (2001).

Capital markets are also affected by agency problems. Agency problems can be partly solved by incentives that help correct inappropriate behavior in using this information, such as management compensation, which takes into account certain key variables. However, no matter how sophisticated the incentives are, it is obvious that design variables have advantages and disadvantages and that none will ever be precisely targeted enough unfailingly to induce a particular type of behavior (Milgrom and Roberts, 1992). In the final analysis, one cannot forget that incentives are necessary but insufficient. Without a clear ethical mindset and behavior, even the best-designed incentive system will eventually fail, as has been shown by recent events in the USA and Europe.

The Banks-based Model

This financial model is not uniform but allows for a great number of possibilities. We will discuss two. The first is the system in which banking plays a major role in non-financial firms, as in Germany, France or Spain.

The second type is found in those countries where the share of banks in total corporate financing is high but consists mainly of short- or long-term lending, not of large holdings in companies' equity. The prototype of this model would be Japan.

Banks as financial intermediaries obtain financial resources from savers by issuing deposits or other financial instruments and channel these resources towards companies that need them to finance their investments. However, this view of financial intermediation seems to have been overtaken by the growing sophistication of financial markets in recent years.

A new approach to financial intermediation has recently emerged (Allen and Santomero, 2001). It explains the existence of banks in terms of the asymmetric information and moral hazard problems that arise between savers and companies that receive funds from them. Savers usually have incomplete information about companies. This makes it more difficult for companies to obtain the funding that they need.

Bank intermediation may mitigate those problems. In fact, when the cost to the providers of financial resources of acquiring information on companies is high, the process of financing companies may be carried out more efficiently if prospective investors delegate the task of obtaining this information to a specialized firm (Diamond, 1984). Therefore, financial intermediation can be justified on the grounds of the information collection and company-monitoring functions that banks can perform.

Moreover, the delegation of this function to banks has significant advantages. Information-gathering is associated with substantial fixed costs that can be absorbed by a greater volume of operations. Therefore, an important aspect of financial intermediation is that banks may enjoy significant economies of scale in information collection and processing (Hellwig, 1991). Besides, banks may be better placed to solve asymmetric information problems and thus reduce transaction costs resulting from the behavior of small shareholders who are not interested in monitoring firms.

Allen (1993) shows that the advantages of financial intermediation over financial markets will depend on the industry concerned and, in particular, on its maturity and degree of technological innovation. In mature markets, with a low level of innovation and, therefore, less uncertainty, financial intermediaries offer clear advantages over capital markets. When there is agreement as to what can and cannot be done to compete in such an industry, banks have advantages over capital markets.[2]

In the case of emerging industries, with significant financial and technological risks, knowledge about the industry is much more unpredictable. In this case, a financial intermediary's opinion will be less reliable. On the other hand, the high volume of information available in financial markets may help to achieve a better allocation of financial resources.

In other words, banks may be the best agents for financing companies' investment or growth projects in consolidated or even mature industries. However, capital markets may obtain better information in the case of emerging industries, where technological, financial and commercial uncertainty is usually greater.

The model based on bank intermediation also has its problems and limitations. The first and most important is the excessive risk accumulated by banks in lending and shareholdings. These holdings were the cause of many bank crises, such as the US crisis in the 1930s, the Spanish crisis in the 1970s and 1980s, or the French crisis in the 1990s.

A second limitation of the banks-based model is that control mechanisms are no longer based on prices set by financial markets but on the bank's ability to monitor the companies with which it has relations. Obviously this requires a much more sophisticated capability and can be a source of rigidity.

Another limitation of the banks-based model is the tendency to overinvest and, therefore, create excess production capacity in industries where companies operate with bank lending. The reason is that the assumption that the company has the continued support of a bank investor may lead to complacency and prolong indefinitely a situation of mediocre management.

Finally, the absence of stricter disciplinary mechanisms such as those provided by capital markets may lead some companies to become complacent. It is always difficult for a bank to pull out of a firm that borrowed money from it.

THE NEW DOMINANT PARADIGM IN BANKING: THE EMERGENCE OF UNIVERSAL BANKS

Some of the largest banks in the world entered the decade of the 1990s with major problems. In the USA, the recession at home and the lasting impact of the Latin American economic crisis, where some US banks had important risks, left banks with some strategic problems and a deteriorated profitability. In Europe, the weakness of the national economies and the coming deregulation of the banking system in the EU raised new threats to the future of European banks.[3] In both regions, new competition coming from insurance firms and capital markets was considered unstoppable.

Today the banking landscape is completely different. Although the world economy was on the brink of a recession in 2001, banks seem to be in reasonably good shape. Moreover, banks have staved off competition coming from financial markets or other financial institutions, have redefined their strategy and are at the epicenter of many changes in the financial system.

Some of the main changes are related to the big consolidation taking place in the national banking industries. Mergers and acquisitions (M&A) have been decisive in reshaping the industry. Although the level of concentration in some countries is still low, most of the big industrial countries have national universal banks able to compete in terms of size in the international arena.

In this section we will describe some major factors behind the transformation experienced by the financial system in recent years and, more specifically, how universal banks have reached the top position in this league. Table 4.3 shows some basic facts about 25 large banks in eight industrial countries, including growth, profitability, market capitalization and internationalization, between 1991 and 2000. All of them can be considered universal banks because, under the same corporate umbrella, they run different business units, all of them in financial services, but with a different structure and a certain degree of autonomy.

Table 4.3   Universal banks in the USA and Europe: some facts

Country	Banks	Currency	Assets 2000	ROE 1991–2000 (average, %)	ROA 1991–2000 (average, %)	Cost/income 1991–2000 (average, %)	Market capitalization (in million)			Revenues from outside the home country (%)	Assets 1991–2000 (average annual rate %)	Revenue 1991–2000 (average annual rate %)
							1991	1995	2000			
Switzerland	Crédit Suisse	€	662.850	7.8	0.3	63.0	4.466	14.891	62.117	56.8	21	21.7
	UBS	€	730.058	7.8	0.4	63.1	32.917	56.553	114.185	45.5	20	21.1
UK	Barclays	€	501.900	14.0	0.5	65.4	8.969	14.964	56.418	30.1	11	6.3
	Lloyds–TSB	€	346.010	19.8	0.9	58.2	9.333	22.213	63.890	18.5	28	19.4
	R.B. of Scotland	€	507.950	12.7	0.6	55.5	5.643	17.716	69.404	16.8	31	30.8
	HSBC	€	715.000	15.9	0.9	55.6	n.a.	37.833	149.583	75.1	22	14.9
France	BNP–Paribus	€	694.037	7.7	0.2	78.9	n.a.	n.a.	41.900	27.5	14	12.8
	Crédit Lyonnais	€	205.500	0.3	0.0	91.5	n.a.	n.a.	12.685	37.3	-2	0.9
	Société Générale	€	455.881	9.5	0.3	72.4	n.a.	8.060	27.626	21.6	11	11.0
Italy	San Paolo	€	172.260	8.8	0.4	63.1	n.a.	6.604	24.216	22.5	3	6.4
	Unicredito	€	182.019	6.2	0.3	69.2	4.652	4.802	27.764	21.1	13	16.8
	Banca Intesa	€	332.270	9.4	0.4	69.9	3.937	4.745	25.691	n.a.	34	30.6
Spain	BSCH	€	348.928	17.1	0.7	62.2	6.941	8.268	51.987	52.7	16	13.5
	Banco Popular	€	31.357	24.6	1.9	42.0	1.806	3.885	8.056	0.0	8	12.8
	BBVA	€	300.416	16.1	1.9	57.7	3.748	5.902	50.654	56.0	21	19.0
	Bankinter	€	19.136	14.3	1.1	50.0	541	887	2.733	0.0	7	1.5
Holland	ING	€	650.000	8.9	0.6	72.4	5.000	14.000	83.000	64.4	19	14.1
	ABN–AMRO	€	543.170	14.1	0.4	68.4	6.910	12.034	35.158	67.6	19	15.7
	Fortis	€	438.083	13.8	0.7	67.0	6.050	12.617	44.780	13.9	32	31.6
USA	Chase	$	715.350	14.7	0.9	60.0	n.a.	25.600	85.860	24.0	15	10.4
	Citigroup	$	902.210	13.6	0.9	57.7	17.559	56.076	273.243	51.7	17	18.9
	Bank of America	$	642.190	14.0	1.0	61.4	32.636	55.933	73.707	n.a.	10	9.2
Germany	Deutsche Bank	€	940.000	9.0	0.3	77.9	20.672	20.968	55.184	56.7	17	16.2
	Dresdner Bank	€	483.498	8.5	0.3	70.4	n.a.	8.692	24.400	38.0	14	13.5
	Commerzbank	€	459.660	8.9	0.3	70.4	6.677	9.437	16.740	26.5	16	10.1

Source: Banks' Annual Reports; Reuters.

The Emergence of Large Banking Groups: Corporate Growth

In the analysis of any industry, corporate growth is an important dimension. Among other things, it shows whether firms have projects for the future and how they are able to capitalize on the growth of the economy or of their industry. The growth of universal banks between 1991 and 2000 was remarkable. Figure 4.1 shows the average annual growth rate in revenue of the banks of the sample analyzed. The range within these groups is striking, from the top average annual growth rate of Fortis to the small annual growth rate of Crédit Lyonnais. Those rates are extremely high, both from a historical perspective within the banking industry, and in any inter-industry comparison.

If instead of analyzing revenue we turn to assets, the picture is relatively similar (Figure 4.2). Again growth rates in assets are extremely high.

Behind this tremendous growth in both revenues and assets, there are several important drivers: first, the need to diversify and capture new opportunities in financial services beyond banking, such as securities, investment funds and insurance; second, the need to grow internationally, which was fostered by the increasing globalization of the world economy; third, the need for consolidation in some countries, whose fragmented financial system meant that domestic institutions did not have the scale, or the efficiency, to compete in an open banking industry; and fourth, the supposed need to increase in size, in order to achieve greater efficiency and lower costs, and to reach a scale in financial markets to lower the cost of capital and fend off unintended proposals for mergers or acquisitions. This question will be discussed in some detail in the next section.

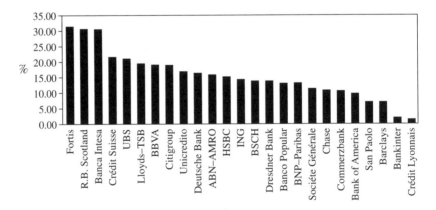

Figure 4.1   Revenue growth 1991–2000 (average annual rate, %)

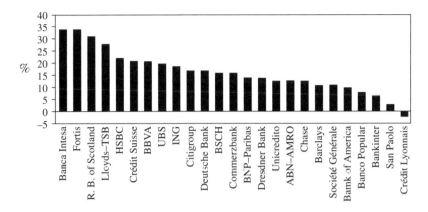

Figure 4.2   Asset growth 1991–2000 (average annual rate, %)

Scale in Banking

The role of the firm's scale in the banking industry has focused on the existence of scale economies. They operate when the average cost of a firm decreases while its volume of operations increases.[4] In the case of retail banks, empirical evidence on this phenomenon, to date, is relatively weak, since economies of scale seem to disappear at a very low level of assets (around US$100 million), although there is scant evidence of some scale economies for banks with assets up to US$25 billion (Berger et al., 1999).

The reasons for the lack of empirical support for scale economies are diverse. First, these economies require that costs must be fixed and not increase with the volume of operations. Scale, however, entails greater complexity, which, in turn, involves higher costs. Therefore, while some costs can be reduced, others may increase with the volume of activity. The existence of scale economies also requires that an increased volume of operations will lead to a proportional increase in revenues. This, however, is not always the case, since margins may decrease.

From a methodological point of view, it is difficult to determine whether economies of scale actually exist through the estimation of cost functions. Retail banks do not have simple cost functions, and the process of confirming empirically the existence of scale economies is difficult.

The effect of scale on the cost of capital, both in terms of diversification of the bank's investments and greater solvency, is another factor. Berger and Mester (1997) obtain some results that could support the hypothesis that business diversification may bring the cost of capital down. However, it is worth bearing in mind that solvency and asset diversification are not attributes of scale, but of good management. Consequently, while a bigger scale can help reduce the cost of capital for a well-managed bank, it is not clear that scale *per se* can guarantee such a reduction.

The search for scale is widespread in the industry, and the fact that scale advantages do not exist in retail banking – although they do seem to exist in corporate and investment banking – does not exclude the possibility that institutions may seek greater operating efficiency from increased size.

This reference of scale in banking can also be approached from another perspective. Gual (1999), using concepts introduced by Sutton (1991), distinguishes between competition based on variable costs and competition based on sunk costs. In terms of the variable cost model, financial institutions compete in some dimensions such as price and service. In this case, a bigger volume of activity results in an increase in variable costs.

The model based on sunk costs assumes that banks compete not on variable costs, but mainly deal instead with fixed investments and sunk costs in order to compete. The costs are independent of the scale that banks plan to achieve. Investment in information technology is one of the factors that suggest that this type of competition can occur in certain businesses, such as investment banking.

The consequences of both models for banking competition are important. If competition is based on variable costs, the scale of banks is not decisive for their efficiency, once a certain minimum scale has been reached. On the other hand, under the model based on sunk costs, scale is key. Empirical evidence is inconclusive in this respect. Nevertheless, both the US and European banking industries seem to confirm that retail banking is still driven by variable costs, which leads to a more fragmented industry. On the contrary, both investment and corporate banking are driven by sunk costs, which explains both the importance of scale and the increasing consolidation in this industry.

M&A in Banking

Mergers and acquisitions are usually related with the search for scale. This is typical in cases of horizontal mergers in the banking industry as well as elsewhere. In the USA and Europe, this type of merger has been frequent in recent years, as shown by the mergers between Banco Santander and Banco Central Hispano, ABN and AMRO, Citicorp and Travelers Group, and Bank of America and NationsBank.

A merger can certainly achieve a greater scale and offer cost reductions (Berger et al., 2001). Nevertheless, one of its hypothesis – that is, that only greater scale can offset declining margins – ignores a fundamental factor, namely, the ability to innovate in the sector. Imitation in the retail banking industry is immediate, and innovations do not last long. Still, certain cases of innovation in European retail banking with spectacular results can be cited, such as the entry of Citibank in telephone banking in Germany, and the development of super-accounts by Banco Santander in Spain.

Another factor, different from scale, propelling mergers and acquisitions is geographical complementarity. The acquisition of Bankers Trust by Deutsche Bank is perfectly in line with this rationale. Complementarity of activities and products is also an important driver of M&A. In this case, a merger or an acquisition is targeted at reinforcing the universal banking strategy, as with the merger of Citibank and Travelers Group (Carow, 2001). Cross-selling of financial products is the implicit objective of this type of merger. This was also one of the aims of Smith Barney's acquisition of Salomon Brothers, or the acquisition of Asesores Bursátiles, the premier Spanish financial asset management group, by Morgan Stanley.

The recent experience in banking shows that mergers and acquisitions in the banking industry do not succeed in producing a substantial increase in efficiency compared to that of the individual banks before the merger (Rhoades, 1998). In most of the cases where such mergers have been successful, the main reason is that the merger has involved major cost reductions and one of the banks has taken the leading role, so that confrontation between management teams has been avoided. In general, the assumed synergies are difficult to realize, and they may more easily be found in the area of cost reduction than in an increase in revenues (Houston et al., 2001).

This conclusion has some implications. Mergers and acquisitions represent a specific decision at a given moment. However, just as important as the decision itself is the implementation process that requires a clearly devised integration plan. It is not surprising that in many cases mergers and acquisitions, having produced high expectations, leave a bad aftertaste. This is because many of these transactions are agreed upon without a clearly defined integration plan. This plan should, among other things, define a strategic vision, the allocation of executive responsibilities within the bank, a new organization and some corporate governance practices. It is common to discover that once the plan begins to be defined, it then becomes clear that the merger will fall short of expectations.

Mergers may be the right strategy for some banks. However, mergers should not hinder the potential for innovation in financial services, which is indispensable for long-term survival. Innovation is generally not driven by large companies, but by innovative ones. Hence, an exclusive emphasis on scale may become dangerous, because it may slow down the process of innovation.

Corporate Diversification

The entry into new financial businesses has been one of the hallmarks of the transformation of banking in the past few years (Berger et al., 2000). What has powered this move has been the attractiveness of some growing segments of financial services beyond traditional banking, such as investment funds, pension funds, securities and insurance. Traditional banks took the lead in offering to their traditional customers new services that were beyond their original reach, appropriating in this process the role of other financial institutions like insurance firms.

On the other hand, the increasing importance of financial markets in the Western world attracted many retail banks to the capital markets, setting up new investment banking, trading and research units, or triggering the acquisition of other small, independent investment banks.

The anecdotal evidence of this trend is clear. Deustche Bank acquired Bankers Trust; Dresdner Bank acquired Kleinwort Benson; Citigroup acquired Schroders; ING acquired Barings; Crédit Suisse acquired Donaldson Lufkin and Jenrette; UBS and SBC merged; Chase Manhattan acquired JP Morgan. But there is also some statistical evidence of the diversification process. Figure 4.3 shows the evolution of non-interest income as a percentage of gross income in the EU. In the 1980s, this ratio was less than 25 percent in most EU countries; in 2000, it was about 40 percent in the eurozone countries. This ratio is not the only indicator of diversification, but shows in a simple way how much banks are going away from traditional intermediation and interest-based transactions to fees-based financial transactions. This means that banks are not only changing the nature of their activities as financial intermediaries, but also the type of capability they need to develop to remain competitive in the new financial landscape.

Geographic diversification has also been an important strategy pursued by many universal banks in response to the increasing globalization of the economy and the world financial system. Many US banks have landed in Europe precisely to take advantage of the new financial market that the euro is bringing about. Spanish banks have become the largest foreign banks in Latin America.[5]

Figure 4.4 shows the growth in international activity by some top universal banks between 1996 and 2000.

The growth and diversification of universal banks in the past ten years is beyond question. There are two tests that universal banks have to pass before one can claim that they are becoming the new paradigm in banking. First, the efficiency test: are universal banks more profitable than specialized banks? Second, the management test: are universal banks better managed than specialized banks?

The first test is difficult to pass today, the main reason being the lack of historical data. Since most of the largest universal banks today are a very recent creation, it is difficult to rate those banks according to profitability or efficiency. They need the test of time.

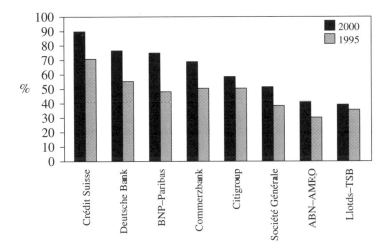

Figure 4.3   Corporate diversification (1995–2000): percentage of earnings different from retail banking

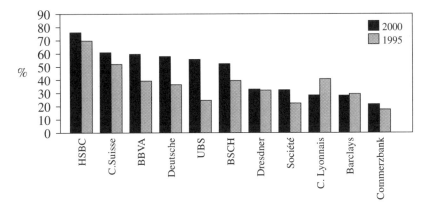

Figure 4.4   Geographic diversification (1996–2000): revenues generated outside the home country

The second test is more of a conceptual one. It has to do with advantages and disadvantages that universal banks have in terms of management and strategy. This discussion will set the framework for a deeper discussion on whether universal banks will be a sustainable organizational form in banking and become the dominant model in financial services in the long term.

WHY HAS THE UNIVERSAL BANKING MODEL BECOME STRONGER?

With financial margins in retail banking narrowing, some banks are trying to follow a universal bank strategy and increase revenues through the diversification of their activities into other financial areas such as asset management or insurance.

The universal bank strategy is based on three major assumptions.[6] The first is the potential to exploit linkages among the bank's business units and, in particular, the advantage of a single point of contact with each customer in order to increase cross-selling of financial services. The creation of banking giants such as the new UBS, HSBC or Citigroup seems to be driven by the goal of offering clients all types of financial services marketed by the bank's different business units.

The opportunities for cross-selling seem to be important in retail banking, asset management, investment funds and insurance. However, experience shows that the volume of cross-selling does not increase as quickly as some banks would wish, for a variety of reasons. First, a bank may not offer the best bundle of financial services, in which case its competitive advantage in cross-selling may be irrelevant. Second, rivalry in each segment makes competition very tough for universal banks, and specialists, as we will see later, may be more competitive. Third, the universal banks' internal organization does not always create an efficient coordination between the business units selling different types of financial services from the clients' point of view. Fourth, the distribution system of universal banks has become increasingly specialized and segmented; the creation of special branches for high-income individuals or special networks for serving the corporate market reflect this trend. This means that fragmentation of distribution channels may work against the integration of financial services that cross-selling may require.

The second reason for the creation of universal banks is the diversification of the sources of earnings and the presentation of the risk of substitution. This risk consists of the threat of innovation that comes from new financial services or alternative distribution channels. The emergence of new products, such as investment funds, or new distribution channels, such as Internet banking, makes this phenomenon evident. Some banks' senior managers also argue that the diversification of earnings may increase earnings stability. This may be true only in those activities in which earnings tend to be stable themselves – for example, they come from recurrent activities – but not in the case of those activities – like capital markets – which are not recurrent by nature.

A universal bank attempting to maintain a presence in many segments of the financial services industry can internalize and reduce the risk of substitution by widening the scope of its activities. However, from a strategic point of view, what really reduces the risk of substitution is innovation – the ability to anticipate the needs of clients, understand new forms of distribution and offer them. In this respect, universal banks do not have in fact a clear advantage over specialized banks. Thus, the differentiating factor is not scale, but rather the ability to innovate. Nevertheless, capital may be an advantage that universal banks can use to speed up entry into new business.

The third reason for the creation of universal banks is their attempt to become 'a one-stop shop' or exclusive providers of a wide range of financial services to individuals, families and firms. Firms may be edging towards dealing with a smaller number of banks. The rationale is that firms are becoming bigger and may want to deal with large banks. However, it is less obvious that a single bank can be superior to others in providing all the financial services that companies might require. In Europe, some universal banks with a strong corporate banking presence have a leading role in lending. However, it is more difficult for them to dislodge US investment banks from advisory functions, mergers or acquisitions. Their problem lies not so much in the size of the market as in the fact that US banks have extensive experience and have developed unique capabilities in this kind of business.

Another reason for the emergence of large universal banks may be their brand equity. A good brand may be an indicator of quality, safety and reliability in the financial services industry. From a marketing viewpoint, their argument makes sense, both from the customers' perspective, since one brand reinforces the message behind a 'one-stop shop', and from the bank's perspective, since this approach may reduce marketing and promotion costs. Nonetheless, some of the most dynamic universal banks, like Citigroup in the USA, or HSBC or Santander Central Hispano in Europe, have moved in the opposite direction, following a multi-brand strategy.

The advantages of universal banks must also be contrasted with certain intrinsic organizational limitations (Canals, 1997). The most important is that universal banks are diversified firms with different business units, whose management is complex and subject to different forces. Cross-selling, a key explanation of the existence of universal banks, requires internal coordination. This task is made even more difficult by the fact that the business units offering these products are different, and their staffs have different backgrounds.

In this context, it is also important to consider that specialized banks still have a role in the financial system. Specialized banks have the enormous advantage of being able to achieve the economies of scale specifically required in each business and to develop the resources and capabilities they need in each of the segments of the financial services industry.

In the next few years specialization may increase for several reasons: first, because increasing competition in each segment of the financial market will lead each bank to focus on those activities where it has the right resources and capabilities and where it can develop sustainable competitive advantages. As a result, many banks will abandon certain activities where they can compete only marginally. The recent experience of banks in shutting down retail business outside their own countries (like Crédit Lyonnais, Barclays, NatWest, Commerzbank) testifies to this. The sale of investment banking units of certain British banks such as Barclays and NatWest, or the restructuring process undertaken by banks such as Crédit Lyonnais and Banesto, speaks volumes.

Another factor that fosters specialization is that greater competition will require a growing commitment of capital to each of the various business units that today are grouped under a universal bank. Business units show different economic performance and compete for capital. It is reasonable to believe that shareholders expect management to allocate capital among business units according to their efficiency. Thus, each unit should be responsible for the capital invested in it, as if it were an autonomous unit. By the same token, the universal bank's corporate center must demonstrate its contribution to the whole organization. As a result, cross-subsidies between business units that currently exist in many universal banks will tend to disappear, since senior managers in each unit will not want to be responsible for capital not allocated specifically to them or which is devoted to financing other, less profitable activities within the banking group.

From the above discussion, the choice between a diversification strategy and a focus strategy in banking has many conceptual dimensions. From an empirical perspective, it is not clear, either, whether financial conglomerates are more efficient than specialists. In a study of the insurance industry, Berger et al. (2000) conclude that there is no evidence that the conglomeration strategy is superior to the focus strategy. On the effects of geographic scope, Berger and DeYoung (2001) also conclude that no particular optimal scope for banks exists. Some banks may operate more efficiently by being geographically focused, while others many operate more efficiently through geographical diversification.

It is important to consider simultaneously two factors when analyzing banks' choice between diversification and focus (Figure 4.5). The first factor is market scale and homogeneity. When there is not a high degree of market homogeneity, geographical specialization can be an important option, as has been the case in European retail banking and some segments of the corporate banking business, which in most countries is concentrated in the hands of local banks.

The second factor deals with the economic nature of competition in the banking industry and the existence of efficiency effects. As has been seen, if the competitive model is increasingly based on variable costs, the fragmentation of financial institutions across countries will remain. On the other hand, if the competitive model is based on sunk costs, the need for scale will force

		Efficiency effects	
		High	Low
Market scale and homogeneity	High	Global strategy	Multinational strategy
	Low	Presence in a few countries	Local strategy

Figure 4.5 Internationalization: some strategic options in banking

many institutions to seek volume. In both cases, there appears to be a future for specialized institutions, provided that they are innovative and have the minimum scale required to reach potential economies of scale in their activities. But this discussion also highlights the attractiveness of a global strategy based on building international universal banks.

IS THE UNIVERSAL BANKING MODEL SUSTAINABLE?

Firms' boundaries in the banking industry have changed over the past ten years. Now, universal banks dominate the competitive landscape in many countries. The nature of banking firms has been transformed, but not the functions that a modern financial system should provide. The challenge for universal banks is to make sure that they can be successful and lasting organizations. We will address this issue from three different perspectives: external threats to universal banks, managerial problems and regulatory constraints.

External Threats

Universal banks – as any company – face a basic threat as organizations: the emergence of a superior type of competitor that might offer customers new products and services that are better, cheaper or both. The likelihood of the emergence of a new competitor in some capital-intensive industries like automobiles or chemicals is low. Nevertheless, in knowledge-based or information-intensive industries like software or financial services new firms have emerged and will emerge.

Technology plays and will play a key role here. The first generation of Internet-based retail banks and brokerage firms in the USA and Europe has not been successful from a financial viewpoint. Nevertheless, the emergence of those competitors has brought about change in traditional banks, because they realized that their market share might be eroding because of the new competition. The new entrants were investing in a technology and developed a business model which was disruptive, if not sustainable. This threat made universal banks change. Institutions like ABN–AMRO, Citigroup, Merrill Lynch, ING, BBVA or SCH realized that they had to embrace the new business model or else be left behind. Their financial muscle was big enough to invest heavily in technology, catch the train and remain in a position of leadership.

It is true that today the market share of e-banking is still small. Nevertheless, in some segments of the financial services industry, in some countries, its market share is already about 20 percent of the new deposits or mortgages. The adoption of any new innovation is slow and takes some time. For this reason, we should not dismiss the already high penetration of Internet-based banking in some segments. Technology has a key role in banking and it is not clear that universal banks will be the first adopters of new technologies. It seems that they can acquire the most innovative and smaller new rivals, rather than pioneering the use of technology or spreading a new banking model. Certainly, first-mover advantages are not always clear; nevertheless, the problem is that no company knows whether a first-mover advantage will be ephemeral or, on the contrary, will redefine the competitive landscape in the next few years.

This is the space where specialists may still have a leading role in the industry. Banks like Bankinter or ING, with their intensive use of the Internet in their activities, may come up with new concepts of distribution of financial services over the Net that could eventually become superior to other traditional ways. Those banks are, by nature and desire, big innovators and well managed. The real challenge for universal banks will not come from mega-mergers, but from well-managed banks, big or small. And technology has played and will play a role in their strategies.

Managerial and Organizational Problems

Although external threats may always be impressive, the most daunting challenge universal banks face is not external, but internal. It has to do with managerial complexity.

A clear argument that top managers at universal banks use to explain the *raison d'étre* of their companies is that their customers have become bigger through internal growth and mergers. Scale has become a relevant factor in serving their customers' needs. Nevertheless, scale brings about internal inefficiencies in terms of coordination, incentives, monitoring, motivation and entrepreneurial mindset. Scale may be necessary, but scale does not mean efficiency or innovation.

There are several battlegrounds where managerial problems display their blocking power. First, coordination problems: universal banks have been created under the assumption that revenue-enhancing activities are both feasible and profitable. Cross-selling has been the mantra. Nevertheless, cross-selling is an elusive phenomenon. It implies an internal level of product innovation and development, marketing and distribution capabilities, and technology that very few banks are able to achieve, so much so that even giants like Citigroup have considered spinning off their insurance division, Travelers, because they realize that the potential for synergies is not very high.

Other financial groups have come to terms with a stern fact: cross-selling may be neither feasible nor profitable. The latter situation appears when the level of internal coordination in order to achieve cross-selling goals is so complex that the benefits that arise from it do not offset the increasing costs.

A second managerial challenge is how universal banks integrate under the same umbrella managers who run very different businesses, like investment banking, private banking or retail banking. Their professional background and experience are completely different, the incentives they expect vary across business units and the level of autonomy they expect is different in each case.

From a theoretical point of view, it is feasible to design organizational structures and incentive mechanisms that take into account those realities. Nevertheless, the fact of the matter is that many of the solutions proposed by universal banks are not sustainable and confirm the hypothesis that running financial conglomerates is more complex than managing a manufacturing conglomerate.

The third managerial challenge is risk allocation. The story about cross-selling could become more sophisticated. Some universal banks argue that they have an incredible advantage in the corporate sector over investment banks, since they can advise customers on very profitable operations such as mergers, acquisitions, alliances or IPOs, and lend them money in the meantime. This argument has been bothering investment banks for a while, because they have always thought that their financial skills and unique experience in deal-making were enough to gain new contracts from large customers. Now, universal banks step in; they may not bring those sophisticated skills, but they do bring capital, which is always a commodity, but a useful one when needed.

In this case, there is a conflict of interest for any universal bank: how much risk in lending money to a customer should be taken up, at a reasonable price, because the prospect of a lucrative fee-based income from advisory services could be astounding? Even if it is suggested that universal banks may not be subsidizing corporate lending through their investment banking operations, it is certainly a situation where a conflict of interest may arise. The recent explosion of the Enron crisis and the involvement of large universal banks like

Citigroup or JP Morgan Chase in the role both of corporate lenders and financial advisors has raised this potentially explosive issue.

Universal banks may be prudent in their lending operations and prevent their marketing efforts from lending recklessly, but during an economic slowdown large universal banks may be hit everywhere. Nonetheless, universal banks' top managers have to come to terms with the fact that they need to be not only prudent but also very transparent about the relationship between advisory services and lending. This means dismantling one of the strong arguments in support of the cross-selling hypothesis. Otherwise, customers, investors and regulators may view this strategy suspiciously. When focus and transparency seem to be again in vogue on financial markets, universal banks like Citigroup, JP Morgan or SCH have problems in convincing investors that their organizational arrangements are better. Investors seem to be unconvinced by these arguments and those banks' market capitalization has fallen steeply over the past 12 months, while more focused banks are commanding higher earnings multiples.

This point leads to another huge challenge for universal banks: how to generate synergies. On the cost side, cutting redundant functions and consolidating and sharing assets and IT infrastructure seem obvious. But as some managers point out, the real challenge for universal banks is to enhance revenues. Cross-selling is not always easy, as we have already discussed.

From the viewpoint of banks, there are further obstacles to cross-selling, besides the risky conflict of interest of lending to and advising companies. Coordination of functions and people across business units requires, very often, a change in the corporate culture and a completely brand new compensation system. Even adopting the same brand could be costly, as Citigroup or Santander Central Hispano are experiencing. Or sharing the same technology infrastructure could be tricky. Some banks have gone ahead with the universal banking strategy, but without a clear view of what advantages this will create and how synergies will come to life. Many bank managers have been good at managing their business unit. Managing an umbrella of business units, or managing one of them in coordination with another, seems simple on paper, but is tough in the real world.

A final managerial challenge that universal banks face is how to speed up corporate growth. Having already achieved a considerable size, becoming bigger is a daunting task. Furthermore, in most of the cases, bigger scale can only be achieved through mergers and acquisitions, because the sheer size of companies like Citigroup or Deutsche Bank makes the impact of any innovation on their organizations too small to be able to propel growth.[7]

Universal banks' strong market capitalization has been decisive in order to achieve a smaller cost of capital and acquire competitors. Nevertheless, stock prices are unlikely to go up for ever – they have actually gone down between

June 2001 and August 2002 in the global banking industry. Moreover, the potential for additional growth through acquisitions diminishes over time. And even though target companies may not be rare, the challenge is that integrating them into an already complex organization is difficult. Only extremely well-managed universal banks will be able to cope in the next few years with the challenge of scale and the need to keep growing.

Regulatory Challenges

Financial authorities keep an eye on universal banks. Their sheer scale is a reason for concern, even if those banks seem to be well managed. But corporate crises like Enron are powerful triggers of additional interest on how universal banks should be monitored or supervised by regulators.

On the other hand, universal banks have become powerful institutions that increasingly seem too big to fail. The moral hazard problem comes in here. Managing risk seems to be cost-free for some of those banks, since the incentives to come up with new innovations are very strong, and the risk of failure seems to have been cushioned by the regulator.

All in all, universal banks seem to be in good financial shape, even after the collapse of companies like Enron. Nevertheless, there is a growing cause for concern, which is bad debt. Banks in general, and universal banks in particular, have become increasingly sophisticated at generating financial innovation. One of the most preferred innovations has been the repackaging of debt. Banks have been selling debt exposure to third parties, like insurance companies or asset management firms, moving assets off their balance sheets. The rub is that when a crisis like Enron erupts, the whole notion of financial innovation and the repackaging of debt come under close scrutiny, and not without a solid argument. The problem is that if credit losses become real, insurance companies and other buyers of the pieces of debt will incur losses, and they may eventually have to go to banks to clear up the mess. But there is also another problem specific to universal banks. They own insurance companies and asset management firms. In the case that those companies have acquired risks from other banks, and those risks turn out to be out of control because the initial company is under financial duress, their owners, a universal bank, will also have a problem, even if they do not have the risk itself.

This situation describes the problem that banks and, in particular, universal banks have. They may reduce risk exposure by selling off part of their debt to other parties. Nevertheless, if they own financial firms that actually buy those risks – even from a rival universal bank – the universal bank will bear this type of risk in its consolidated accounts. This implies that the whole notion of risk management by selling off risk to other companies as a safe policy for banks may be put into question.

This situation is a special one for universal banks. In the case of a commercial bank that has been selling off debt to other firms, the overall risk because of this operation actually decreases. This is not the case with a universal bank that owns the buyers of that risk, and that makes a world of difference.

Accelerated financial innovation is widening a second problem for universal banks: the conflict of interest between the commercial side of the bank and the advisory side. Universal banks have the financial muscle to lend capital while advising companies to follow a certain strategy, like merging with another company. This attribute sets them apart from traditional investment banks. They may not make a lot of money in lending operations, but could generate lucrative fees from the advisory function. This is a clear conflict of interest that universal banks try to manage in the best possible way.

This problem becomes more complex when the advisory function involves creating new financial instruments to fund some operations, or the setting up of new companies that trade risk. In this case, the conflict of interest becomes bigger, since the lending function by the commercial business unit looks at risk in a particular way, while the advisory business unit looks at it from a different perspective. And in order to win the second – managing risk for your customer you may need to have the first – lending capability. And the risk-aversion nature of the second collides with the risk-appetite nature of the first.

Certainly, there is no clear solution to this conflict of interest, and finding a way out of this conundrum will not come from more regulation or a reintroduction of the old division of functions that the Glass–Steagall Act brought about for several decades in the USA. In the short term, the best strategy for both universal banks and regulators seems to be to enforce additional financial disclosure, which sheds light on the problem of preparing financial statements that could be useful in this respect and to make sure that audit firms can do a good job. This challenge is not the exclusive domain of universal banks.

Other conglomerates, like General Electric, share the same problem. But in the case of financial institutions there are two factors that make the challenge greater: financial risk management, and the stability of the financial system. The failure of an industrial conglomerate may have big, but limited effects. The failure of a universal bank may have ripple effects across the financial system and the rest of the economy.

There is no clear solution for universal banks. The nature of their activities is intrinsically risky and the efficient use of financial innovation seems to be indispensable. Nevertheless, it is in their best interests, and in the interest of the financial system, to keep risk management under control, and to strike a delicate balance between innovation and marketing aggressiveness, on the one hand, and financial prudence, on the other. Disclosing information on time and setting very clear rules for corporate governance that can also be made public, so that investors know how universal banks run their risks, may seem a high price to pay in the short term, but a condition for the viability of universal banks in the long term. If universal banks do not learn how to manage risk and show to regulators and investors that they are very good at it, there is the risk of a growing tide in public opinion in support of re-regulating universal banks, perhaps excluding them from some of their most attractive business opportunities.

UNIVERSAL BANKS AND THE FUTURE OF THE FINANCIAL SYSTEM: SOME FINAL REFLECTIONS

The emergence of large and powerful universal banks over the past decade should be viewed as an answer that some financial firms have chosen in order to cope with the new challenges of globalization, deregulation and the use of technology in financial firms.

This trend should not be considered as the only option for financial firms, nor a dominant force in the financial system as a whole. From the previous discussion on the role of financial specialists in a modern financial system, the conclusion seems to be clear: there is a role for focused institutions, with a clear mission, strategy and implementation skills. There is no danger that the 'one-size- fits-all' type of universal bank approach becomes the only possible and efficient way to operate in the financial services industry today. We are going to see very successful, well-focused financial institutions, both domestic and international, in this industry in the next few years, as we have seen in the past ten years.

The increasing weight of universal banks may seem to put in jeopardy the role of financial markets in a modern financial system, tilting the balance between markets and banks towards the latter. The special attribute of the new universal banks, as opposed to the classic universal banks of Germany or France, is that their functions are much more integrated with and much more dependent on financial markets than in the past.

On the other hand, financial markets are also dependent on financial innovation, which is driven in part by universal banks and their capital-markets divisions. In some ways, the emergence of the new universal banks has created a different balance between financial markets and financial institutions. Markets without banks would be less vibrant and less operational. Banks without markets would not be able to be as innovative as they are.

In a nutshell, universal banks do not have the ultimate power over financial markets, nor will they replace their role. Nevertheless, financial markets owe a lot to the new developments that universal banks are fostering. The case of the USA is clear. With new universal banks like JP Morgan Chase, Bank

America or Citigroup, the potential for innovation of its financial system is extraordinary. The role of financial markets gets an additional boost with universal banks. And this is a trend that, at another scale, can also be perceived in other countries, like France or Spain.

Nevertheless, this trend will be sustainable as long as two conditions are met. The first is that universal banks' top managers never lose sight of the fact that this business model is not necessarily superior to the specialist model. The second is that universal banks' top managers realize that the sustainability of this business model depends on their capability to handle the three threats that we have discussed in the previous sections: first, the increasing rivalry coming from other specialists; second, the managerial challenge of pulling together a complex organization, making sense of it, giving it a unified mission and being able to implement the strategy successfully; and third, tackling the challenge of the huge regulatory problem that universal banks have to face in managing risk and balancing the different attitudes to risk within the different business units.

NOTES

1.   For a wider picture on this topic, see Allen (1993), Canals (1997) and Dobson and Hufbauer (2001).
2.   Diamond (1984) also stresses this point: providing that the uncertainty is low, banks can diversify the risk among a number of companies, so that their respective yields are relatively uncorrelated.
3.   For an overview of the financial system in the EU, see Scott-Quinn (2002).
4.   From a methodological viewpoint, scale economies should be attributed to individual business units within a universal bank, for instance retail banking. Scope economies may refer to both business units and the whole universal bank.
5.   Bartlett and Ghoshall (1989) and Bryan et al. (1999) discuss some of the drivers behind this international expansion.
6.   For a deeper discussion, see Canals (1997) and Saunders and Walter (1994).
7.   The level of concentration in the banking industries in Europe is likely to increase in the next few years, mainly because of the effort to cut costs and gain a stronger presence in more than one country. Nevertheless, it is far from clear that bigger banks will become better banks.

REFERENCES

Allen, F. (1993), 'Strategic management and financial markets', *Strategic Management Journal,* special issue, 11–22.
Allen, F. and A.M. Santomero (2001), 'What do financial intermediaries do?', *Journal of Banking and Finance*, **25**, 271–94.
Bartlett, C. and S. Ghoshal (1989), *Managing Across Borders*, Boston, MA: Harvard Business School Press.
Belaisch, A., L. Kodres, J. Levy and A. Ubide (2001), 'Euro-area banking at the cross-

roads', working paper 01/128, International Monetary Fund.

Berger, A.N. and R. DeYoung (2001), 'The effects of geographic expansion on bank efficiences', working paper, Washington, DC: Federal Reserve Board.

Berger, A.N. and L.J. Mester (1997), 'Inside the black box: what explains differences in the efficiencies of financial institutions?', *Journal of Banking and Finance*, **21**, 895–947.

Berger, A.N., J.D. Commins and M.A. Weiss (2000), 'Conglomeration versus strategic focus: evidence from the insurance industry', *Journal of Financial Intermediation*, **9**, 323–62.

Berger, A.N., R.S. Demsetz and P.E. Straman (1999), 'The consolidation of the financial services industry: causes, consequences and implications for the future', *Journal of Banking and Finance*, **23**, 135–94.

Bryan, L., J. Fraser, J. Oppenheim and W. Rail (1999), *Race for the World*, Boston, MA: Harvard Business School Press.

Bryan, L.L. (1991), 'A blueprint for financial reconstruction', *Harvard Business Review*, May–June, 73–86.

Canals, J. (1997), *Universal Banking*, Oxford: Oxford University Press.

Carow, K.A. (2001), 'Citicorp–Travelers Group merger: challenging barriers between banking and insurance', *Journal of Banking and Finance*, **25**,1553–71.

Diamond, D.W. (1984), 'Financial intermediation and delegated monitoring', *Review of Economic Studies*, **51**, 393–414.

Dobson, W. and G.C. Hufbauer (2001), *World Capital Markets*, Washington DC: Institute for International Economics.

Gual, J. (1999), 'Implicaciones de la moneda única para la banca española', in R. Caminal (ed.), *El euro y sus repercusiones sobre la economía española*, Bilbao: Fundación BBV.

Hellwig, M.F. (1991), 'Banking, financial intermediation and corporate finance', in A. Giovannini and C. Mayer (eds), *European Financial Integration*, Cambridge: Cambridge University Press.

Houston J.F., C.M. James and M.D. Ryngaert (2001), 'Where do merger gains come from? Bank mergers from the perspective of insiders and outsiders?', *Journal of Financial Economics*, **60**, 285–331.

Milgrom, P. and J. Roberts (1992), *Economics, Organization and Management*, New York: Prentice Hall.

Rhoades, S.A. (1998), 'The efficiency effects of bank mergers: an overview of case studies of nine mergers', *Journal of Banking and Finance*, **22**, 273–91.

Saunders, A. and I. Walter (1994), *Universal Banking in the United States*, New York: Oxford University Press.

Scott-Quinn, B. (2002), 'The EU in world finance', in T.L. Brewer, P.A. Brenton and G. Boyd (eds), *Globalizing Europe*, Cheltenham, UK and Northampton, USA: Edward Elgar.

Sutton, J. (1991), *Sunk Costs and Market Structure*, Cambridge, MA: MIT Press.

5. International banking regulation

Maximilian J.B. Hall and George G. Kaufman

Banks have traditionally been regulated by their domestic or host countries for a wide variety of reasons. In more recent years, as advances in technology and communications have both reduced the cost of banking services across greater distances, including across national boundaries, and increased the demand for such services, banks have both expanded physically (bricks and mortar) across national boundaries and conducted business across such boundaries without a physical presence. In response, many of the same concerns that led governments to regulate domestic banks have given rise to pressures for harmonizing bank regulation among countries. This chapter first reviews and evaluates the historical reasons for domestic bank regulation and the reasons more recently offered for transnational or international regulation. It then discusses both the specific international prudential regulations developed by the Basel Committee on Banking Supervision, which have been adopted by many countries, and the modifications and extensions recently proposed by the Committee. Lastly, the chapter reviews the structure of government-provided or -sponsored deposit insurance in the USA, which both provides a basic justification for government regulation of banks and interacts with such regulation to determine the ultimate effectiveness of the regulations. The chapter concludes by making recommendations on how international regulation should be structured to best achieve efficient, safe and competitive domestic and international banking systems.

WHY BANKS ARE REGULATED DOMESTICALLY

Banks are regulated because the regulations are perceived to benefit one or more targeted groups. Banks are the oldest type of financial institution and have been regulated by their domestic governments almost from the beginning. But the nature of the regulation has changed over time with changes in the state of economic development and in the form of economic organization of the home country. The most common rationales for the regulation of banks by home governments are discussed below.

Government Benefit

In the early stages of industrial countries and currently in emerging economies, many governments view banks as a readily available source of financing, particularly during periods of war. In return for serving as a reliable source of funding, perhaps even at below market rates of interest, governments were frequently willing to grant banks monopoly or near-monopoly powers in particular geographic regions, including in the extreme the country as a whole, or in product lines, for example, demand deposits with checking privileges. This was accomplished by requiring banks, unlike most other corporations, to obtain special charters from the government and limiting the parties to whom these charters were granted. This was the *quid pro quo,* for example, for the chartering of the Bank of England in 1694, before it became a modern central bank.[1] Through time, the dedicated source of credit was expanded beyond the government *per se* to its friends and allies and to industries and sectors favored by the government for economic, political or social reasons. Some governments also viewed competitively protected banks as a handy source of revenue and imposed special taxes on their activities or profits. In the extreme, governments assumed partial or complete ownership of the banks.

In the USA, a number of states in the era before the Civil War in 1860, when effectively all banks were chartered by the states, received more than one-quarter of their annual revenues from taxing banks to whom they had granted monopoly powers through restricting chartering or other privileges in order to enhance their profitability.[2] One observer concluded that early banks in the USA 'were commonly thought of by legislators, shareholders, bankers, and the general public as public utilities'.[3] Indeed, it was the heavy political use of banks that led many states to introduce 'free banking' policies in this period in which any person or organization with sufficient initial capital could obtain a bank charter from the state. This policy was carried over by the federal government when it began to charter banks after the National Bank Act of 1863. But many countries, including some industrial countries, have retained partial government ownership or control in the form of state-owned banks (SOBs) or state-controlled banks (SCBs). These include France, Italy and Germany, in which SOBs and SCBs compete with private banks of large or near equal size, as well as China and Russia, where the largest banks are SOBs. In Japan, the government-owned Postal Savings System is a major competitor of private banks, some of which are currently insolvent and effectively kept in operation only by implicit government-provided capital and thus represent a form of SOB and SCB.

In addition, even if governments do not explicitly own or control private banks, they are frequently able to use them to influence, if not direct, credit through regulation. For example, in the USA, from the 1930s through the

1980s, the federal government used the privately owned savings and loan associations to channel funds into the residential mortgage market by encouraging the institutions to make long-term 20- to 30-year fixed-rate mortgages financed by short-term and thus effectively variable rate federally insured deposits. As a result, these institutions assumed very large interest rate exposures and were 'an accident waiting to happen' if interest rates rose sharply, which they did in the late 1970s. This increased their costs but left their revenues basically unchanged. The aggregate losses from the subsequent insolvency of many of the institutions exceeded the resources of the government insurance agency and required an infusion of some $150 billion of public or taxpayer funds.[4] In the absence of deposit insurance, it is unlikely that many depositors would have maintained their funds in such risky institutions, or, if they had, it would have been only at sharply higher interest rates to compensate them for the high risk. This may have discouraged the institutions from making such long-term fixed-rate loans. Indeed, in the period before the introduction of federal deposit insurance in 1934, savings and loan associations rarely made fixed-rate loans beyond five years in maturity and offered effectively longer-term, less liquid deposits. Similar structures exist in many other countries for similar reasons and are kept in operation only by government guarantees to the depositors.

Another form of credit allocation imposed through banks is to direct credit to 'underserved' groups, frequently including low-income and minority groups. It is argued that banks often fail to realize the profitability of loans to these sectors, in part because it is more difficult to evaluate the credit-worthiness of these borrowers. The credit standards applied to other groups do not apply as easily to these groups, for example, employment turnover may be more frequent but net unemployment no longer relevant and 'family' income may include more extended family members than for more traditional borrowers. As a result, these groups are perceived to be either unfairly denied credit or charged higher interest rates than may be socially warranted for credit or the borrower can afford. Because banks receive special charters from the government that are valuable, they are perceived by some to owe an obligation to serve the community in which they are chartered. Thus, regulators feel justified in using regulations to help direct credit to these communities until the perceived barriers to open credit markets are eliminated. In the USA., such regulations are classified under the rubric of 'Community Reinvestment' regulations.

Many of these regulations effectively make the institutions conduct government activities, but the costs are recorded off-budget and thus harder for the public to measure and evaluate. In the absence of the banks engaging in these activities, they would be recorded directly on the government budget, if conducted, and the risks and associated potential costs would be more transparent.

Structure and Competition

Bank regulation is, at times, justified by the need to maintain competition in banking by preserving numbers and preventing excessive concentration. But there is no empirical nor theoretical evidence to indicate that banking is either a natural monopoly or, in the absence of government restrictions on charter- ing, an industry with sufficiently large economies of scale to operate with only a small number of firms relative to other industries. In almost all countries, small banks appear to be competitive with large banks. Thus, the number of banks should not differ greatly from the number of firms in similar industries and, in large countries, domination by a few very large banks does not appear to be a lasting equilibrium. On the other hand, as noted in the previous section, governments have often restricted entry of new competitors to foster monop- oly, either to further their own objectives directly or in response to pleas from in-place bankers to reduce the threat of future competition and thus enhance current profitability. Thus, bank charters are frequently endowed with monop- olistic franchise value. On balance, regulation generally appears to restrict competition in banking rather than to enhance it.

Payments System

In many countries, banks operate much of the retail and wholesale payments system through the provision, clearing and settlement of checks, credit and debit cards, and large-value electronic interbank transfers. An efficiently operating payments system is a prerequisite for an efficiently performing economy and breakdowns in the payments system are likely to significantly reduce trade and thereby also aggregate income. In the absence of an effi- cient system, it may require government intervention to encourage the devel- opment of the basic infrastructure. But once established, there is little evidence that a continued government presence, outside a lender-of-last- resort function that provides emergency liquidity to the banking system, improves either efficiency or safety. Indeed, in some countries, including the USA, governments tend to underprice their own risk exposures in the payments process and thereby encourage excessive risk-taking by banks. Any resulting losses are borne by the government. In the USA, this occurs for daylight overdrafts by banks on transferring funds on the Federal Reserve's fedwire (transfers of not-currently-available funds that are paid in good funds before day end), where the Federal Reserve charges significantly below market rates of interest. Private parties providing this service would demand appropriate compensation, full collateralization, or transfers only in good funds to reduce their potential for losses.

One role that regulation may perform efficiently in the payments system extends beyond banks and is really a consumer protection issue, which is discussed later. That role may involve providing some protection against fraud for prepaid stored-value cards sold to the public, for example, required bonding or periodic examination of providers.

Consumer Protection

Understanding finance is not easy. Thus, there is widespread fear that 'more sophisticated' bankers may take advantage of 'less sophisticated' bank customers and force them into commitments and contracts that would not be entered into by equals. To the extent this is true, and there is no evidence that bankers are or are not 'smarter' in protecting their own interest than are bank customers, regulation focusing on education, simplification of terms, and disclosure may serve to enhance the understanding of customers and improve the efficiency and fairness of financing markets. Such regulations may also protect against fraud and misrepresentation.

Another consumer protection concern focuses on fair and equitable treatment of all consumers of equal economic standing regardless of their other characteristics, such as race, color, religion, or country of national origin. Although there is no evidence that such discrimination is more widespread among banks than elsewhere in the economy, regulations may discourage if not halt discrimination of this type by banks.

Safety and Soundness

Banks are widely perceived to be more fragile than other firms and thus more subject to failure, and bank failures to be more adverse for customers, other banks and the community as a whole. Because of the potentially strong and broad negative externalities associated with bank failures and the widespread fear they ignite, bank safety is a major public policy concern that appears amenable to be pursued through regulation. The excessive fragility of banks arises from three sources:

- High proportion of demand to total deposits;
- Low ratio of cash to assets; and
- Low ratio of capital to assets.

The adverse implications for failure result from the interaction of these three factors. The high proportion of demand deposits is seen as potentially likely to lead to rapid withdrawals and runs when depositors rightly or wrongly perceive their banks to be in financial trouble. Because banks hold only low ratios of cash on hand (engage in fractional reserve banking), they are likely to be unable to meet all the deposit losses with cash if and when runs occur and to be forced to sell earning assets quickly on which they may suffer fire-sale losses. If these losses are sufficiently large, they may exceed the relatively low capital (high leverage) that banks maintain and drive them into economic insolvency. To reduce the risk of individual bank failure and thereby financial fragility, regulation has traditionally focused on maintaining bank capital and leverage (gearing) ratios at perceived safer levels.

But fragility *per se* does not necessarily signal breakage or failure. Rather, it signals 'handle with care'. Thus, fragile fine wine glasses or chinaware often have lower breakage rates than less fragile ordinary drinking glasses or dishware, which are typically handled with considerably less care. And before deposit insurance, private banks, at least in the USA, had a better safety record than non-banks. From 1870, shortly after the end of the Civil War, to 1913, the year the Federal Reserve Act was enacted, the failure rate for commercial banks averaged 0.91 percent per year.[5] In contrast, the average annual failure rate for non-banks was 1.01 percent. But bank failures were more variable; banks failed more often in clusters and clusters of any undesirable event, be they bank failures or fires or cancer, tend to be scary. Thus, bank failures were widely viewed to be more adverse than failures of other firms and gave rise to calls for greater government intervention to reduce the failure rate.

In addition, bank failures were perceived as more damaging to the community than other failures and more likely to spread to other banks. Bank failures not only impose credit losses on depositors, but generally also liquidity losses, as the depositors at failed banks may not be able to access the recovery value of their deposits until the bank assets are sold and the funds recovered. This often took many years to complete, so that even though the loss rate in bank failures was, on average, considerably lower than for creditors of failed non-banks, sizeable proportions of the accounts were effectively frozen. The resulting illiquidity both greatly increased the fear of bank failures and greatly reduced the money supply in the community, as short-term deposits were suddenly transformed involuntarily into longer-term deposits. If the bank was of large size, the efficiency of the payments system was likely to be significantly affected. Loan relationships were also likely to be, at a minimum, interrupted and the availability of new loans limited unless other geographically nearby banks could take up the slack. These adjustments may reasonably be expected to occur more slowly for banks than for the failure of many other types of firms, for example grocery stores, which are less relationship-based, although the direct reduction in employment may be less severe. Nevertheless, the evidence from US history suggests that any adverse effects from bank failures on the macroeconomy were less important than the adverse effects of poor macroeconomic performance on bank failures.

The failure of one bank is also perceived to spread easily and quickly to other banks, both because banks tend to be closely interconnected through interbank deposits and loans and because banks may appear to be more homogeneous, so that if one or a group of banks encounters problems, depositors at other banks may start to doubt the financial health of their banks and run. Thus, a default on an interbank exposure by one bank may, in turn, trigger defaults by the counterparty bank on its interbank exposures and so on down the chain. But the loss from default by the initial failed bank will only cause other banks to fail if it is larger than the capital of the counterparty banks. The low bank failure rate noted above suggests that this was often not the case. Bank capital, although relatively low, was high enough to protect almost all banks against such domino-type losses. Indeed, the low level of capital at banks before meaningful capital regulation appears to have reflected the market's perception of less risk assumed by banks rather than more risk. Although bank runs were relatively frequent in the USA before deposit insurance, they rarely were a primary cause of bank failures.[6] Except when insolvent, the banks were able to meet the outflows without suffering sufficiently large fire-sale losses on their assets to exhaust their capital. Most depositor runs also were to other, perceived safer, banks rather than into specie (currency) and caused primarily a churning in deposits among banks rather than a multiple contraction of deposits from all banks. But the introduction of government-provided or -sponsored deposit insurance increased the fragility of banks and, as is discussed in the next section, required an accompanying increase in regulation to offset the reduction in depositor concern about the safety of their banks.

Deposit Insurance

The existence of explicit or implicit deposit insurance is an important contemporary rationale for prudential regulation of banks, because it exposes the government to losses from bank failures either directly or indirectly. In addition, because it weakens depositor and market discipline on the banks, deposit insurance requires an offsetting increase in government regulation to maintain the same degree of overall discipline on the banking system. Similar to private insurers, government insurers need to impose conditions that will minimize moral hazard behavior by the insured banks and thus their potential losses. These conditions, in the form of government regulations, may involve periodic examinations of a bank's risk exposure, appropriate pricing of risk, risk-sharing arrangements through deductibles, co-insurance, coverage ceilings, and prompt corrective actions before insolvency and legal closure and resolution at insolvency at least cost to the insurance agency. Because currently all countries effectively have some form of deposit insurance, be it explicit or implicit, all countries impose regulation for this purpose. If imposed correctly, unlike regulations imposed for the other purposes reviewed above, regulations imposed to minimize government losses from bank failures should improve aggregate economic welfare unambiguously. Unfortunately, as is discussed in a later section, the regulations are rarely imposed correctly and more often than not through time increase rather than minimize government losses. Moral hazard excessive risk-taking by the banks, particularly in the form of lower capital-to-asset ratios and higher leverage, is not minimized and the insuring agency itself frequently engages in forbearance in imposing effective but painful sanctions on troubled banks and acts as a poor agent for the ultimate at-risk taxpayer.

Costs of Bank Regulation

But bank regulations, like any restrictions, have costs as well as benefits and these costs for any particular regulation must be quantified and weighed against the benefits in order to determine the net benefit (desirability) or net cost (harm) of that regulation and thus whether it should be imposed or not. Because regulations are generally imposed to assist particular sectors, it is important that the cost–benefit analysis includes the implications for other sectors and the economy as a whole as well as for the targeted sectors. In his analysis of the costs and benefits of financial markets regulation, Benston (1999) distinguishes between two types of costs – 'intended' and 'unintended'. This is a useful distinction. The latter costs occur because the supporters and drafters of the regulation either did not foresee or failed to disclose all the possible responses in changed behavior by the regulatees or others affected by the regulation. In part, this reflects both the complexity of markets and the drive of individual units to find ways around imposed barriers that may interfere with their ability to maximize their own welfare.

Intended costs

Economic regulations are imposed to change the economic behavior of targeted units. They give rise to two foreseen or intended potential costs: (1) administrative costs to the regulators of drafting, monitoring, supervising and enforcing the regulations; and (2) costs to individual sectors and the aggregate economy of foreseen possible reductions in economic welfare resulting from the targeted changes in behavior net of the foreseen benefits to the targeted sectors. Some governments have recently required bank regulators to estimate both the administrative costs to the agencies of promulgating, disseminating, monitoring and enforcing their regulations and the

administrative costs to the banking industry of complying with the regulations. These costs have been estimated not to be insignificant. The costs of any
reduced aggregate or sector welfare arising from the modified behavior has
been less well quantified, in large part because these costs are often minimized
or denied altogether by supporters of the regulations, who frequently propose
them as a 'free lunch' generating only benefits. Thus, many resulting reductions in aggregate economic welfare become unintended costs by either oversight or willful neglect.

Unintended costs
Unintended consequences and costs of regulation occur when policymakers do
not foresee all the responses to any particular regulation or which otherwise
arise from the interaction with other regulations imposed for other purposes.
This occurs either because the policymakers have given insufficient time to
analyze the complete implications of the particular regulation or because of
lack of knowledge or concern by the regulators. In addition, when governments provide banks with deposit insurance or other forms of a safety net, they
frequently feel justified in viewing the banks as benefiting from this and in
collecting 'payment' for this benefit. They may do so by imposing regulations
that are intended to direct credit to socially or politically 'desirable' sectors or
that restrict the prices that may be charged on such credit. This is likely to
contribute to an economic misallocation of resources with the associated
losses in aggregate economic welfare.

Lastly, all the objectives of regulation discussed in the previous section
may not be mutually consistent and attainable concurrently. For example,
encouraging institutions to extend credit to sectors favored by the government
or to risky, socially desirable, but perceived 'underserved' sectors may endanger the safety and soundness of the institutions, particularly if the credit is
granted at below market rates, in excessive quantities, and without sufficient
capital being maintained by the bank. Conversely, increasing the safety of
institutions by limiting their risk-taking in order to reduce losses to the Federal
Deposit Insurance Corporation (FDIC) may discourage them from assuming
otherwise acceptable risks, including dampening their incentive to innovate.
Similarly, preventing banks from expanding to a larger size through merger
and acquisition or entering additional product lines may prevent them from
attaining their optimal size to maximize any benefits from economies of scale
or scope.

Unintended costs are generally difficult to quantify, but casual observation
suggests that they are high. Countries with strong regulations have, on average. experienced slower economic growth and higher costs of bank failures,
although these costs were not always evident in the short run (Nosal and
Rupert, 2002; Sapienza, 2002). The cost of bank failures frequently became

evident only after explicit or implicit government guarantees to bank stake-holders lost their credibility in the eyes of the general public and the accumu-lated unbooked losses from insolvencies were officially booked. In the USA, as was noted earlier, the cost of government intervention in the savings and loan industry in the 1950s through 1970s to channel additional funds into the residential mortgage market was a major factor in creating the costly thrift crisis of the late 1980s. Likewise, the costly collapse of the banks in Japan in the early 1990s and in many East Asian countries in the mid-1990s can be largely traced to government intervention to channel credit to socially desir-able or otherwise favored sectors by, among other things, effectively guaran-teeing the source of the funding so that depositors were not concerned over their banks' risky lending.

It is likely that the unintended costs of most bank regulations far exceed the intended costs and have a far longer-lasting adverse effect on aggregate economic welfare. This is not to argue that all or any regulation is unwar-ranted, but rather to note the importance of computing and disclosing all the costs associated with a particular proposed regulation, as well as its benefits to the economy as a whole, and weighing the results to obtain the net benefit or cost before adopting the regulation.

Why International Banking Regulation?

When banking systems in a number of industrial countries weakened in the late 1980s, pressure developed for harmonizing bank regulation among indus-trial countries, at least for large internationally active banks in these countries. The harmonization was intended both to enhance safety by reducing the like-lihood of individual failures that could spread the adverse effects across national boundaries and to provide for a more level playing field, so that banks in different countries would not benefit from any competitive advantages due to subsidies from their governments, such as lower capital ratios in an envi-ronment of explicit or implicit deposit insurance or other government support. In large measure, the call for such transnational regulation reflects both the limited market discipline on banks in most countries because of the existence of actual or conjectural government guarantees and the greater difficulty in monitoring banks in non-home jurisdictions by both private stakeholders and government regulators. This is particularly true if the regulations differ signif-icantly across jurisdictions. The international regulations would resemble domestic prudential regulations, but take into account any differences in insti-tutional and legal structures in the different countries that, in particular, impact the quality of regulatory supervision and private market discipline.

The design of the cross-border or transnational regulations was delegated to a newly established Basel Committee on Banking Supervision, housed at the Bank for International Settlements in Basel, Switzerland and comprising representatives of central banks and banking regulators in developed economies. The first capital accord was completed in 1988 and implemented by member countries at year-end 1992. Its major contributions were to focus on capital relative to the risk exposure of individual banks as measured by risk-weighted assets and to encourage higher capital ratios. Through time, the desirability of standardized capital regulations was accepted by other countries, including emerging economies, which adopted some or all of the Accord in their countries and achieved representation on the Basel Committee. But afterwards, the initial proposal was viewed as overly simple and crude. By attempting to apply a 'one-size-fits-all' policy, the Committee encouraged substantial arbitrage among risk classes by the banks, which weakened the effectiveness of the regulations.

As a result of this criticism, the Basel Committee began to work on a broader and more sophisticated capital accord that was both tailored to the particular risk exposures of individual banks and recognized the need for supervisory review and market discipline to enforce the designated minimum capital requirements. The resulting proposal was issued for public comment in mid-1999, revised on the basis of the comments received, and reissued in early 2001 for additional comment. It is currently in the process of further refinement. Implementation of any final agreement is now scheduled for 2005. The major features of both the initial and modified capital accords and the pros and cons of the salient features are discussed in the next section.

Description and Analysis of the Basel Capital Accord and Proposed Modifications

One of the main initiatives undertaken by the Basel (previously termed 'Basle') Committee on Banking Supervision (henceforth, the 'Committee) was the development of 'rules of the game' for the capital adequacy assessment of internationally active banks.[7] These were ratified by the major industrial countries represented in the Group of Ten (G10) in July 1988[8] for adoption by G10 banks by end-1992 at the latest.[9] They were subsequently amended in 1996[10] (effective 1 January 1998) to accommodate market risk alongside credit risk. Following widespread criticism of the original Accord, however, the Committee proposed, in June 1999, a complete overhaul of the assessment regime. A further set of reform proposals was published in January 2001 to take account of the submissions received from the banking industry during the consultation period, which followed publication of the Committee's initial ideas. As noted above, the Committee was continuing to develop its proposals with a view to producing a final, definitive version by end-2002, for possible adoption in 2005. These developments, and their implications, are examined in more detail immediately below.

The current 'rules' applying under the Accord ('Basel 1')

Since 1 January 1993, internationally active banks incorporated in G10 countries have been obliged to comply with a minimum 'risk asset ratio' (RAR) requirement of 8 percent.[11] A bank's RAR – see Exhibit 5.1 – is derived by expressing its (adjusted) regulatory capital, comprising so-called 'Tier 1' and 'Tier 2' capital,[12] as a percentage of risk-adjusted, on- and off-balance-sheet activities.[13] And since January 1998, the same banks have been required to embrace market risks alongside credit risks within the assessment regime, while remaining subject to the same minimum RAR requirement – see Exhibit 5.2.[14] Those satisfying their national supervisory authorities,[15] however, are allowed to use internal models (that is values at risk – VaRs)[16] to generate their (general) market risk capital charge rather than the 'standardized' RAR approach. Most other (that is, non-G10-incorporated) significant international banks have been induced to comply with the spirit if not the letter of the agreement as they wish to avoid incurring the market's wrath and the inevitable sanctions (in terms of price and availability of external capital) that would accompany this.[17]

Problems with Basel 1

Evidence of material flaws and weaknesses in the current assessment regime has existed since the Accord's inception. Whilst this is not to decry the undoubted benefits that have arisen from the adoption of the Accord – such as the contribution to systemic stability[18] resulting from all major banks being forced to hold more and higher quality capital than would otherwise have been the case and to link this, albeit in a fairly arbitrary fashion, to the main risks to which they are exposed – it does call into question the cost-effectiveness of the current approach adopted in respect of capital adequacy assessment and vindicates the Committee's quest for a replacement regime.

Typically, concerns have centered on the following:

- the voluntary nature of the agreement (outside the EEA);[19]
- the flawed methodology inherent in the 'standardized' assessment approach;
- the market distortions[20] and concomitant induced resource misallocation; and
- the potential danger of exacerbating global or regional 'credit crunches'.[21]

The Basel Committee's proposals for change

In response, somewhat belatedly, to the above criticisms and with a desire to accommodate market developments and industry practices, especially in the field of risk management, which have evolved since the promulgation of Basel 1, the

EXHIBIT 5.1　THE RISK ASSET RATIO
METHODOLOGY EMPLOYED BY BANKING
REGULATIONS UNDER THE G10 CAPITAL ACCORD

Under the Accord, the internationally active banks authorized by G10 countries have to observe a minimum risk asset ratio (RAR) of 8 percent. The RAR is calculated as follows:

$$RAR\ (\%) = \frac{ACB}{TOWRA}$$

where ACB is the adjusted capital base

and TOWRA (the total of weighted risk assets) $= \displaystyle\sum_{i=1}^{s} \sum_{j=1}^{t} (A_{ij}\,W_j)$

$$+ \sum_{i=1}^{u} \sum_{j=1}^{v} \sum_{k=1}^{w} (B_{ijk}\,X_k\,W_j)$$

$$+ \sum_{i=1}^{u} \sum_{j=1}^{y} \sum_{k=1}^{z} [(C_{ijk}\,X_k + M)W_j]^*$$

A_{ij}　being the value of the ith asset with risk weight, W_j,

B_{ijk}　being the notional principal amount of off-balance-sheet activity i with risk weight W_j and conversion factor X_k, and

C_{ijk}　being the notional principal amount of the interest or exchange rate related activity i with risk weight W_j and conversion factor X_k,

s　the number of different asset components,

u　the number of distinct off-balance-sheet activities (excluding interest rate and exchange-rate-related activities),

x　the number of distinct interest and exchange rate related off-balance-sheet instruments, and

M　the 'mark-to-market' value of the underlying contract.

where $x < u < s$; $v \le t = 5$; $y \le t = 5$; $w = 4$; and $z = 4$.

*'Current exposure' assessment method employed.

EXHIBIT 5.2   THE RISK ASSET RATIO METHODOLOGY EMPLOYED BY G10 BANKING REGULATORS SINCE THE IMPLEMENTATION OF THE AMENDED CAPITAL ACCORD ON 1 JANUARY 1998

Under the 'Amendment to the Capital Accord to Incorporate Market Risks' (Basel Committee, 1996), all G10-incorporated internationally active banks have to observe, continuously, a minimum capital requirement derived as follows:

$$RAR\ (\%)^1 = \frac{ACB^2}{TOWRA^3 + [12.5 \times Market\ Risk\ Capital\ Charge]^4}$$

1   This remains subject to a minimum of 8 percent.
2   The capital items which may be included in the capital base (CB) are the same as those which were eligible for inclusion (subject to limits and deductions) within the capital base under the original accord. However, national regulators are empowered to permit banks to adopt an alternative definition of capital, subject to limits and restrictions, but only in respect of satisfying the risk-based requirements arising from trading-book activities.
3   This now represents the 'total of weighted risk assets' arising from banking-book activities only (although, note, it covers credit counterparty risk on all over-the-counter derivatives, whether or not they are included in the trading book) and is calculated using the general methodological approaches set out.
4   This represents notional risk-weighted assets on the trading book.

Committee proposed, in June 1999,[22] a fundamental overhaul of the original Accord. Under these proposals, the new capital adequacy assessment framework would comprise three mutually reinforcing 'pillars' covering:[23]

- minimum regulatory capital requirements (Pillar 1 and the sole focus of Basel 1);
- supervisory review of an institution's capital adequacy and internal assessment process (Pillar 2); and
- greater market discipline (Pillar 3).

The main changes to be implemented under Pillar 1 embrace the proposal that an amended[24] 'standardized' approach, involving the use of external credit assessments, continue to be used by the vast majority of international banks, with more sophisticated banks being allowed to use internal ratings (and, possibly, portfolio credit risk models at some future date) to set capital charges, subject to supervisory approval and adherence to quantitative and qualitative guidelines. Wider supervisory recognition of credit risk mitigation techniques would also be given.

Under the Pillar 2 requirements, early supervisory intervention is encouraged, and supervisors would be required to set bank-specific capital charges that reflect each bank's particular risk profile and control environment, and which may exceed the 8 percent minimum RAR requirement.

Finally, under the Pillar 3 requirements, which emphasize disclosure, banks would be forced to reveal additional information about capital structure, risk exposures and capital adequacy, although the precise requirements had yet to be formulated.

In aggregate, the June 1999 proposals represented a considerable improvement on what is currently in operation. For example, *stability of* the international banking system may increase as a result of, *inter alia:*

- the removal of some of the 'perverse' incentives currently facing the banks;
- the focus on additional bank risks;
- the promotion of the further development of risk mitigation techniques;
- the reduction of the bias in favour of short-term interbank lending;
- the introduction of a higher (that is, 150 percent) risk weight for lowly rated (that is, below 'B–') borrowers of a given sector;
- the abolition of the 50 percent cap on the risk-weighting of derivative exposures;
- the incentives provided to most borrowers to seek higher credit ratings;
- the demand for greater information disclosure; and
- the new obligations placed on bank supervisors (for example to engage in 'prompt corrective action', to impose bank-specific capital charges that more closely reflect the risk exposures actually assumed, and to take explicit account of an individual bank's relative importance in national and international markets and its potential to trigger systemic instability).

Likewise, *economic efficiency* may increase because of, *inter alia:*

- the use of external credit ratings, which take account of, among other things, the characteristics of the obligor, to determine risk weights;
- the possibility of banks obtaining supervisory recognition of internal credit ratings (and, perhaps, at some future date, portfolio credit risk models), which would align regulatory capital requirements more closely with the internal allocation of economic capital;
- the removal of the bias in favour of loans to OECD countries and OECD banks;

- the reduction in the bias in favour of short-term (that is, for less than 365 days) interbank lending;
- the introduction of a 150 percent risk weight for lowly rated borrowers;
- the incentives created for most borrowers to seek improved ratings;
- the attempts to block the use of securitization as a means of circumventing capital requirements through the risk-weighting of securitization trenches; and
- the enhanced information disclosure requirements, which will lead to improved market transparency and greater market discipline.

And, on balance, and notwithstanding the comparative advantages enjoyed by the large, sophisticated banks, the proposals are likely to contribute to a further *levelling of the regulatory playing field*[25] because of:

- the enforced geographical spread of 'prompt corrective action' and the application of bank-specific capital charges;
- the induced convergence in information disclosure standards and supervisory practices; and
- the removal of the bias resulting from OECD membership/incorporation.

Despite the positive features of the new proposals, however, a number of concerns were raised. The most significant are summarized immediately below.

1. Too much power would be vested in the hands of far-from-infallible *credit rating agencies*. The main anxieties relate to: their previous track record, especially in relation to the recent Asian crisis; the degree of concentration in the industry; the absence of an agreed industry standard for ratings procedures, and hence the opportunities created for regulatory arbitrage; their potential to act in a destabilizing fashion and to intensify the procyclicality of bank lending; and fears about how they will react to the commercial and political pressures they will face in the new environment (their goal of profit maximization may not sit easily alongside the desire to maximize social welfare).

2. *Perverse incentives* are also apparent in the proposed new framework. For example, those banks, sovereigns and corporates currently without a rating and fearful of being awarded a rating of below 'B–' would have a positive disincentive to seek a rating as they would end up being worse off if their fears were realized (because unrated borrowers typically incur a 100 percent risk weight whereas those rated below 'B–' incur a 150 percent risk weight). Also, given the failure to differentiate adequately between corporate borrowers (those with a rating of between 'A+' and 'B–' all incur the same risk weighting of 100 percent), banks would still

have an incentive to court the higher-risk corporate borrowers if they believed that they could extract sufficiently high loan charges to more than offset the costs associated with the increased risk of default.

3. Similarly, inexplicable *anomalies* also feature in the proposed new framework. For example, it is not clear why sovereign borrowers are generally favored by the new risk framework proposed. Moreover, why is such little differentiation made in respect of corporates and, to a lesser degree, between banks, a factor which reduces incentives to seek higher ratings?

4. The imposition of additional flat rate capital charges to cover 'other' risks, such as *operational risk,* is widely believed to be ill conceived.

5. As the Committee acknowledges, insufficient attention has been paid to the *maturity of claims* in the promulgation of risk weights, militating against accurate assessment of underlying risks.

6. The scope for *national discretion* is still too great, militating against a leveling of the playing field.

7. The proposals imply a significant, and possibly untenable, increase in the *burden placed on* most *supervisory authorities.*

8. In terms of the overall impact on compliance costs, the proposals are *inequitable.* A small group of highly sophisticated global players would probably enjoy significantly reduced costs while the vast majority of banks would probably incur significantly increased costs.

9. In respect of the treatment of *bank claims,* both 'options' are flawed.

10. Although the introduction of *'prompt corrective action'* has been enshrined in statute in the USA and Japan, where it is seen as an important device for limiting supervisory 'forbearance', poor design use of the policy instrument could, potentially, be destabilizing.

11. In so far as the *standardized approach,* which the vast majority of banks would still adopt, would still treat credit risks as being addictive, the basic flaw in the risk assessment methodology would remain, notwithstanding the greater supervisory recognition of risk mitigation techniques.

12. Finally, the Committee's *desire to at least maintain the current level of capital* within the international banking system does not sit easily alongside the primary objective of the reform exercise, namely, to refine the credit risk assessment process, linking capital requirements more closely to the 'true' (in an actuarial sense) levels of risk run by individual banks, which may require higher or lower capital.

In the light of these observations and the comments received during the consultative period which followed the publication of its June 1999 proposals, a revised set of proposals was released for discussion by the Basel Committee in January 2001.[26] A final, definitive version was promised by year-end 2001 for adoption in 2004 although both deadlines have since slipped by one year.

As expected, the Committee confirmed that its new approach would be based around the previously identified three pillars of minimum regulatory capital requirements, supervisory review and market discipline. The approaches to be adopted under each of these pillars, however, have been substantially revised and extended, as explained below. In general, the changes reflect the Committee's greater emphasis than hitherto on providing banks and their supervisors with a range of options for the assessment of capital adequacy, in an attempt to move further away from prescription and a 'one-size-fits-all' approach; and a greater willingness to allow banks to deploy their own assessments of the risks to which they are exposed in the calculation of regulatory capital charges is also evident (for example in their proposals for the use of internal ratings-based (IRB) approaches).

The main changes made under Pillar 1 embrace the following:

1. A *more risk-sensitive standardized approach* is proposed, embracing a revised set of risk weights derived from the use of the credit assessments of eligible external credit assessment institutions or, for the first time, the risk scores of export credit agencies.
2. A set of *operational requirements* must now be satisfied when the standardized approach is adopted: national supervisors must ensure that banks do not assign risk weights based on external credit assessments in a mechanical fashion; to gain supervisory recognition of their credit assessments, external credit assessment institutions (ECAIs) must satisfy six criteria, covering issues of 'objectivity', 'independence', 'international access'/'transparency', 'disclosure', 'resources' and 'credibility'; supervisors are responsible for mapping the ECAIs' assessments with the risk weights, for ensuring the risk weight assignment is consistent with the level of credit risk involved, and for preventing banks from 'cherry-picking' from the available assessments; and banks are expected to apply the assessments consistently for both risk-weighting and risk management purposes.
3. With respect to *credit risk mitigation* under the standardized approach, the use of collateral, credit derivatives, guarantees and netting arrangements are all now recognized. Recognition, however, is subject to minimum operational standards being adhered to and to the fulfillment of certain disclosure requirements set out under Pillar 3. Credit risk mitigation is also available under a foundation IRB approach and an advanced IRB approach.
4. Under its revised approach to *asset securitization,* the Committee has published for consultation standardized and IRB approaches for treating the explicit risks that securitization creates for banks, be they issuing banks, investing banks or sponsoring banks. And, within each approach, operational requirements, disclosure requirements and minimum capital requirements are laid down.

5. As regards the *IRB approaches,* as foreshadowed in the June 1999 consultation paper, banks with more advanced risk management capabilities are to be able, at national discretion, to use internal assessments of credit risk (now set out as IRB approaches) provided they satisfy rigorous supervisory standards. To be eligible to use the so-called *'foundation'* approach, banks must satisfy the following *minimum* requirements, both at the outset and on an ongoing basis, relating to:

   (i)   a meaningful differentiation of risk;
   (ii)   completeness and integrity of rating assignments;
   (iii)   oversight of the rating system and processes;
   (iv)   criteria and orientation of the rating system;
   (v)   estimation of the probability of default (PD);
   (vi)   data collection and IT systems;
   (vii)   use of internal ratings;
   (viii) internal validation; and
   (ix)   disclosure requirements (as set out in Pillar 3).

   A bank using its own estimates of any components of the *'advanced'* IRB approach – that is, in respect of 'loss given default' (LGD), 'exposure at default' (EAD) and the treatment of guarantees and credit derivatives – must satisfy all of the above as well as the additional minimum requirements for the relevant risk component it is estimating.

6. Finally, in connection with the treatment of *operational risk,* the Committee has confirmed its intention to require banks to establish an explicit capital charge to cover operational risk, which it defines as 'the risk of direct or indirect loss resulting from inadequate or failed internal processes, people and systems or from external events'. All internationally active banks and banks with significant operational risk exposure are expected to use one of the last two-mentioned approaches. And, based on industry experience, the Committee has proposed that a figure of 20 percent of regulatory capital be used as a first approximation in developing the minimum capital charge. As additional loss data become available, the minimum capital requirements will be adjusted accordingly.

As far as the changes made under Pillar 2 are concerned, the Committee has now identified four 'key principles' of supervisory review which are designed to complement the extensive supervisory guidance already established.

The first key principle is that:

Banks should have a process for assessing their overall capital adequacy in relation to their risk profile and a strategy for maintaining their capital levels.

The Committee argues that the main features of such a process should comprise the following:

- a sound risk management process subject to effective board and senior management oversight;
- sound capital assessment;
- a comprehensive assessment of risks;
- an adequate system for monitoring and reporting risk; and
- adequate internal control review.

Guidance given under this principle is designed to ensure that banks are able to demonstrate that chosen internal capital targets are well founded and that these targets are consistent with their overall risk profiles and current operating environments.

The second key principle, associated with internal control review, is that:

> Supervisors should review and evaluate banks' internal capital adequacy assessments and strategies, as well as their ability to monitor and ensure their compliance with regulatory capital ratios. Supervisors should take appropriate supervisory action if they are not satisfied with this process.

Under this prompt corrective action principle, the Committee is seeking to ensure that supervisors regularly review, on the basis of published criteria, banks' capital adequacy assessment processes, banks' risk positions, and the resultant amounts and quality of capital held by the banks. Supervisors are also expected to evaluate the soundness of the banks' internal capital adequacy assessment processes. The Committee believes that the emphasis of the review should be on the quality of the banks' risk management and controls, and should comprise some or all of the following:

- on-site examinations or inspections;
- off-site review;
- discussions with bank management;
- review of relevant work done by external auditors; and
- periodic reporting.

The third key principle, which is designed to ensure *all* banks operate above the minimum regulatory capital requirements, states that:

> Supervisors should expect banks to operate above the minimum regulatory capital levels and should have the ability to require banks to hold capital in excess of the minimum.

This may involve, as in the UK, setting bank-specific 'target' and 'trigger' capital ratios or, as in the USA, defining categories above minimum regulatory capital ratios (for example 'well-capitalized' and 'adequately capitalized') when identifying the capitalization level of a bank. Alternatively, countries may choose to set higher ratios for the banking system as a whole. Maintenance of an operational buffer, over and above the Pillar 1 standard, is deemed necessary to take account of:

- the banks' own preferences for greater credit-worthiness;
- fluctuations in the type and volume of business activities undertaken;
- potential future difficulties faced when raising additional capital;
- the severity of the impact of sanctions/remedial action triggered by breaches of the relevant laws; and
- the risks not captured by Pillar 1 requirements.

At the individual bank level, supervisors are also expected to clearly explain their reasons for setting capital requirements above the minimum requirement.

Finally, the fourth key principle, designed to ensure that prompt supervisory intervention and remedial action are taken, states that:

> Supervisors should seek to intervene at an early stage to prevent capital from falling below the minimum levels required to support the risk characteristics of a particular bank, and should require rapid remedial action if capital is not maintained or restored.

Under this prompt corrective action principle, supervisors are expected to range of options if they feel banks are not meeting the requirements embodied in the principles outlined above. These actions may include:

- intensifying the monitoring of the bank;
- restricting the payment of dividends;
- requiring the bank to prepare and implement a satisfactory capital adequacy restoration plan; and
- requiring the bank to raise additional capital immediately.

Last, but by no means least, the Committee has also proposed major changes to its Pillar 3 requirements. Building on the six broad recommendations set out in its January 2000 paper (Basel Committee, 2000), the Committee has developed a set of more specific qualitative and quantitative disclosures in four key areas: scope of application; composition of capital; risk exposure assessment and management processes; and capital adequacy. It also now distinguishes between disclosure 'requirements', which serve as pre-conditions for the use of a particular methodology or instrument, and 'strong recommendations'; and between 'core' and 'supplementary' disclosure requirements, in recognition of the disclosure burden placed on some institutions. Core disclosures are defined as those which convey vital information for all institutions and are important to the basic operation of the market discipline (all institutions are expected to disclose such information, subject to 'materiality'); while supplementary disclosures, in contrast, are important for some, but not all, institutions depending on the nature of their risk exposure, capital adequacy and methods adopted to calculate the capital requirements. Sophisticated, internationally active banks are expected to make the full range of core and supplementary information publicly available, again on the basis of materiality.

In respect of the 'strong recommendations' made in relation to the disclosure on capital structure, 'core' disclosure recommendations are both quantitative and qualitative in nature. The former cover disclosure of:

- the amount of Tier 1 capital held, with separate disclosure of paid-up share capital/common stock, disclosed reserves, minority interests in the equity of subsidiaries, innovative Tier 1 capital instruments grandfathered, innovative Tier 1 capital instrument not grandfathered, and goodwill and other amounts deducted from Tier 1;
- the total amount of Tier 2 and Tier 3 capital held;
- deductions made from Tier 1 and Tier 2 capital; and
- overall eligible capital held.

The latter cover, in turn:

- accounting policies used for the valuation of assets and liabilities, provisioning and income recognition;
- information on consistency of accounting principles used between years;
- whether unrealized gains are included in Tier 1 capital;
- whether unrealized loses have been deducted from Tier 1 capital;
- what influence deferred taxes have on Tier 1 capital; and
- the nature and functions of innovative Tier 1 capital instruments.

'Supplementary' disclosures, meanwhile, are expected to cover the amount of Tier 2 capital (split between 'Upper' and 'Lower' Tier 2), with separate disclosure of material components; and the amount of Tier 3 capital.

Summary disclosure of information about the terms and conditions of the main features of all capital instruments, especially in the case of innovative, complex or hybrid capital instruments, is also expected under both core and supplementary disclosures. And this information should provide a clear picture of the loss-absorbing capacity of each instrument, and highlight any conditions (for example, 'trigger' events) that may affect the analysis of banks' capital adequacy.

Similarly, with respect to capital adequacy disclosures, 'core' disclosure recommendations (to be made on a consolidated basis by each internationally active bank within a banking group, and by holding companies of banking groups) embrace:

• capital requirements for credit risk for balance-sheet assets;
• capital requirements for credit risk for off-balance-sheet instruments;
• capital requirements for market risk, including disclosure of capital charges for component risk elements;
• capital requirements for operational risk;
• total capital requirements;
• total eligible capital; and
• the percentage of total eligible capital to total capital requirements.

Banks using the internal models approach should also disclose their individual capital requirements for component elements of market risk.

Under the 'supplementary' disclosure recommendations, banks are also expected to provide an analysis of factors impacting on their capital adequacy position and economic capital allocations. This would include:

• changes in capital structure and the impact on key ratios and the overall capital position;
• information about contingency planning;
• its capital management strategy, including, where appropriate, future capital plans; and
• the amount of economic capital allocated to different transactions, products, customers, business lines, or organizational units.

Banks are also invited to consider disclosing a summary comparison/analysis of internal estimates of aggregate economic capital requirements versus reported capital amounts versus regulatory requirements.

Finally, in connection with the frequency of disclosure, the Committee believes that it is desirable for the disclosures covered on its paper to be made on no less than a semi-annual basis, subject to proper verification on no less than an annual basis. For certain categories of disclosure, and, in particular, for internationally active banks, quarterly disclosures are expected.

In many ways, the January 2001 package of proposals represents a major advance on the June 1999 package because of the increased cost-effectiveness likely to result from, *inter alia*:

• the increased choice (subject to national supervisory approval) now offered to a wider range of banks as a result of the Committee's more concerted attempt to move away from the current 'one-size-fits-all policy';
• the promulgation of a more risk-sensitive standardized approach which

addresses the concerns raised about the lack of specifics in the treatment of corporates, the operation of a sovereign floor for bank/corporate exposure risk weights, and the assignment of a 100 percent risk weight to unrated borrowers;

- the reduction, from six to three months, in the original maturity of interbank claims before they qualify for preferential treatment under 'Option 2';
- the additional safeguards built into the use of external credit assessments and internal assessments (under the IRB approaches);
- the new IRB framework for credit risk explicitly recognizing more elements of credit risk (that is, the credit-worthiness of the obligor, the structure and maturity of the transaction, and the concentration of loans to a particular borrower or borrower group) in the regulatory capital calculation;
- the increased financial stability induced by the extension of the supervisory review process;
- the enhanced market discipline deriving from the adoption of a much broader range of disclosure requirements and recommendations, the former now extending to the provision of prerequisites for the supervisory recognition of internal methodologies for credit risk assessment, credit risk mitigation techniques and asset securitization; and
- the attempts made to lighten the overall burden placed on banks and supervisors alike by the decisions taken to, respectively, distinguish between core and supplementary disclosure requirements/recommendations under Pillar 3, and to phase in the new requirements (under the Committee's transitional arrangements).

This does not mean, however, that all the previously expressed fears and concerns have dissipated. As far as the Committee's stability objective *is* concerned, concerns persist because of the following:

- notwithstanding the greater supervisory recognition to be given to credit risk mitigation techniques, credit risks will still be treated in an additive fashion under the standardized approach, with no account being taken of the degree of portfolio diversification secured;
- the fear that the more risk-sensitive framework might amplify business cycles;
- the danger that some banks will be allowed to operate the IRB approaches prematurely;
- the very real fear that, because of limited skills, expertise and experience and/or a lack of professional standing, supervisors in a number of jurisdictions will not match up to the Committee's expectations (indeed, the Committee has acknowledged this, promising that it, together with the

BIS's 'Financial Stability Institute', will stand ready to provide assistance and will serve as a forum for information dissemination and exchange among supervisors);

- the feeling that the 'safeguards' introduced to assuage the fears of the dissenters concerning the use of external credit assessments still do not do enough to ensure that the public interest prevails;
- some perverse incentives remain in the new framework;
- the Committee's failure to provide sufficient incentives, *via* the credit risk calibration process, to encourage take-up of the IRB approaches;
- the Committee's failure to take account of a bank's liquidity and access to future funding when assessing the value of its loan portfolio (a 'fair-value' approach may overstate true worth as the latter may depend on its liquidation value);
- a belief that both external ratings and IRB approaches are too blunt an instrument to reflect the day-to-day riskiness of credit portfolios;
- the Committee's failure to resist more forcefully the 'special pleading' from certain governments[27] and other interested parties;
- the Committee's decision to treat operational risk under Pillar 1 rather than Pillar 2; and
- continuing fears about the overall burden – reporting and otherwise – to be placed on the banks.

Similarly, in connection with the Committee's level playing field objective, a number of fears persist. The main one relates to the wide range of opportunities available to national supervisors to exercise their discretion under the latest set of proposals (particularly under Pillar 2) and the fear that, despite the Committee's promise to monitor the use of discretion, serious competitive distortions will materialize. In a similar vein, bankers are anxious about the possible further loss of market share to non-bank financial service providers active in certain markets yet not subject to comparable regulation (for example insurance companies involved in credit derivatives).

Continuing developments
Notwithstanding the substantial refinements in its ideas through time, the Committee is continuing its work in the following areas: the treatment of asset securitization; the treatment of operational risk; assessing the potential impact of provisioning practices on capital adequacy; the development of the IRB approach; the mapping of external credit assessments to the standardized risk brackets; and the development of the information disclosure requirements and recommendations. The results of the more detailed analysis are likely to lead to further changes to the Committee's set of proposals.[28]

Deposit Insurance in the USA[29]

To better understand the interconnection between bank regulation and govern-ment-sponsored deposit insurance, this section reviews the development and features of deposit insurance in the USA. In 1934, the USA was the second country after Czechoslovakia to adopt federal government deposit insurance. The insurance has had major effects on both banking and the economy, some good and some not so good. On the good side, it stopped most runs, and, in particular, runs into currency immediately by reducing the need for insured depositors to be concerned about the financial condition of their banks. On the bad side, it reduced the intensity of depositor monitoring and disciplining of their banks. In the longer run, deposit insurance has resulted in a smaller number but eventually equally, if not more, costly bank and thrift institution failures. This occurred both because the weaker monitored banks assumed greater risk exposure than before, both in their asset and liability portfolios and in their capital positions – moral hazard risk-taking by banks – and because regulators practiced increased forbearance, particularly in crisis periods and on larger banks, and often failed to impose and enforce either meaningful sanctions on troubled solvent institutions or timely resolution on insolvent institutions – poor agency behavior by regulators. Unfortunately, the 'good' effects of the halt in bank runs was observed first and was easily associated by the public with the introduction of the insurance and the 'bad' effects of moral hazard risk-taking by banks. Poor agent behavior by regulators was observed only later and was not as readily associated by the public with the introduction of the insurance some time, in some cases many years, earlier. Thus, deposit insurance is a typical time-inconsistency problem in economics, whose contri-bution is measured primarily by the favorable short-run outcome rather than the unfavorable long-run and longer-lasting outcome.

The regulators frequently acted as poor agents for their taxpayer principals for a number of reasons, including: being overwhelmed by the number and large size of the insolvent institutions, particularly in period of crises; fear that official recognition of the insolvencies and official booking of the accumu-lated losses would both tarnish their reputations as protectors of bank safety and possibly ignite panic among the public; reluctance to deal harshly with members of the industry with whom they were well acquainted and possibly endanger future lucrative employment opportunities with them; and strong political pressures exerted by bankers, who tend to be leading members of their communities and significant financial contributors to their elected or appointed representatives. Until the late 1980s, the maximum premium rate that the deposit insurance agencies could charge banks was set by law. As a result, as the cost of the insolvencies officially recognized and booked increased during the thrift and banking crisis of the 1980s, the stated reserves of the insurance agencies declined. At the same time, the economic but not booked reserves of the agencies declined even faster and quickly turned negative from the even larger unbooked cost of the many unbooked bank economic insolvencies. Thus, when the accumulated unbooked bank losses were finally booked in the late 1980s and early 1990s, the resulting losses exceeded the agencies' stated reserves and were paid for by the taxpayer rather than the surviving insured institutions. Not until insolvency became a realistic possibility did the insurance agencies petition Congress for permission to increase the premiums on banks. In response to what was perceived to be poor performance by the regulators that led to more and costlier failures than perceived necessary, Congress reversed its course and attempted to reduce the discretion of regulators to forbear, particularly on larger banks, in 1991 in the Federal Deposit Insurance Corporation Improvement Act (FDICIA).

FDICIA significantly changed both the structure of bank regulation and the coverage and financing of deposit insurance. The major, although not the sole, focus of bank performance for prudential regulatory purposes was put on capital. The lower a bank's capital-to-asset ratio (defined in three ways – Tier 1 and total capital to total risk-weighted on- and off-balance-sheet assets and Tier 1 to total on-balance-sheet assets), the progressively harsher and more mandatory are the sanctions that the regulators first may and then must impose on the bank. The corrective sanctions to be imposed are modelled on those that the market typically imposes on troubled non-regulated firms, such as reductions in dividends, limits on acquisitions and growth, and changes in senior management. The more important sanctions that regulators may or must impose as banks decline through five capital tranches or tripwires and the definitions of the tranches are shown in Table 5.1. Regulatory discipline is designed to mimic market discipline.

The progressively harsher structure of the sanctions under prompt corrective action as a bank's financial position deteriorates is intended to reduce the incentive for moral hazard risk-taking by the insured banks by increasing the cost of such behavior. The progressively more mandatory structure of the sanctions is intended to reduce the ability of regulators to engage in unwarranted forbearance from poor agency behavior. The mandatory sanctions supplement the regulators' discretionary sanctions. Indeed, to the extent that the threat of mandatory harsher sanctions reinforces the incentive of targeted banks to respond to less harsh discretionary sanctions on a timely basis, the mandatory sanctions strengthen the discretionary effectiveness of the regulators.

If, despite the actions of the regulators to try to turn a troubled bank around, the bank approaches insolvency, FDICIA encourages the regulators to resolve institutions before their reported capital is completely exhausted. In FDICIA, the minimum legislated capital ratio for legal closure is 2 percent equity to total assets. But regulators may place a bank in receivership earlier if there is

Table 5.1 Summary of corrective action provisions of the Federal Deposit Insurance Corporation Improvement Act of 1991

| Zone | Mandatory provisions | Discretionary provisions | Capital ratios (%) | | |
| | | | | Risk-based leverage | |
			Total	Tier 1	Tier 1
1. Well-capitalized			>10	>6	>5
2. Adequately capitalized	1. No brokered deposits except with FDIC approval		>8	>4	>4
3. Undercapitalized	1. Suspend dividends and management fees 2. Require capital restoration plan 3. Restrict asset growth 4. Approval required for acquisitions, branching and new activities 5. No brokered deposits	1. Order recapitalization 2. Restrict inter-affiliate transactions 3. Restrict deposit interest rates 4. Restrict certain other activities 5. Any other action that would better carry out prompt correction action	<8	<4	<4
4. Significantly undercapitalized	1. Same as for Zone 3 2. Order recapitalization*	1. Any Zone 3 discretionary actions	<6	<3	<3

119

Table 5.1 Continued

Zone	Mandatory provisions	Discretionary provisions	Capital ratios (%) Risk-based leverage		
			Total	Tier 1	Tier 1
	3. Restrict inter-affiliate transactions* 4. Restrict deposit interest rates* 5. Pay of officers restricted	2. Conservatorship or receivership if fails to submit or implement plan or recapitalize pursuant to order 3. Any other Zone 5 provision, if such action is necessary to carry out prompt corrective action			
5. Critically undercapitalized	1. Same as for Zone 4 2. Receiver/conservator within 90 days 3. Receiver if still in Zone 5 four quarters after becoming critically undercapitalized 4. Suspend payments on subordinated debt 5. Restrict certain other activities				<2**

*Not required if primary supervisor determines action would not serve purpose of prompt corrective action if certain conditions are met.
**Tangible equity.

Source: Board of Governors of the Federal Reserve System.

an obvious threat to solvency. This requirement is intended to reduce the losses to the insurance agency and uninsured creditors and depositors. Indeed, if a bank (or any firm) is resolved before its capital becomes negative, losses accrue only to shareholders, not to depositors, other creditors or the insurer. Deposit insurance is then effectively redundant. Any positive capital in the resolved institution is returned to the shareholders, so that there is no expropriation of property. However, as a bank's reported capital tends to progressively overstate its actual or market value capital as it approaches economic insolvency, because of a tendency to underreserve for loan losses and engage in other inappropriate accounting practices, regulators are frequently unlikely to succeed in resolving most institutions without a loss.

To further reduce the magnitude of any loss to the FDIC, FDICIA requires that the FDIC resolve an institution in such a way as to minimize the cost to itself – least cost resolution (LCR). The FDIC is effectively prohibited from protecting deposits in excess of the maximum legal insurance limit if doing so increases the cost of resolution. This appears to have brought an end to the former frequently used policy of 'too big to fail' (TBTF). Under this policy, although large insolvent banks were generally legally failed, shareholders wiped out, senior management changed, and the bank sold or merged, *de jure* uninsured deposits (currently those in excess of $100 000 per account) were generally fully protected – provided with implicit insurance – at a high cost to the FDIC and eventually the economy as a whole.[30]

But an exemption to LCR was provided if not protecting uninsured deposits 'would have serious adverse effects on economic conditions or financial stability and . . . assistance [to these depositors] . . . would avoid or mitigate such adverse effects'. However, evoking such a 'systemic risk exemption' (SRE) is not easy. It requires a written recommendation to do so to the Secretary of the Treasury by a two-thirds vote of both the directors of the FDIC and the Board of Governors of the Federal Reserve and a determination by the Secretary after consultation with the President that the above conditions exist. Written notification of such a determination must be provided to the House and Senate Banking Committees and the Secretary must maintain all documentation. The reasons for the determination and the purposes and effects of any actions undertaken must be reviewed by the General Accounting Office. Moreover, if the FDIC suffers any loss in providing assistance to the uninsured depositors, the cost must be paid by a special assessment on all banks according to their total assets. Thus, it appears highly likely that these provisions will significantly dampen the enthusiasm of both the regulators and the healthy banks for protecting uninsured depositors at insolvent large banks, although it may not eliminate it altogether.

The structure of deposit insurance was further changed to shift the liability for losses from failure almost entirely from the government and the taxpayer to the insured banks. As noted earlier, before FDICIA, the maximum insurance premium the FDIC could charge insured banks was set by law. This constraint contributed to the insolvency of the old Federal Savings and Loan Insurance Corporation (FSLIC) and the near-insolvency of the FDIC when losses from insured institution failures mounted in the late 1980s. FDICIA changed this. It established a minimum reserve to insured deposit ratio for the FDIC, currently 1.25 percent. If losses drive this ratio below this minimum, the FDIC is required to increase premiums to recapture the amount within one year or be required to impose a very high premium until the minimum reserve ratio is regained. In effect, this provision requires all losses to the FDIC to be borne by the banking system until its aggregate capital is exhausted to the extent that it cannot pay the premiums. To the extent this reduces the potential liability of the taxpayer for losses, it reduces the need for as intense and comprehensive government regulation as before. If this provision is credible, the greater at-risk banks will assume a greater responsibility for monitoring and disciplining their fellow banks to reduce their own liabilities.

Because few and not very large banks have encountered serious financial difficulties in the USA since the enactment of FDICIA in 1991, it is too early to tell whether the new structure is successful or not in strengthening the banking system and in reducing or eliminating altogether the protection of uninsured depositors at insolvent large banks. On the one hand, the number of bank failures has been very small by historical standards, as has been the increase in the number of failures during the recent recession. Uninsured depositors have not been protected at any of the post-1992 bank failures when doing so was expected to impose an additional cost on the FDIC. On the other hand, losses to the FDIC in some of the failures exceeded 25 percent of bank assets and have been as high as 75 percent. This is hardly consistent with the intentions of the designers of the prompt corrective action and least cost resolution provisions of the Act. Nevertheless, if these large losses turn out to be outliers due to massive fraud and contained to relatively small banks, much of the regulatory structure of FDICIA could well be incorporated into the Basel structure, as is partially proposed in the latest recommendations for strengthening of the second pillar of supervisory discipline and the third pillar of market discipline, although probably on a country-specific basis. Indeed, if this is correct, these two new pillars may well reduce the necessity for the excessively complex structure of the capital regulations in Pillar 1.

CONCLUSIONS

This chapter has reviewed the rationale for government regulation of banks and how regulation has expanded from being domestic to transnational, particularly for large, internationally active banks. Although, throughout history, regulation has been imposed on banks for a wide variety of reasons, the primary current rationale is safety. Ironically, the concern over safety is, in part, the result of the introduction of explicit or implicit government guarantees, particularly deposit insurance, that has reduced the intensity of market monitoring and discipline. That is, government regulation needed to be increased to offset the induced decline in private market discipline. In addition, as they will be financing part of any losses from insolvencies, the government guarantees give governments a direct financial interest in the solvency of their banks.

Advances in communications and computer technology that have increased the speed and reduced the cost of transferring funds across even large distances and across national borders have significantly broadened both the market areas of individual banks and the interconnections among banks. Thus the fear that problems at one large bank or in one country will quickly spill over to other countries has increased.

But designing effective regulations is not easy and is even less easy if they affect different jurisdictions. Moreover, regulations have unintended as well as intended effects, and the costs of some of the unintended effects may offset in part, in full, or more than in full the benefits of the intended effects. In particular, government guarantees to enhance safety have often also encouraged excessive risk-taking by banks and excessive forbearance by regulators. The design of the new international regulations has been delegated to the Basel Committee on Banking Supervision, which has been working and developing such a structure since the mid-1980s.

The Basel Committee is to be congratulated for, albeit belatedly, moving to address some of the long-standing flaws inherent in the original 1988 Capital Accord, for seeking to embrace financial innovation and encouraging the development of advanced risk management practices, and for responding in a positive fashion to the comments received following the publication of its original reform proposals in June 1999. While the January 2001 package of proposals addresses some of the criticisms made concerning the earlier proposals, the residual concerns outlined in this chapter, however, call into question the overall increases in cost-effectiveness and economic efficiency likely to result from its adoption. Although the Committee still has time to further refine its blueprint for reform – implementation is not now being called for until after 2005, following the launching of a final 'impact study' in October 2002 and the issuing of a definitive set of proposals towards the end of 2003 – some serious concerns are likely to persist. Nevertheless, the Committee's work has not been wasted; on the contrary. Banks are more conscious of the risks they run today than they have ever been, and their focus is now correctly on risk-adjusted capital and rates of return. But one needs to recognize that all possible forms of assessment regime have their own attendant benefits and costs. The theory of the 'second-best' highlights the danger of assuming that continued progress towards the 'first best' solution – a regime which perfectly corrects for market failure – ultimately delivers increased social welfare.[31]

NOTES

1. West (1997).
2. Wallis et al. (1994); Sylla et al. (1996); and Sylla et al (1987).
3. Sylla (1995, p. 212.
4. Kaufman (1995).
5. Kaufman (1996).
6. Kaufman (1996).
7. Others include, *inter alia*, the development under the so-called Basle Concordat of the principles which should underpin the allocation of supervisory responsibilities between parent and host supervisors of international banks, and the promotion of a set of 'Core Principles for Effective Banking Supervision' which the Committee hopes will eventually be adopted by all supervisory authorities around the globe. (For further details see Hall, 1999, chs 3 and 7.)
8. See Basel Committee (1988).
9. A set of transitional arrangements applied in the run-up to this deadline although not all countries (for example,the UK) found it necessary to avail themselves of the temporary freedoms afforded – see Hall (1992).
10. See Basel Committee (1996).
11. In some jurisdictions, for example in the UK and USA, national supervisors set higher minimum RAR requirements on a bank-by-bank basis.
12. The distinction is drawn to reflect the Committee's concern with both the quality and quantity of capital held by international banks – for further details see Hall (2001), Exhibit 1.
13. See ibid., Exhibits 2 to 5.
14. For further details on the adjustment to the RAR methodology necessitated by the reform see ibid., Exhibit 7.
15. The supervisory authorities have first to satisfy themselves that their banks comply with six sets of 'safeguards' relating to their usage, covering general criteria, qualitative standards, quantitative standards, the specification of risk factors, stress testing and external validation of the models (see Basel Committee, 1996).
16. For further details see Hall (2001), Exhibit 8.
17. It is worth noting that, in the European Economic Area (EEA), compliance with European Commission Directives on the subject is mandatory for all member states.
18. This has always been the major objective of the Committee, although a subsidiary objective of the Accord was to contribute to a 'levelling of the regulatory playing field' for internationally active banks.
19. See note 18.
20. The most serious risk is that the assessment framework may actually be perverse and hence destabilizing as banks engage in various forms of 'regulatory capital arbitrage' in order to negate or mitigate the undesirable consequence, in terms of increased compliance costs, that ensue its adoption. (For further details see Jones, 2000.)
21. For a more detailed discussion see Hall (2001), pp. 121–6.
22. See Basel Committee (1999).
23. For further details see Hall, 200 1, pp. 126-35.
24. For a summary of the proposed amendments see ibid., Exhibit 10.
25. Whether or not this is desirable is another matter – see Shaefer (1992), and Bowe and Hall (1998).
26. See Basel Committee (2001).

27. Most notably the German government in respect of the treatment of loans to small- and medium-sized entities (SMEs).
28. Changes already announced since publication of the January 2001 consultation paper embrace the following:

   (i) a revised credit calibration has been issued by the Committee to encourage take-up of the IRB approaches;
   (ii) in respect of the treatment of operational risk, a Working Paper on the subject was issued by the Committee on 28 September 2001 refining the definition of operational risk and foreshadowing a future recalibration of the associated capital charge (the proximate 'target' for the minimum capital charge was cut from the initially proposed 20 percent of total regulatory capital to 12 percent);
   (iii) in respect of disclosure requirements, a Working Paper on market discipline was also released on 28 September 2001 proposing a number of changes to required disclosures with the intention of reducing the overall burden placed on banks (although the Committee also suggested that the proposed streamlined disclosures become 'requirements' rather than recommendations);
   (iv) as regards the treatment of credit risk mitigation, the Committee announced in September 2001 that it would drop the idea of applying a 'w factor' to account for residual risks (which have now to be addressed under Pillar 2); and
   (v) on 25 June 2001 the Committee issued a press release following submissions from the German government and other interested parties, foreshadowing lower capital charges for loans to SMEs, provided the loan portfolios are sufficiently well diversified.

29. Deposit insurance is one part of the safety net under depository institutions in the USA. The other two parts are the Federal Reserve discount window and the Fed's guarantee of funds transferred on its fedwire.
30. Benston and Kauftman (2000) and Kaufman (2002).
31. 'The increased complexity deemed necessary to accommodate demands to more closely align capital charges with the underlying risks facing banks does not, unfortunately, necessarily deliver increased precision. Accordingly, it can be argued that adoption of appropriate Pillar 2 and Pillar 3 requirements reduces the need, especially in developed countries where the skills base of supervisors is so much higher and market discipline so much more deeply ingrained, for an overly complex Pillar 1 set of requirements.

REFERENCES

Basel Committee (1988), *International Convergence of Capital Measurement and Capital Standards*, Basel, July.

Basel Committee (1996), *Amendment to the Capital Accord to Incorporate Market Risks*, Basel, January.

Basel Committee (1999), 'A new capital adequacy framework', consultation paper, Basel, June.

Basel Committee (2000), 'A new capital adequacy framework: pillar 3', consultation paper, Basel, January.

Basel Committee (2001), 'The new Basel capital accord', consultative document, Basel, January 2001

Benston, George J. (1999), *Regulating Financial Markets: A Critique and Some Proposals*, Washington, DC: American Enterprise Institute.

Benston, George J. and George G. Kauftman (2000), 'Deposit insurance reform in the FDIC Improvement Act,' *Economic Perspectives*, Federal Reserve Bank of Chicago, second quarter, pp. 2–20.

Bowe, M. and M.J.B. Hall (1998), 'A comparison of capital standards and proprietary surveillance as mechanisms for regulating financial market risk in the EU', *International Journal of Finance and Economics*, **3**(4), 303–20.

Hall, M.J.B., (1992), 'Implementation of the BIS "rules" on capital adequacy assessment: a comparative study of the approaches adopted in the UK, USA and Japan', *Banca Nazionale del Lavoro Quarterly Review*, **45**(180), 35–57.

Hall, M.J.B. (1999), *Handbook of Banking Regulation and Supervision in the UK*, Cheltenham, UK and Northampton USA: Edward Elgar.

Hall, M.J.B., 'The Basle Committee's proposals for a new capital adequacy assessment framework: a critique', *Banca Nazionale del Lavoro Quarterly Review*, No. 217, June, 111–79.

Jones, D. (2000), 'Emerging problems with the accord: regulatory capital arbitrage and related issues', *Journal of Banking and Finance*, **24**, 35–58.

Kaufman, George G. (1995), 'The U.S. banking debacle of the 1990s', *Financier*, May, 9–26.

Kaufman, George G. (1996), 'Bank failures, systemic risk, and bank regulation', *Cato Journal*, spring/summer, pp. 17–45.

Kaufman, George G. and Steven A. Seelig (2002), 'Post-resolution treatment of depositors at failed banks', *Economic Perspectives*, Federal Reserve Bank of Chicago, second quarter, 27–41.

Nosal, Ed and Peter Rupert (2002), 'Infrastructure and the wealth of nations', *Economic Commentary*, Federal Reserve Bank of Cleveland, 15 January.

Sapienza, Paola (2002), 'What do state-owned firms maximize? Evidence from Italian banks', working paper, Northwestern University, 7 January.

Shaefer, S.M. (1992), 'Financial regulation: the contribution of the theory of finance', in J. Fingleton (ed.), *The Internationalization of Capital Markets and the Regulatory Response*, London: Graham and Trotman.

Sylla, Richard (1995), 'The forgotten private banker', *The Freeman*, April, 210–14.

Sylla, Richard, John B. Legler and John J. Wallis (1987), 'Banks and state public finance in the republic: The United States, 1790–1860', *Journal of Economic History*, June, 391–403.

Sylla, Richard, John J. Wallis and John B. Legler (1996), 'Historical economics: U.S. state and local government', *NBER Reporter*, Spring, 11–16.

Wallis, John 1, Richard E. Sylla and John B. Legler (1994), 'The interrelationship of taxation and regulation in nineteenth-century U.S. banking', in Claudia Goldin and Gary D. Lidecap (eds), *The Regulated Economy*, Chicago: University of Chicago Press, pp. 121–44.

West, Edwin G. (1997), 'Adam Smith's support for money and banking regulation: a case of inconsistency', *Journal of Money, Credit, and Banking*, February, pp. 127–34.

6. Technology, productivity and structural change

Sarianna M. Lundan

In this chapter we will explore the consequences of the internationalization of corporate research and development (R&D) for the locational patterns of innovative activity. The process of innovation has been characterized as a coupling activity by comparing it to a pair of scissors, with demand–pull representing one blade and innovation–push representing the other blade.[1] We employ this metaphor in a slightly different form to represent the process of industrial innovation as the coupling of innovative ideas on one side, and financing and marketing capability on the other side. While we are not suggesting that this approach is particularly novel, it allows us to discuss the two essential aspects of the innovation process that make the role of multinational enterprises (MNEs) in this process a critical one.

We know from existing research that innovations are concentrated within large firms, and that although the number of research-intensive small firms continues to grow, both in terms of output as measured by patent citations as well as input as measured by R&D expenditures, large firms claim the lion's share of innovative activity in many sectors, although sectoral differences are substantial (Freeman and Soete, 1997). It should also been noted that, in the USA, the share of federally funded research has continuously declined in the aftermath of the cold war, while corporate investment in R&D has become by far the most important source of research financing. In fact, this is the case in all the G8 countries, with the exception of Italy, where industry provides research funding for 44 percent, while government-funded research accounts for slightly over a half of the total (National Science Board, 2002, pp. 4–48).

To address the issue of where innovative ideas come from, since they are not a simple function of R&D efforts, we need to look at the institutional influences on innovative activity. To describe such institutions on the national level, the literature on national systems of innovation helps us to identify the central features, such as programs of technical and vocational education, levels of university education, public funding of R&D, and the existence of public research institutions (Nelson, 1993b). However, as useful as this literature is in helping to appreciate the variety of institutional systems in existence, an approach concentrating solely on the national level almost inevitably results in an equal number of systems as countries (see Amable, 2000), so to overcome this problem we propose to disaggregate the discussion to the level of the firm.

At the lowest level of aggregation, individual entrepreneurs, due to their tolerance of risk and ambiguity, create markets by bringing together previously disparate segments of the economy. Consequently, differences in the rates of entrepreneurship across borders are one part of explaining differences in innovative activity. However, since we are concerned specifically with the marriage between sustained financing and innovative activity, we will focus on the role of multinational firms in exploiting the innovative capabilities available in local clusters of activity. Indeed, the key aspect of the transformation of the multinational firm over the past decade has been the changing of focus away from the exploitation of home-based capabilities towards the establishment of corporate networks aimed not only at the diffusion, but also at the exploitation of disparate knowledge-based resources. We will argue that multinationals have a unique capability of combining both sources of funding and sources of innovation into the successful commercial introduction of new innovations.

The superior financial resources of multinational firms may be path-dependent; in other words, they may rest on a past inheritance, but for most multinationals global competition entails mandated reinvestment (Milberg and Gray, 1992), that is, the generation of sufficient cash flow to feed competitive levels of R&D on a sustainable basis. The source of this cash flow at least in the case of some of the largest multinationals is undoubtedly partly attributable to market power and market domination, as only firms that can rely on a brand name, superior distribution, and in final consumer markets, extensive advertising, can generate the required cash to run a successful R&D program. But having the resources to invest in R&D, and in particular to invest in the commercialization of innovation, does not guarantee a regular source of inventions. We will argue that the ability of the multinational not only to exploit its market power, but also its superior access to knowledge-based resources around the world gives MNEs a key place in the generation of new technology. We will also present some aggregate evidence on the patterns of innovative activity within Europe, and particularly on the extent of American direct investment in European R&D.

From a policy perspective, facilitating the ability of the multinational to attach itself to local innovative networks requires a policy of non-discrimination towards foreign investors, and results in an exacerbation of differences between regions. Thus while the competitive clusters develop at the regional (subnational) level, any efforts to reduce the effects of regional disparities are more likely to occur at the supranational (EU) level. Since locational competition is to an extent unavoidable, we will argue that policy efforts should focus on encouraging regions to invest in revealing their true competences in order to avoid market distortion as a result of misdirected investment.

KNOWLEDGE AND LOCATION

The literature on so-called national systems of innovation has produced some interesting research on the connections between firms and the local national and regional institutions that support them, such as independent research centers, universities and the like (see, for example, Nelson, 1993a, 1993b on the national level and Cooke and Morgan, 1998 on the regional level). A well-functioning network of firms and institutions not only encourages domestic economic activity, but also creates an attractive hotspot for foreign multinationals, eager to benefit from the interaction.[2] However, the same virtuous cycle of the right institutional climate attracting the right kind of firms that makes the region even more attractive, also risks locking the region into a particular trajectory of growth. In a sense, the lack of variety of options available to the generalist is the price one pays for increased specialization. More specialized resources are also more unusual, which makes investing in them both a high-risk and high-return type of activity.

In a recent special issue of *Industrial and Corporate Change* on the geography of innovation and economic clustering, the editors point to a couple of interesting lessons learnt from the literature so far (Breschi and Malerba, 2001). First of all, there seems to be a wide consensus that the availability of a highly skilled labor force and the quality of the human capital coming from leading universities is likely to be one of the most important factors encouraging the growth of innovative clusters. Another point of commonality is that there is clearly a difference in trying to understand the dynamics of well-established clusters like Silicon Valley, and understanding the dynamic growth of emerging clusters. Nonetheless, external linkages appear to be important both for emerging and established clusters, and of particular interest to us here is how such linkages are established. While linkages can result from the repatriation of foreign-educated engineers and scientists, or the movements of key scientists within a firm or between firms, we are particularly interested in the extent to which multinational corporations initiate the establishment of such linkages in distant clusters of innovation.

Not surprisingly, on the public policy front, the editors conclude that there is indeed a consensus for policy to be in the first instance broadly supporting of the infrastructure of innovation. This means primarily investment in education, while more directed programs such as the establishment of science parks and various kinds of technopolis are not likely to be very successful. With the government playing a supporting role, and we would argue with multinationals playing a facilitating role, it would appear that the more 'organically' grown clusters such as the case of Baden-Württemberg (Cooke, 2001), where the interactions involve both public and private sectors, appear to be more successful. In another example, in the development of a new high-technology region around Washington, DC (Feldman, 2001), entrepreneurial activity in response to external shocks set in motion the beginnings of the development of a cluster. While government policy was broadly supportive, it followed the establishment of a proto-cluster rather than bringing it about in the first place.

If clustering is fundamentally an issue of employment, and the right kind of human resources in the right place at the right time, it is also an inherently local phenomenon, particularly in Europe, where the labor mobility of highly skilled labor is very low. This is partly due to institutional impediments that still remain after the creation of the common market, for example in the lack of mutual recognition of professional qualifications for doctors and lawyers, and the difficulty of transferring pension rights across borders. But it is also because the idea of a Europe-wide labor market has not yet featured in any meaningful way in the minds and career paths of professionals. Thus the highly trained resources that lie at the heart of clusters are relativity immobile, and require that in one form or another, economic activity is drawn to them rather than the other way around.

Furthermore, if at the heart of knowledge creation lies a system of education and specialized human resources, the question is raised as to what extent this is an extension of agglomeration or urban economies, or to what extent it relies on the existence of knowledge spillovers. Breschi and Lissoni (2001) tackle this question in an interesting paper, where they argue that what would have been labeled as spillovers in the innovation literature, are not necessarily spillovers of the technical variety, but should perhaps more appropriately be classified as pecuniary externalities of the Marshall type.[3] Such externalities arise because the increasing availability of specialized skilled labor and specialized suppliers in a given area allows local firms to become more efficient, and might also allow firms to charge higher prices in the market. Such externalities are pecuniary, as they are experienced either through the price mechanism or the labor market in wage costs. Non-pecuniary externalities, on the other hand, are the result of a genuine spilling over of knowledge, which is of course much harder to quantify, but which may nonetheless have suffered somewhat from an over-attribution in the recent literature. We agree with Krugman (1991) that before trying to use pure technological externalities in our explanations, it would be useful to see how far the story could be told by reference to pecuniary externalities, which lend themselves more easily to measurement.

In other words, while there is no question that innovative activity is spatially concentrated, to what extent actual knowledge spillovers account for much or any of the concentration is an open question. Part of the problem here is that knowledge spillovers are difficult to define in a way that would not lead to contradictory conjectures. In other words, if the essence of a spillover is that knowledge is a public good, with the characteristics of non-excludability and non-rivalry, such spillovers should be equally appropriated by all firms with the capacity to utilize such information. However, this in itself does not dictate whether the receiving firms would be near or far. One contention is that such knowledge would only spill over in close proximity, that is, with the possibility of face-to-face contact. In this connection, many authors make the distinction between knowledge that includes a tacit component, and is difficult to transmit, and information that is codified, and easier to transmit over distances. However, the distinction between tacit versus codified knowledge doesn't really help to address the issue of why, in practice, knowledge seems to be simultaneously both difficult and easy to transmit. Thus, for example, there is a great deal of research studying knowledge management within multinational firms, or the ability of the firm to transfer knowledge, some tacit and some codified, within the firm. At the same time, there is a great deal of research directed at inadvertent spillovers of knowledge, particularly within collaborative ventures between firms.

An alternative way of looking at the flow of knowledge is to change the focus away from the amorphous knowledge and its inherent properties, and instead to look at the institutional context within which the knowledge transfer occurs. Breschi and Lissoni (2001) suggest by reference to some recent literature that it is possible that contractual activity underlies much of the transfer of knowledge within high-technology clusters, particularly in connection with university research, or that, at the very minimum, the institutional context within which the transfer takes place is essential in determining the extent to which knowledge spills over, or is carried over on purpose.

We will argue here that the participation of firms within networks of local firms and institutions is in itself an effort to appropriate a part of the market, and it is in a way similar to the participation of firms in business groups and associations. Each association develops its own norms and language to promote the objectives of its members, and it is possible that, as suggested by Breschi and Lissoni (2001), such conventions also extend to the transfer of knowledge within high-technology clusters. Rather than being a product of the inherent characteristics of knowledge, successful transfer is the outcome of a process of exclusion. To effect such exclusion, it is possible that scientists and other groups of practitioners develop their own jargon which at the same time is highly specific and specialized, and yet dependent on the context within which it is transmitted in order for it to be deciphered correctly.

But exclusion can also take much more mundane forms, such as reciprocal obligations for exchanging information and norms about sharing within the group, and correspondingly not sharing outside of the group. Such a system can function on trust and mutual forbearance, or, like any successful cartel, it can also function on mutual monitoring and effective punishment of defectors. Either way, the knowledge that is transmitted does not really spill over like a true public good, but it is shared more like common property or a club good. This implies that the goal of knowledge management is perhaps partly how to prevent the accidental spilling of knowledge, but at least as importantly, it is about how to be included within the clubs that are sharing knowledge. For example, the success of new clusters described in Bresnahan et al. (2001) was strongly influenced by specializing in a niche underserved by leading firms, but linked to the activities of US firms (India, Israel, Ireland and Taiwan). (See also Teece, 1992 for a classic argument about the importance of a dominant design.)

The influence of organized social contact through industry associations, research consortia and such also tends to reinforce the basic finding that systems of innovation are sectoral, with similarities within industries and across borders (Breschi, 1999; Malerba, 2002). Malerba's (2002) suggestion that the appropriate units of analysis are not firms, but individuals, or units of firms (or indeed groups of firms) suggests that the inclusionary or exclusionary effect of clubs should play a role in the study of industrial innovation. In a way, trust relationships and group culture are just a means of defining the inside and outside. In some cases, the exclusion is not absolute, as an outside firm taking on the behaviors and characteristics of a local firm can eventually be accepted within the network. On the other hand, monitoring and punishment systems are also likely to work much more effectively when the actors within the club are well known. A very interesting example of institutionalizing such inclusion (and exclusion) is provided by Cooke (2001), who describes the emergence of private clusters or EcoNets in Silicon Valley. These are groups of start-up firms, set up by venture capitalists like Kleiner Perkins, who manage them in *keiretsu*-like manner, with a strong sense of an inside and outside group of firms.[4]

KNOWLEDGE-BASED RESOURCES AND MNES

Evidence of the importance of foreign sourcing of competitive assets by Fortune 500 multinationals, particularly in high-technology sectors, has been presented by a number of authors, including survey-based evidence by Dunning et al. (Dunning and Lundan, 1998; Dunning and Wymbs, 1999). They argue that, in addition to size and consequent oligopolistic rents resulting from market domination, one element contributing to the advantage of multinationality is the ability of multinationals to source various competitive resources around the world. In particular, the recent decades have witnessed a tremendous increase in various cooperative efforts by firms in order to gain access to various geographically dispersed resources. However, the patterns of partnering activity present a picture of concentration, both in terms of a sectoral concentration in high technology, as well as a geographical concentration within the Triad. While in the earlier stages of internationalization, the tendency was for firms to keep their R&D-related activities closer to home, the increased partnering activity is an outgrowth of the internationalization of the R&D function, which has resulted in the establishment of corporate R&D centers abroad (Lundan and Hagedoorn, 2001).

The underlying reasons for the expansion of cross-border cooperative activity are related to intensified global competition and the consequent shortening of product life cycles, and the need to keep the costs of new product development under control by collaborating with other firms. Thus, a firm may hope to partner in order to gain experience in a field where its current competencies are minimal, and where in-house development would be exceedingly expensive and time-consuming. On the other hand, a firm might wish to access the locally developed resources as an intact package, and the dramatic increase in mergers and acquisitions in recent years can be at least partially attributed to this desire.

Hagedoorn and Lundan (2001) present evidence of partnering activity since the 1980s, and argue that there is a clear shift, whereby companies seem to prefer contractual partnerships to joint ventures, and there is an explosion in high-technology partnerships. However, such trends mask a great deal of inter-industry variation, since the information technology and chemicals sectors alone account for slightly under and slightly over half of all new alliances in the high- and medium-technology sectors respectively. It should also be noted that over the past ten years the vast majority of alliances in the two most active sectors, namely information technology and biotechnology, have been alliances between American firms. In fact intra-American alliances have been twice as numerous as the second largest group, which are alliances between American and European firms (National Science Board, 2002, pp. 4–40).

There is therefore an increased interest on the part of multinationals to access different elements of the local network of institutions in their host locations, and to combine such elements within the multinational network of the firm. Recent research on knowledge management within MNEs has indicated that efforts to link the subsidiaries to the local institutional structure, and in particular to the system of innovation, promote learning within the subsidiary, and to the extent that knowledge is transmitted within the MNE, this makes the subsidiary more secure within the MNE network (Simoes et al., 2002). In some cases, such subsidiaries can grow to form the basis for a center of excellence within the multinational network (Holm and Pedersen, 2000).

The evidence on the influence of multinational corporations on the further development of regional clusters has been explored extensively by Cantwell and his colleagues (Cantwell and Iammarino, 2001; Cantwell and Noonan, 2001). In their research using US patent statistics as indicators of innovative activity, they have charted the role of multinational firms in the leading innovative clusters within Europe. Their results reveal that, depending on the industrial sector, multinationals sometimes attach themselves to existing local centers of excellence, while in other instances there is a complementarity between the firms' existing skills and those prevalent in the location. In general, multinationals appear to be more technologically diversified than the regions they enter into. (Only three of the 33 EU regions studied by Cantwell and Iammarino, 2001 experienced a broadening of technological specialization over time.)

The fact that in the science-based sectors, corporate research seems to be strongly concentrated in the domestic market (Cantwell and Santangelo, 2000) may be an indication of the tacitness of the underlying knowledge and the consequent need for face-to-face communication. Alternatively, it can also be seen as an indication of the exclusion of foreign firms from existing groupings and knowledge-sharing communities. The assumption there would be that it is easier in the first instance to form clubs with local firms of the same nationality, and that some clubs can perpetuate themselves for quite a while, if there is sufficient critical mass to sustain the innovative activity without the intrusion of foreigners. Of course, in this sense the question of investment in high-technology sectors is quite different from market-seeking or resource-seeking investment, because in the first case this is a question of what motivates the multinational in the search for foreign locations, while in the case of high-technology industries it is also a question of which locations would be both better suited and willing to receive such investment, keeping in mind that the costs and potential long-term implications of a wrong decision are quite substantial.

In terms of attracting a multinational into a local cluster, a high-quality infrastructure is necessary, but not sufficient, in ensuring that from among many potential investors, the investor with the best long-term potential will undertake the investment. But even if the right firm is attracted, without a degree of exclusivity arising from membership in the local network, the means governments have of tying the multinational into the local network amount to little more than moral persuasion. We would argue that rather than offer monetary incentives, the host government can play an important role in facilitating the entry of the foreign investor into the local network, including research consortia and other collaborative ventures involving local firms. This contrasts with the overall provision of high-quality infrastructure in terms of a highly educated workforce, for example, in that there should be asymmetrical benefits accruing to the firm that enters early into the network. The more fully the multinational participates in the local network, the more it is in its interest to keep the network functional and exclusionary, which in the long run should result in the kind of value-adding collaboration governments are hoping to achieve.

MNES AND 'MANDATED REINVESTMENT'

In spite of the extensive literature devoted to high-technology investment, clustering and alliances, very little has been written on the origins of funding for R&D investment. For most multinationals, global competition entails mandated reinvestment (Milberg and Gray, 1992), that is, the generation of sufficient cash flow to feed competitive levels of R&D on a sustainable basis. We would argue here that the critical ability of a multinational to combine financial resources with geographical reach is made possible by combining the multinational's ability to derive profits based on higher prices and lower wages (market power), and to reapply these in sectors where innovative or entrepreneurial profit can be generated.[5] We agree with Cantwell and Santangelo (2000) that, in principle, unlike standard profits, which are based on market power, and tend to shift income from wages to profits, entrepreneurial profits are at least compatible with increasing wages, albeit linked to productivity and an increase in profits, and are in that sense preferable to profit derived from market power. The point we are making here is to question whether the latter kind of profit is possible without financing from the first kind.

Entrepreneurial profits are clearly preferable if innovation is thought to be a positive sum game, resulting in improvements in the processes of production and the introduction of new products. But of course there is no guarantee that all innovative activity is genuinely productivity enhancing. In extremely competitive markets, multiple simultaneous efforts to achieve the same result can easily take place, and assessing whether this is a case of 'healthy variety' or 'wasteful duplication' is a difficult distinction to make. Furthermore, since the ability to market and distribute products effectively is crucial in the process of appropriating returns from innovation, superior financial resources can lead to the market adoption of a technically inferior product. While virtue may be its own reward, if innovative activity doesn't result in improved productivity or entirely new products, the origin of the profit remains suspect.

It is suggested here that there is a trade-off between the two kinds of profit, where continued innovation is paid for to an extent by increasing market power. Of course, a virtue of international production is that the payers and the beneficiaries do not have to be in the same markets, since profits derived from elsewhere or from different activities can be used to finance innovative activities in another location. We also agree with Cantwell and Santangelo (2000) that increased competition in many markets has set definite limits to the ability of multinationals to derive profits based on market power, and that part of the spur to innovative activities is the need to find new sources of profit. However, at the same time we wonder what proportion of such profits are a by-product of spurious (marketing) innovation and market power as discussed earlier.

There are of course other issues in the financing of high-technology investment, particularly regarding the existence of so-called funding gaps in the financing of small, high-technology firms.[6] While the argument can be made that entrepreneurship within large firms can overcome the information asymmetry and consequent adverse selection related to risky projects, lending criteria can also become distorted through internal interference and politics. More broadly, any form of relationship lending, where the lender is in a long-term relationship with the innovative firm, can improve the functioning of the market. For example, Cooke (2001) emphasized how the German-style regional credit-based system, which is an institutionalized form of relationship lending, can be very valuable for start-up firms, particularly if the private sector is not very keen on risk-taking.

INVESTING IN INNOVATION

A problem with much of the empirical research on the geography of innovation is that while the central ingredient identified in nearly every study as critical to the process, namely the locally specialized human resources, are immobile and location-specific, the means used to measure the extent to which local and foreign firms exploit these locational resources is disconnected from location to various degrees. The literature that looks at innovation counts and the influence of university-industry spillovers is by its nature more locationally specific, and has moved to progressively lower levels of aggregation, from the level of the nation or state to regions and sub-regions. However, the extensive research that looks at patenting as the outcome of innovative activity, or the literature that looks at alliance formation as a proxy for innovative activity, suffers from the problem of not being able to link the general outcome to the local context. This is not to say that the focus on patenting would not be important in the sense that they are ultimately related to firm profitability. But from the point of view of the location hosting the innovative activity, while patents (or alliances) contribute to corporate success, they are not necessarily indicative of the money being spent on R&D and, more specifically, on employing research scientists in a particular region.

In this connection, we would like to highlight a few specific aspects of the extent of R&D activities of US multinationals in Europe. These data are drawn from the 1994 benchmark survey of US direct investment abroad conducted by the Bureau of Economic Analysis, and they represent the most recent comprehensive data on the activities of majority-owned foreign affiliates of US firms.[7] These data reveal that of the $11.88 billion worth of R&D performed by foreign affiliates, 73 percent was performed in Europe, and within Europe 78 percent of this money was spent in only four countries, namely Germany, the United Kingdom, France and the Netherlands. Furthermore, 58 percent of the investment was concentrated in only three sectors: pharmaceuticals, computers and automotive investment.

By contrast, the latest available figures for the R&D activities of US affiliates of foreign firms come from the preliminary results of the 1997 benchmark survey of foreign direct investment in the USA. Of the total of $19.7 billion spent on R&D, 69 percent came from European firms, dominated by Switzerland, and the same four major EU investors, namely Germany, the United Kingdom, France and the Netherlands. More than half of the R&D funded by these affiliates was in chemicals (mostly pharmaceuticals) and computers (mostly communications equipment). Altogether, the research performed by the US affiliates of foreign firms accounted for 12 percent of all the R&D performed in the USA (Zeile, 1999).

In the evidence presented by Cantwell and Santangelo (2000), we note that between 1991 and 1995, the share of US patents attributed to the research efforts by American firms abroad was only 8.62 percent, while as a share of the overall R&D effort the research performed abroad varied between 10–12 percent (National Science Board, 2002, pp. 4–60). Also the reverse seems to be true of European firms, where a high proportion of US patenting, 16.47–55.69 percent, depending on the industrial sector, is due to the research performed outside Europe (mostly in the USA). During the same period, the R&D spending accounted for by US affiliates of foreign firms rose from 10 percent to 14 percent (National Science Board, 2002, pp. 4–60). The differences in the two sets of measurements are due to differences in how firms patent, and how they spend money and integrate themselves into local networks of innovation. Again, this is not to say that the extent of US patenting resulting from research abroad is not important, but it is to say that for questions that concern the growth in the innovative ability of a particular region, they alone are not a sufficient proxy for describing the impact of multinational activity.

What is particularly interesting is the extent to which American direct investment has been financed for quite some time to a large extent by retained earnings, which has not been true of European investment abroad. According to the balance-of-payments statistics available from the Bureau of Economic Analysis, between 1992 and 1999, 42 percent of US direct investment was in the form of reinvested earnings (35 percent for US investment in Europe). By contrast, during the same period, reinvested earnings accounted for only

4 percent of European direct investment abroad, and only 6 percent of European investment in the USA.

Indeed, from 1992 onwards, European investment in the USA has been primarily equity investment, and in mergers and acquisitions rather than in greenfield investment. From 1992, when greenfield investment accounted for 31 percent of foreign direct investment in the USA, this proportion has diminished steadily to a low of 1 percent in the year 2000. Of course, part of this dramatic decline is due to the increasing role of mega-mergers (each worth $5 billion or more) in the past few years, but even in 1997, when no cross-border megamergers took place, the ratio of US businesses established to US businesses acquired by foreign investors and their existing affiliates was only 13 percent.[8] In other words, it would appear that while Europeans have been buying their way into markets and specialized capabilities in the USA, Americans have been building more gradually on their existing investments in Europe.

While these aggregate statistics should not be taken too far, in the first instance the acquisition of research capability within the USA by European firms does not increase the amount of research performed or research personnel employed, as it merely shifts ownership from one firm to another. By contrast, sustained reinvestment of earnings in the research-intensive sectors would seem to indicate the presence of a different dynamic, possibly of the kind we have been discussing in this chapter. Multinationals that had been initially attracted by an existing base of innovative research and highly skilled labor are gradually becoming more integrated into the local network, and are growing 'organically' within the cluster. Of course it is possible that this is happening within the European investment in the USA as well, but the aggregate picture doesn't give much indication that this is the case. (At a later stage, we aim to complement the figures presented here with evidence on alliance formation, which would offer a richer picture of the linkages between innovative firms in the US and Europe.) It should be pointed out, however, that there is no direct link between reinvested earnings and investment in R&D. The contention here is simply that reinvested earnings for American firms have been of sufficient magnitude to finance their R&D activities abroad. For example, within the European chemical sector (mostly pharmaceuticals), American investment in R&D from 1994 to 1998 was $13.5 billion, while the cumulative reinvested earnings over the same period within the same sector amounted to $13.2 billion.

CONCLUSIONS

In this chapter we have discussed the role of the multinational enterprise in connection with industrial innovation, and in particular MNE participation in high-technology clusters in Europe and the USA. We have argued that multinational firms are in a privileged position due to their ability to tap into localized resources in different markets. The benefits of clustering arise from structural upgrading in a particular location or region, which gives rise to pecuniary externalities in the form of access to a specialized workforce and specialist suppliers. Some of the benefits enjoyed by firms in such a cluster may also be due to pure knowledge spillovers, although these are difficult to track empirically. We have argued that the ability of multinationals to establish themselves in attractive clusters, and to secure their presence by substantial financial resources, makes them critical to the process of industrial innovation. We believe that the ability of large multinational firms to maintain steady levels of R&D investment is contributing to higher rates of innovation than would otherwise be possible. On the other hand, the ability of the multinational to do so is dependent on its ability to derive profits from other activities. Consequently, one might suspect that the origins of financing for investment in innovation lie in profits based on the exploitation of market power.

The fact that nearly half of American foreign investment in the past decade has consisted of reinvested earnings points to two things. The first is that in order to have reinvested earnings it is necessary to have earnings in the first place, and the second is that high levels on reinvested earnings indicate a desire by American multinationals to gradually build on their existing investments abroad. This is in stark contrast to the behavior of European multinationals during the same period, whose investment consists almost entirely of equity investments in mergers and acquisitions. The structural implications of the American type of investment have been discussed at some length in this chapter. This is a process of gradual upgrading of innovative capacity based on the exploitation of highly skilled human resources attached to a particular location. The European type investment, on the other hand, has very few short-term implications for structural upgrading. Some R&D capacity has changed hands from the Americans to the Europeans, and depending on how these resources are managed, this may improve the long-run competitive position of European firms.

We know that American firms are already well integrated with each other through strategic alliances in the key high-technology sectors. The critical question for European multinationals is to what extent European firms can become insiders in the markets that they have entered. Assuming that knowledge does not in fact typically spill over, but that its transfer is mediated by a web of relationships that places firms on the inside and outside, many large takeovers will neither enhance the acquiring firm's capabilities, nor enrich the existing relationships in the market. On the other hand, American multinationals attached to European clusters of knowledge and capabilities may in fact have become better integrated into the local networks, possibly due to their longer presence in the key markets.[9] From a public policy perspective, every effort should be made to ensure that foreign multinationals are able to continue this process, and to take part in local as well as EU-wide research networks. Allowing success to breed more success in any given location will naturally also result in greater disparities between regions. It would appear, however, that a policy to compensate poorer regions for being left behind may in the end be less costly that trying to orchestrate high-growth regions where they have not arisen under existing conditions.

NOTES

1. Schmookler (1996), cited in Freeman and Soete (1997).
2. 'Sticky places in slippery space', as Markusen (1996) put it.
3. While Marshallian economies are generally seen as intra-industry, and urbanization economies as inter-industry, understandably in empirical work such definitions can be difficult to sustain.
4. See also Teece (1991) on Japanese acquisitions in Silicon Valley in the 1980s.
5. A firm that can finance its growth organically is of course also less dependent on the external market, and therefore also more protected from turmoil in world financial markets.
6. See, for example, a special issue of *The Economic Journal* (Cressy, 2002).
7. Both the financial and operating data pertaining to US direct investment abroad and to foreign investment in the USA, as well as the balance-of-payments data, have been downloaded from the Bureau of Economic Analysis, US Department of Commerce (www.bea.gov).
8. The figures for affiliate investment reflect investment both by their foreign parents in terms of retained earnings and intercompany debt and local financing arranged by the affiliate. Data from Howenstine (2001).
9. Mudambi (1998) offers evidence that firms with a longer investment duration are more likely to make further investments.

REFERENCES

Amable, B. (2000), 'Institutional complementarity and diversity of social systems of innovation and production', *Review of International Political Economy*, **7**(4), 645–87.
Breschi, S. (1999), 'Spatial patterns of innovation: evidence from patent data', in Alfonso Gambardella and Franco Malerba (eds), *The Organization of Economic Innovation in Europe*, Cambridge: Cambridge University Press.
Breschi, S. and F. Lissoni (2001), 'Knowledge spillovers and local innovation systems: a critical survey', *Industrial and Corporate Change*, **10**(4), 975–1005.
Breschi, S. and F. Malerba (2001), 'The geography of innovation and economic clustering: some introductory notes', *Industrial and Corporate Change*, **10**(4), 817–33.
Bresnahan, T., A. Gambardella and A. Saxenian (2001), '"Old economy" inputs for new economy' outcomes: cluster formation in the new Silicon Valleys', *Industrial and Corporate Change*, **10**(4), 835–60.
Cantwell, J. and S. Iammarino (2001), EU regions and multinational corporations: change, stability and strengthening of technological comparative advantages', *Industrial and Corporate Change*, **10**(4), 1007–37.

Cantwell, J. and C.A. Noonan (2001), 'The regional distribution of technological development – evidence from foreign-owned firms in Germany', in M.P. Feldman and N. Massard (eds), *Knowledge Spillovers and the Geography of Innovation*, Dordrecht: Kluwer.

Cantwell, J. and G.D. Santangelo (2000), 'Capitalism, profits and innovation in the new technoeconomic paradigm', *Journal of Evolutionary Economics*, **10**, 131–57.

Cooke, P. (2001), 'Regional innovation systems, clusters, and the knowledge economy', *Industrial and Corporate Change*, **10**(4), 945–74.

Cooke, P. and K. Morgan (1998), *The Associational Economy: Firms, Regions, and Innovation*, Oxford: Oxford University Press.

Cressy, R. (2002), 'Funding gaps: a symposium', *The Economic Journal*, **112** (February), F1–F16.

Dunning, J.H. and S.M. Lundan (1998), 'The geographical sources of competitiveness of firms: an econometric analysis', *International Business Review*, **7**(2), 115–33.

Dunning, J.H. and C. Wymbs (1999), 'The geographical sourcing of technology-based assets by multinational enterprises', in D. Archibugi, J. Howells and J. Michie (eds), *Innovation Policy in a Global Economy*, Cambridge: Cambridge University Press.

Feldman, M.P. (2001), 'The entrepreneurial event revisited: firm formation in a regional context', *Industrial and Corporate Change*, **10**(4), 861–9 1.

Freeman, C. and L. Soete (1997), *The Economics of Industrial Innovation*, 3rd edn, London: Pinter.

Hagedoorn, J. and S.M. Lundan (2001), 'Strategic technology alliances: trends and patterns since the early eighties', in A. Plunket, C. Voisin and B. Bellon (eds), *The Dynamics of industrial Collaboration*, Cheltenham, UK and Northampton, USA: Edward Elgar.

Holm, U. and T. Pedersen (eds) (2000), *The Emergence and Impact of MNC Centers of Excellence*, Basingstoke: Macmillan.

Howenstine, N.G. (2001), 'Foreign direct investment in the United States: new investment in 2000', *Survey of Current Business* (June), 27–34.

Krugman, P. (1991), *Geography and Trade*, Cambridge, MA: MIT Press.

Lundan, S.M. and J. Hagedoorn (2001), 'Alliances, acquisitions and multinational advantage', *International Journal of the Economics of Business*, **8**(2), 229–42.

Malerba, F. (2002), 'Sectoral systems of innovation and production', *Research Policy*, **31**, 247–64.

Markusen, A. (1996), 'Sticky places in slippery space: a typology of industrial districts', *Economic Geography*, **72**(3), 293–313.

Milberg, W.S. and H.P. Gray (1992), 'International competitiveness and policy in dynamic industries', *Banca Nazionale del Lavoro, Quarterly Review*, **180** (March), 59–80.

Mudambi, R. (1998), 'The role of duration in multinational investment strategies', *Journal of International Business Studies*, **29**(2), 239–62.

National Science Board (2002), *Science and Engineering Indicators–2002,* Arlington, VA: National Science Foundation.

Nelson, R. (1993a), *The Co-evolution of Technologies and Institutions*, New York: Columbia University Press.

Nelson, R. (ed.) (1993b), *National Innovation Systems: A Comparative Analysis*, New York: Oxford University Press.

Simoes, V.C., R. Biscaya and P. Nevado (2002), 'Subsidiary decision making autonomy: Competences, integration and local responsiveness', in Sarianna M.Lundan (ed.), *Network Knowledge in International Business*, Cheltenham, UK and Northampton, USA: Edward Elgar.

Teece, D. (1992), 'Strategies for capturing the financial benefits from technological innovation', in N. Rosenberg, R. Landau and D.C. Mowery (eds), *Technology and the Wealth of Nations*, Stanford, CA: Stanford University Press.

Teece, D.J. (1991), 'Foreign investment and technological development in Silicon Valley', in Donald G. McFetridge (ed.), *Foreign Investment, Technology and Economic Growth*, Calgary: University of Calgary Press.

Zeile, W.J. (1999), 'Foreign direct investment in the United States: preliminary results from the 1997 benchmark survey', *Survey of Current Business* (August), 21–54.

7. Cracks in the façade: American economic and financial structures after the boom

William R. Emmons and Frank A. Schmid[*]

Many observers of the boom in the USA during the late 1990s concluded that a 'new era' had arrived. Real economic growth averaged almost 4 percent annually during the five years ending March 2000, compared to about 3 percent per year during the preceding 20 years. Inflation-adjusted increases in stock prices (measured by the Wilshire, 5000) averaged nearly 19 percent annually during the five years ending March 2000, compared to about 3 percent annual increases during the preceding 20 years. The prestige of the Federal Reserve and its chairman, Alan Greenspan, rose along with faith in the US economy, the dollar, and its stock market.

During the nine quarters following March 2000, however, the US economy fell into its first recession in ten years; the annualized rate of real economic growth during those nine quarters was only 1.4 percent. Real stock prices fell at a 21 percent compounded annual rate, wiping away about $4.9 trillion of paper wealth ($5.2 trillion after inflation adjustment). Corporate profitability and business investment – especially in high technology and telecommunications – collapsed. Bankruptcy and bond default rates increased as the huge debt loads taken on by optimistic entrepreneurs and established firms alike became crushing burdens unsupportable by dwindling revenues. Corporate-governance scandals threatened to undermine the prestige of the American financial system.

Meanwhile, federal government budget deficits re-emerged as tax revenues plunged and spending commitments – especially relating to the aftermath of the 11 September terrorist attacks – soared. The Federal Reserve slashed short-term interest rates by almost five full percentage points during 2001. Despite the abrupt shift toward stimulative fiscal and monetary policies, the economic and financial vital signs of the US economy remained unusually fragile during mid-2002.

Was there ever really a 'new era' in the USA, as suggested by its outstanding economic and financial performance during the late 1990s? Will the boom quickly resume after the current interruption? More specifically, will corporate profitability, business investment, productivity growth and the stock market pick up where they left off before the recession? Can the Federal Reserve's prestige survive the collapse of the 1990s boom?

This chapter describes several key aspects of the US economy and its financial system both before and after the great boom of the 1990s. In the first section of the chapter we briefly sketch some of the international background against which US economic and financial structures should be assessed. This is followed by an assessment of the efficacy of financial markets in allocating scarce resources to their best use. The next section discusses risk-sharing and financial systems. We then discuss the role of monetary policy in financial markets and its implications for business investment decisions. Before concluding, we discuss ongoing imbalances in the US economy and their implications for financial markets.

INTERNATIONAL COMPARISON OF FINANCIAL SYSTEMS

Compared to other countries, one of the more striking characteristics of the US economy is its highly sophisticated set of financial markets. As reported in Dimson et al. (2002, p. 12), the ratio of stock market capitalization to GDP at the beginning of the year 2000 amounted to 182 percent in the USA. This was lower than in Switzerland (267 percent of GDP) and the United Kingdom (203 percent), but was higher than the 105 percent of Japan or the 68 percent of Germany. Market capitalization of the US bond market amounted to 159 percent of GDP at the beginning of 2000, highest among all countries (Dimson et al., 2002, p. 15). In fact, most industrialized countries rely more heavily on the banking system than either the stock or bond markets for allocating savings into investment capital.

There are two possible (not necessarily mutually exclusive) explanations for why the USA has a comparatively greater financial-markets orientation than other countries. First, similar to the United Kingdom, the USA is a common-law country and organized as an individualistic society, compared to the more communitarian and somewhat paternalistic civil-law countries typified by Germany and France. Second, the USA, like the United Kingdom, became a democracy early on. Democracy and a market economy with private ownership are isomorphic because both are manifestations of self-determination. The ideal of the self-determined individual, which was born during the period of the Enlightenment, manifested itself most significantly in the Declaration of Independence in 1776, Adain's Smith *Wealth of Nations* of the same year, and the French Revolution, beginning in 1789.

Unlike France, however, the USA did not slip back into an authoritarian regime as the nineteenth century began. And unlike England, the USA was able to expand economically on its own territory and hence did not suffer from loss of territory and resources during the period of de-colonization. Finally, unlike Germany and Japan – neither of which embraced democracy until the twentieth century – the USA was able to struggle with and develop its own form of democratic rule over many generations. It bears emphasizing that American democracy is an unusually long-lived 'survivor' in global historical terms, a fortunate experience that allowed its economic and financial structures to mature at their own pace. By way of contrast, in one of the greatest political, humanitarian, and not least, economic disasters of modern times, Germany voluntarily relinquished its fledgling democracy originating in 1918 after only 25 years – receiving, in return, a catastrophic 13-year dictatorship. Japan, of course, lacked even this fleeting early taste of democracy. It was not until the end of World War II that democracy became widely accepted in Germany and Japan, and modern economic and financial institutions finally could establish themselves. A 'head start' of a century and a half certainly provided American institutions some advantages.

Success tends to feed on itself – at least for some time. In order to understand the economic and financial structures of the USA, it is essential to realize that the US stock market is an extraordinary survivor. Arnott and Bernstein (2002) report on four stock markets that realized catastrophic losses of minus 100 percent in the twentieth century: China, Russia, Argentina and Egypt. It should be noted that Russia was a significant economic and military power at the beginning of the twentieth century and, therefore, would have been a significant component of any globally well-diversified stock market portfolio at the time. Furthermore, the stock markets of two other countries, Germany and Japan, came close to extinction after World War II. As reported by Dimson et al. (2002), the German stock market suffered an inflation-adjusted loss of 91 percent during the period 1945–48, while the Japanese market plummeted by 97 percent during the 1944–47 period. In comparison, between September 1929 and June 1932, the inflation-adjusted value of the US S&P (Standard & Poor) Composite Index fell by 80.6 percent, as reported by Shiller (2000). Other countries' stock markets have 'melted down' at various times for a wide variety of reasons, and many others – including perhaps even the US market – will do so in the future. As Bennett (1998) and Taleb (2001), among others, point out, a rare but plausible event is virtually certain to occur if we extend the time horizon long enough into the future.

LEGAL INSTITUTIONS AND ASYMMETRIC INFORMATION IN FINANCIAL SYSTEMS

In a seminal paper, La Porta et al. (1998) suggest that cross-country differences in financial systems are related to legal differences across countries.

Different legal systems offer different degrees of investor protection. Investor protection has several dimensions. First, there are different types of investors, such as creditors and shareholders. Creditors hold the primary claims on the firm's assets, while shareholders hold the secondary, or residual, claims.

Two finance and governance issues highlight the importance of stakeholder legal protections. Various stakeholders have divergent interests and capabilities; in broad terms, we can characterize some stakeholders as firm insiders and others as firm outsiders. Insiders, by definition, possess information about the firm that is not publicly available. If firm insiders have an economic interest in the firm, outside investors are at risk of being exploited when trading financial claims with insiders if they do not recognize the information asymmetry they face.

Asymmetric information and lack of enforceability of property rights are likely to cause underinvestment. When property rights are not enforceable, opportunistic behavior abounds. Opportunistic behavior leads to a redistribution of existing claims, which has no serious welfare implications in the first instance. However, when opportunistic behavior is anticipated, there will be negative welfare implications. The party that anticipates the possibility of being 'held up' (exploited due to weak bargaining power) hesitates to trade. Similarly, asymmetric information, if anticipated, leads to underinvestment, because the party with inferior information hesitates to trade. In this way, information asymmetries can lead to risk premiums, which manifest themselves in wide bid and ask spreads. More generally, information asymmetries open a wedge between the potential buyer's willingness to pay and the potential seller's willingness to accept an offer (Milgrom and Roberts, 1992).

The second issue relates to incentive conflicts arising directly from the firm's capital structure. When a hitherto all-equity-financed firm issues debt, the shareholders effectively sell the firm to the creditors. At the same time, the creditors effectively issue a call option on the firm's assets to the shareholders. Exercising this call option is tantamount to reclaiming the firm's assets by paying down the debt (principal plus interest). Default is the option of the shareholders to walk away from the firm, leaving its assets in the hands of the creditors.

Both problems highlighted here imply that different types of investors have different incentives. Creditors, for instance, prefer low-risk projects because they share in the negative outcomes but not in the positive ones. This is because creditors' returns can be less than promised, but not more. The shareholders, on the other hand, prefer greater risk. Recall that shareholders hold a call option on the firm's assets. All else equal, the more volatile the underlying asset, the more valuable is the call. Thus, while creditors prefer low risk, shareholders prefer high risk (Hart, 1995).

In order to internalize the consequences of decisionmaking at the firm level, shareholders hold both the residual cash flow rights and the residual control rights over the firm's assets. Thus, in order to protect the creditors from being held up by the shareholders through excessive risk-taking, debt covenants and other instruments are installed to restrict the shareholders' choice set. Yet such measures are imperfect and costly, and fail to achieve the first-best situation in which creditors are not exposed to potentially opportunistic behavior of the shareholders. Moreover, in times of financial distress, the conflict between the shareholders' interests and the creditors' interests is particularly pronounced. Situations of debt overhang and asset substitution abound – with adverse welfare implications (Brealey and Myers, 2000).

La Porta et al. (1998) argue that civil-law countries, such as Germany and France, tend to have weaker shareholder protection than common-law countries, such as the UK and the USA. As a result of poor shareholder protection, civil-law countries tend to have thin stock markets. Also, shareholder concentration in publicly traded firms tends to be higher in civil-law countries than in common-law countries. Concentrated shareholders become firm insiders; this is a way to overcome the asymmetric information problem. Also, only large shareholders have an incentive to exercise shareholder control. In common-law countries, on the other hand, small shareholders are better protected and therefore don't need to exercise control to ensure adequate returns on their investments.

One aspect of civil-law countries that appears to be superior to common-law countries is their ability to provide durable intertemporal smoothing contracts (Allen and Gale, 1995, 2000). Contracts offered by financial intermediaries such as depository institutions, insurance companies and pension funds smooth consumption risk by providing returns that differ systematically from current-period returns in spot markets. That is, the institution can commit to paying a 'smoothed' or averaged return by building up surpluses (or accumulating deficits) on its balance sheet and distributing them gradually to members or policy-holders. In this way, no particular generation is unduly disadvantaged by retiring at the 'wrong' time. A financial system with robust intertemporal and intergenerational risk-sharing mechanisms may also be more resistant to devastating asset-market crashes.

There is, of course, an incentive for any generation of members to break intertemporal contracts when accumulated surpluses are large. The market power of financial intermediaries in civil-law countries appears to counteract these incentives. A financial-markets-oriented financial system, on the other hand, may be unable to sustain such welfare-enhancing arrangements as defined-benefit pension plans or annuities. For example, there has been strong pressure to 'demutualize' many mutually owned savings and insurance associations in the English-speaking countries during recent decades in order to unlock the accumulated surpluses that had built up over generations.

CORPORATE FINANCE AND CORPORATE INVESTMENT

For the period 1900–2001, Dimson et al. (2002, p. 52) report an average annualized return on US stocks of 6.7 percent after inflation adjustment. This average annualized return accelerated to 7.4 percent during the last 75 years of the 101-year period, to 8.2 percent during the last 50 years, and to 10.2 percent during the last 25 years. The magnitude of these stock market returns is astounding when compared to the average annualized rates of return on default-risk-free securities. Government bills returned only an average annualized 0.9 percent for the period 1900–2000, while long-term US government bonds returned an average 1.6 percent, inflation-adjusted.

What is a 'reasonable' expected return? Gordon (1962) showed that the maximum long-term return stock investors can reasonably expect is the sum of the dividend yield (that is, ratio of the sum of annual dividend payments and net share repurchases to stock market value) and the rate of dividend growth. These two components correspond to the current cash payments investors receive (say, 2 percent of invested capital) plus the average annual increment to that payment (say, 3 percent). Note first that the rate of dividend growth cannot exceed the rate of growth of the economy overall, at least not indefinitely. A reasonable expected inflation-adjusted return on stocks in excess of ten-year government bonds for the period 1926–2000 was in the neighborhood of 2.4 percent. This figure – which was calculated by Arnott and Bernstein (2002) – stands in sharp contrast to the actual, or realized, excess return on stocks – the realized equity risk premium – of around 5 percent per annum.

Figure 7.1 shows the market-to-book value of equity of the US non-farm, non-financial corporate sector beginning in 1952. A high market-to-book ratio can be interpreted in three ways; only one of these three interpretations represents an equilibrium state. First, the sharp appreciation of the market-to-book ratio of equity during the 1980s and 1990s may reflect intangible capital that is not represented on the firm's balance sheet. Second, the corporate sector may be overvalued in the stock market – that is, stock prices are so high that the reasonable real rates of return discussed above are not achievable – which would represent a disequilibrium situation. Third, the market-to-book value of equity, which is closely related to Tobin's q, may reflect unusually favorable investment opportunities.

The first explanation – a large increase in intangible capital – is plausible, but it is difficult to prove independently of the appreciated market values we are attempting to explain. Under the assumption that organizational and technological knowledge is unlikely to be significantly more important today than it was yesterday, this explanation is not terribly compelling. As for the possibility of many new investment opportunities suddenly becoming available,

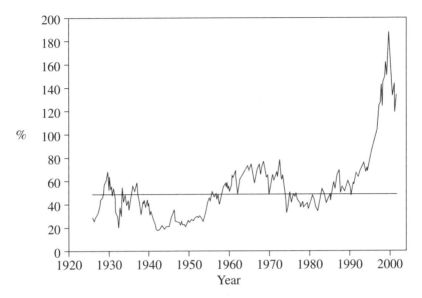

Note: Quarterly observations. First observations: 1925:4; last observation: 2001:4; median: 48.10.

Sources: CRSP (Center for Research in Security Prices): total US stock market capitalization (provided on request); Haver Analytics (GNP from 1984:1 to 2001:4), and Nathan S. Balke and Robert J. Gordon (1986), 'Appendix B: Historical Data', in Robert J. Gordon (ed.), The American Business Cycle: Continuity and Change, Chicago: University of Chicago Press, 781–850 (GNP prior to 1984:1).

Figure 7.1   Stock market valuation as a percentage of GNP

finance theory suggests a firm should expand if (and only if) the value of its marginal Tobin's q is below one. An appreciation of the market-to-book value then would mean that the US corporate sector underinvested in the late 1990s. This interpretation is difficult to reconcile with the data, however, as business investment was very strong. Consequently, the dramatic rise in the market-to-book value of equity simply may reflect overvaluation of the US corporate sector.

The possibility of increasing overvaluation of the US corporate sector during the 1990s has important implications for the US economy. As the equity of US corporations appreciated, the borrowing capacity of the corporate sector increased. Companies could easily take on more debt, using their inflated asset values as collateral. When these assets started to depreciate in March 2000, leverage ratios in the corporate sector increased sharply and borrowing capacity dropped.

At the time of writing, the US economy is characterized by excessive leverage at three levels: the corporate level, the household level and the national level. Households are highly leveraged both because the rising stock market encouraged greater consumption and because a brisk appreciation of home equity during the late 1990s and early twenty-first century provided greater borrowing capacity. A wave of mortgage refinancing effectively loosened the liquidity constraints facing many US households.

It should be remembered also that the USA is a large borrower *vis-à-vis* the rest of the world on a per capita basis – a result of many years of current-account deficits. The net foreign-investment position of the USA *vis-à-vis* the rest of the world was a negative $2.3 trillion at the end of 2001 (over 20 percent of GDP, measured at market values), almost $10 000 per US citizen. Net holdings of credit-market instruments – including Treasury, agency and corporate bonds plus commercial paper, that is, fixed-income claims rather than equity – represented virtually all of that amount. Portfolio equity investments and direct (equity) investments held by US residents abroad are nearly equal to foreign residents' holdings of US equities and direct investments. Thus the net foreign-investment deficit indeed represents an ongoing debt-service obligation owed by US residents.

Leverage is a risky bet – the riskier the project, the more valuable the financial claim of the party in control of the assets, all else equal. In other words, high leverage is a big bet leaving little room for error. This high-risk situation is the most significant characteristic of the US economy today.

THE STOCK MARKET AND FIXED INVESTMENT[1]

A recurring topic of debate among central bankers and academic experts is the role of financial markets in cycles of boom and bust in the real economy. This discussion has flared up once again in the wake of the recent economic slowdown. The performance of the US economy in the 1990s was remarkable, as was the performance of the stock market. Starting in April 2000, both the stock market and real economic activity weakened considerably. In the real economy, we observed a sharp drop-off in private business fixed investment. In the financial sector, we witnessed the stock market delivering disappointing returns for two consecutive years. The number of initial public offerings – or IPOs – fell dramatically, and the market for venture capital dried up.

The link between the real economy and the financial sector is currently most visible in the telecommunications industry. Between April 2001 and March 2002, eight major telecommunications services providers went bankrupt; the total pre-bankruptcy book value of assets of these companies amounted to about $55 billion. (The bankruptcy of WorldCom in July 2002 nearly doubled this amount.) It is noteworthy that all eight of these corporations went public between 1990 and 2000, a time when the telecom sector enjoyed spectacular growth rates. Between 1990 and 2000, private fixed investment in communications equipment as a share of GDP increased by 52 percent, adding 0.41 percentage points (41 basis points) to GDP growth during this period. In comparison, during the prior 30 years the share of investment in telecom equipment in GDP grew by only 33 basis points. As the telecom industry expanded, the stocks of telecom services providers and equipment makers were in high demand. From December 1990 through March 2000, the Nasdaq Telecommunications Index increased by more than 816 percent, compared with an increase of 317 percent in the Wilshire 5000 Stock Market Index. Then, in April 2000, the Nasdaq Telecommunications Index began a steep decline in which it shed about 75 percent by the end of January 2002. By comparison, the Wilshire 5000 Price Index dropped only 26 percent over the same time period.

The parallel performance of the telecom industry in the real economy and in the stock market raises several questions about the interaction between financial markets and the real sector. Were the financial markets driving the boom and subsequent bust in the telecom industry? What does the interaction between the real economy and financial markets imply for the efficiency of resource allocation?

Market Sentiment

The history of banking and financial markets is littered with bouts of investor optimism that have led to extraordinary and temporary appreciation of financial and real assets. Famous asset-price bubbles include the Dutch 'tulip mania' of the 1630s, the first British railway boom of the mid-1840s, and the bubble in Argentine loans in the 1880s, to name but a few. Recently, the field of behavioral finance has begun to investigate market sentiment and other investor biases in more detail (Shleifer, 2000).

Asset-price bubbles start with good news and substantial profits for early investors in the boom. For instance, the seventeenth-century tulip mania had its origin in a mosaic virus, which generated interesting-looking tulips that fetched high prices among tulip growers. Because the virus-infected tulip bulbs were difficult to reproduce, they appreciated sharply. This generated a windfall profit among those who happened to own them. The initial capital gains sowed the seeds for overly optimistic expectations of the profitability of growing and trading these strains of tulip bulbs. There are reports of extensive trading in derivative contracts written on tulip bulbs. Eventually, the formerly interesting-looking tulips lost their appeal and the price of the erstwhile highly valued bulbs fell, ending the speculative bubble.

The British railroad boom was unleashed by a major technological advance. There was not only excitement about the new means of transportation, but the British also welcomed the economic stimulus of the railroad boom because it marked the end of a period of economic depression.

The bubble in Argentine loans in the 1880s began with increased demand in the world market for Argentine agricultural products. This led to an economic boom in Argentina, which gave the Argentine government easy access to the world debt market. Argentina also raised equity capital through initial public offerings of corporations that specialized in developing land. When one of these IPOs failed in 1888, the Baring Brothers helped out with credit. Two years later, the Argentine government failed to meet these debt obligations because of falling prices for raw materials in the world markets. This led to the famous Baring crises, which gave rise to an early example of the central bank – in this case, the Bank of England – acting as a lender of last resort.

All three bubbles – and history has recorded many more – started with good news that created high hopes that eventually ended in tears. In general, bubbles are driven by positive market sentiment, that is, widespread and excessive investor optimism. Positive market sentiment gives rise to a sharp appreciation of asset prices, which eventually regress to their fundamental values. Regression to the fundamental value is often followed by unwarranted asset depreciation as market sentiment turns overly negative. Hence, market sentiment causes both asset mispricing and excessive volatility.

The consequences of asset mispricing and excessive volatility are not confined to financial markets, but also affect fixed investment and production. Financial markets are critical for directing scarce resources to their most productive use. The efficiency by which financial markets achieve this goal depends on the accuracy of the prices that financial markets signal to investors. The price signals of the stock market allow corporations to calculate their cost of equity capital and to evaluate the profitability of potential projects.

In his seminal book, *A General Theory of Employment, Interest, and Money*, John Maynard Keynes discussed several factors that bear on the accuracy of the stock market's price signals. He recognized an important role for the stock market in guiding investment and stimulating growth. In brief, Keynes hypothesized that market sentiment is carried into financial markets by uninformed investors, causing mispricing and excessive volatility. Although it appears that mispricing and the ensuing excessive volatility offer arbitrage opportunities for informed investors, arbitrageurs may be unable to exploit these opportunities due to liquidity constraints. Clearly, if informed investors were able to exploit these arbitrage opportunities, the opportunities would not be there in the first place.

In a 1981 study, Yale University economist Robert Shiller showed that the valuation of the US stock market exhibits pronounced fluctuations around its fundamental value, defined as the discounted value of future dividends. Multi-year periods of stock market overvaluation alternate with equally extended periods of stock market undervaluation. An example of a period of bearish market sentiment was the early 1970s, when the four-quarter trailing price-to-earnings (P/E) ratio of the S&P 500 stock price index was as low as 7. During the late 1990s, on the other hand, the trailing P/E ratio climbed well above 30. This was remarkable because corporate profits (the denominator of the ratio) were rising; the P/E ratio subsequently rose even further when earnings dropped beginning in late 2000. Such an elevated stock market valuation might be viewed as excessively optimistic, given that the median value of the postwar P/E ratio in the S&P 500 was around 15.

The Limits of Arbitrage

Recognition of market sentiment as a potent force in financial markets warrants the question, 'Why don't arbitrageurs bet against it?' This question needs to be answered before one accepts the possibility of stock market overvaluation (or undervaluation, for that matter) and its implication for the allocation of resources.

Keynes attributes the persistence of asset mispricing and excessive volatility to a lack of liquidity. This is another way of saying that there is a dearth of traders who lean against the prevailing market sentiment. Why don't arbitrageurs – hedge funds, for instance – put on aggressive trades that push the market back to its fundamental value?

There are two answers to the question of why arbitrageurs do not bet aggressively against market sentiment (Shleifer, 2000). First, arbitrageurs have limited wealth and limited time horizons. Asset prices might take a long time to regress to their fundamental value. Worse yet, asset mispricing might even deepen along the road. Furthermore, rare events – such as an 'overvalued' stock market rising strongly, or an 'undervalued' market crashing – can and do happen more often than is predicted by standard models such as the 'value at risk' (VaR) approach (Scholes, 2000). In the meantime, arbitrageurs who invest their own money might develop liquidity needs as they near retirement. Also, hedge funds might be faced with withdrawals as investors become impatient and start doubting the arbitrageur's talent as gains are long in coming and losses mount. As Keynes remarked, 'Markets may stay irrational longer than you remain solvent.' There is also the old stock market adage that a man can lose his shirt betting on fundamentals.

Another reason why informed investors might not bet aggressively against the prevailing market sentiment is uncertainty about the assets' fundamental values. Even the most sophisticated investor cannot rule out the possibility that the way he looks at financial markets is inadequate. The Nobel Prize-winning economists who helped run Long Term Capital Management could not prevent a meltdown of the hedge fund during September 1998 when completely unexpected market movements undermined their precisely calibrated trading strategies. This unknowable complexity is termed Knightian uncertainty (Knight, 1921). The possibility that the world in which we live is not well charted, if recognized, leads informed investors to tread cautiously when putting on their trades.

The Recent Spell of Bullish Market Sentiment

A compelling object of study for the interaction between financial markets and the real economy is the market for initial public offerings (IPOs). In countries with sophisticated financial markets, periods of excessively optimistic market sentiment tend to be accompanied by extraordinarily strong activity in the IPO market. During these so-called 'hot issue' markets, the vast majority of companies going public have been established only recently and they operate in the very industries that are exciting the exuberant investors.

Hot issue markets are characterized by high volume, unusually high returns on the first trading day – known as 'initial returns' – and very poor long-run performance in the secondary market. Empirical evidence for long-run underperformance of IPOs in the wake of hot issue markets was provided in a seminal study published by Jay Ritter in 1991. Hence, the poor performance of IPOs in the secondary market was public knowledge long before the frantic IPO activity in the US stock market during the late 1990s, yet the IPOs with the highest initial returns during the hot issue market of the late 1990s were (predictably) among the worst-performing stocks in the secondary market. From 1998 to early 2000, the top ten IPOs – ranked by initial return – climbed between 400 and 700 percent on the first day of trading. As of August 2001, nine of these ten stocks had depreciated by at least 80 percent; one stock was delisted after a competitor acquired the company.

The recurrence of hot issue markets leads to the question of why history repeats itself in such an obvious manner. Academia has tried to find an answer to this puzzle by devising the concept of the noise trader – a concept that is related to Keynes's notions of uninformed investors and speculators. Noise traders are unable to separate information from noise, forming erroneous beliefs about the fundamental value of financial assets. Successive generations of noise traders fall prey to the same old fallacies.

The first academic treatment of noise traders in financial markets was a 1953 paper by Milton Friedman. Friedman assumed that the beliefs of noise traders are idiosyncratic. Noise traders, because they trade both on information and noise, trade excessively. The introduction of noise into asset prices makes these assets riskier than they would be otherwise. However, if noise traders' beliefs are idiosyncratic, noise-trader risk can be eliminated through diversification, and hence the risk is not priced. Consequently, noise traders do not distort asset prices in a sustained manner. Also, because noise traders trade on erroneous beliefs, they tend to lose money when trading with informed investors and they eventually throw in the towel. Sure enough, there are always pockets of noise traders in financial markets as new noise traders keep entering the market, and some noise traders return with fresh funds.

Half a century after Friedman's paper, the academic view of noise traders is less sanguine. Given the empirical evidence we have today, we recognize noise traders as a potent force in financial markets. Noise traders matter because their beliefs might be systematic, rather than idiosyncratic. Just think of the recurrence of hot issue markets and the aforementioned rise and fall of telecom stocks. To be sure, these are phenomena that are driven by systematic errors in the beliefs of large groups of investors – a manifestation of market sentiment. Informed investors, for the aforementioned reasons, yield to market sentiment rather than betting aggressively against it. This way, market sentiment 'creates its own space', obtaining the capacity to distort asset prices in a sustained manner. Noise-trader risk becomes a source of systematic risk because the informed investors are unable to eliminate it through diversification.

A valuable gauge of market sentiment in the stock market is the P/E ratio. In March 2000, the Nasdaq 100 – which accounted for more than 10 percent of the US stock market – traded at a P/E ratio of about 100. Certainly, there have always been a handful of stocks that trade at elevated levels. However, when 10 percent of the entire market trades at such a lofty level, some questions might be in order. Chan et al. (2001), who study the earnings growth rates of US corporations, drew up the following examples. Assume the P/E ratio of a company takes ten years to revert from 100 to 20, which is still a fairly generous level given that historically the P/E ratio of the S&P 500 has averaged 16. If we assume that the annualized real return on this stock over the next ten years is zero, then the company's real earnings have to grow at an annualized rate of 17.5 percent. Alternatively, if the investor demands an annualized 10 percent real return on the stock over the next ten years, the real earnings of this company have to grow by an average 29.2 percent per year. Of course, it was illusory to assume that the companies that comprise the Nasdaq 100 would average such growth rates in real earnings. At the same time, the returns expected by avid investors in these companies were most likely not as modest as assumed in the numerical examples.

Investors are willing to hold stocks with high P/E ratios if they expect these companies to grow at an above-average rate. Given that investors disagree about which companies will be the fast-growing ones, many companies may trade at elevated prices at the same time. This brings us to the question of how predictable earnings growth at the company level really is. Chan et al. (2001) show that there is virtually no predictability of earnings growth rates at the company level at the five- and ten-year horizons. Thus, it is no more likely to pick the next Microsoft from the population of fast-growing companies through rational deliberation than by chance.

The unpredictability of earnings growth was known long before the Nasdaq 100 (Keynes, 1936). Given that there is no predictability in earnings growth beyond the very short horizon, it is not surprising that stocks with high P/E ratios tend to underperform the market, as many academic studies have shown.

Before returning to the link between stock market valuation and resource allocation, it is important to be more specific about noise traders. It might appear an easy way out to blame asset mispricing and excessive volatility on anonymous noise traders. Who are these noise traders, anyway? Typically, when we think of noise traders, we think of small investors. Admittedly, small investors may play a bigger role in the stock market than in the market for Treasury securities. But consider this little-appreciated fact: the real yield to maturity on ten-year Treasury inflation-indexed securities – the safest security in the world – reached a high of 4.42 percent in January 2000. This astonishingly high yield is difficult to reconcile with historical returns or prospective risks. For instance, the inflation-adjusted buy-and-hold return on long-term US government securities between the end of 1925 and the end of 2000 averaged only about 2.2 percent per annum (Ibbotson Associates, 2002) – half the January 2000 level. During the same 75-year time period, real GDP grew at an annualized rate of 3.16 percent. Given that Treasury inflation-indexed securities contain no inflation risk and should yield less than the historical average of long-term nominal bonds less inflation, a yield of 4.42 percent is astoundingly optimistic. The point is that institutional investors, who hold the bulk of the Treasury inflation-indexed securities, appear to have been overly optimistic about the growth prospects of the economy at that time, also. This points to the conclusion that swings in market sentiment affect not only small investors, but institutional investors as well.

Stock Market Valuation, Investment and Growth

In the 1990s, the issuance of excessively valued stocks, along with an overvaluation of existing securities, led to an appreciation of the US stock market that makes the run-up to the September 1929 market peak look like a hiccup. The median annual ratio of stock market valuation to nominal GNP in the period 1920 to 2000 runs at 48 percent. Between 1990 and the first quarter of 2000, this ratio increased from its median value to an unprecedented 186 percent. By comparison, in the third quarter of 1929, the ratio of stock market valuation to GNP amounted to only 68 percent. The historic peak before the run-up to the 1990s was recorded in the fourth quarter of 1972 at a value of 78 percent.

Certainly, such excessive stock market valuation leaves its mark on the real economy. By depressing the cost of capital, the stock market appreciation of the 1990s fuelled the longest investment boom in postwar history. From a trough in the first quarter of 1990, the fraction of fixed private non-residential investment in (nominal) GDP increased from 9.7 percent to a peak value of 13.2 percent in the third quarter of 2000. By comparison, the median postwar value was 10.5 percent.

As a result of the investment boom, the real capital stock of the economy expanded sharply. After hitting a trough in 1992 at 1.5 percent, the rate of increase in real capital stock climbed steadily to 4.2 percent in 2000. When the economy slowed, it became evident that a capital overhang had developed. In the fourth quarter of 2000, non-residential business fixed investment recorded its first decline in nine years. Although the decline was a modest 3.2 percent at an annual rate, it initiated a string of seven consecutive quarterly declines through the second quarter of 2002. Investment in information processing equipment and software was hit particularly hard, declining in each quarter of 2001. The level of real investment in information processing equipment and software was 10.5 percent lower during the fourth quarter of 2001 than it had been a year earlier – representing the sharpest four-quarter decline during the 40 years for which data are available. As estimated by President Bush's administration (Council of Economic Advisors, 2002, p. 41), the growth rate of real capital stock dropped to 2.6 percent during 2001 as a whole.

Like other investment booms in history, the rapid expansion of the capital stock in the 1990s followed on the heels of a major technological advance – the digital revolution. In the early stages of the boom in computers and communications, there were extraordinary corporate success stories, as epitomized by the rise of Microsoft. On the financial side, these admirable corporate achievements were reflected in equally impressive capital gains in the stock market. The new technology, which gave rise to new, fast-growing corporations, created expectations of a 'new era' in the real economy and high returns in the stock market. During a boom, investors rarely remember Schumpeter's dictum of creative destruction – namely, that the benefits of technological advances are passed on to the consumer. This is the nature of competition. Busts are the inevitable consequence of mean-reverting rates of growth and of the erosion of corporate profits through competition.

Clearly, no company can produce an earnings growth rate that exceeds the growth rate of potential GDP forever. Inevitably, earnings growth rates of individual companies revert toward the mean of all companies' growth rates; otherwise, this fast-growing individual company eventually would become larger than the economy itself – an impossibility. Against this background, a P/E ratio of 100 in the Nasdaq 100 is difficult to explain without some kind of new-era thinking. There is a risk in new-era thinking because it is an attempt to rationalize, rather than explain, high stock market valuation. Although the productivity growth of the US economy has been impressive over the last couple of years, including the most recent period of recession, bursts of productivity growth have happened before – for instance, during the 1960s and mid-1980s. More importantly, past technological innovations had no lasting impact on the growth rates of corporate earnings. In fact, the median share of corporate profits in GDP in the 1990s ran at 8.2 percent, which was 1.3 percentage points lower than the postwar median value of 9.5 percent.

Over the last couple of years, the decline in corporate profits has been accompanied by a rise in corporate leverage. The ratio of total liabilities to net worth for non-farm non-financial corporations soared from a recent trough of 94 percent during the fourth quarter of 1997 to a near-record 113.2 percent during the first quarter of 2002. By comparison, the median postwar value is only 63.8 percent. Note also that this figure understates the actual rise of debt obligations at the company level because of the increased use of leasing and the proliferation of special (off-balance-sheet) financing vehicles.

The rise of corporate indebtedness is in part a consequence of the soaring stock market of the 1990s. As the market values of firms' equity appreciated, their borrowing capacity increased. Corporations that dipped deeply into their borrowing capacity in the days of the boom found themselves highly leveraged after their equity depreciated in the stock market. Excessive use of debt, along with overcapacity, has contributed significantly to the current wave of bond defaults and bankruptcies – in particular in the telecom sector. Another implication of high leverage is the increased share of interest payments in current income. At a time of tightening lending standards and debt downgrades in the bond market, high debt obligations might put a drag on capital spending as corporations find it difficult to finance investment projects out of current cash flow.

MONETARY POLICY AND FIXED INVESTMENT

The Federal Reserve is an important link between the financial sector and the real economy. Legally, the Federal Reserve has two important mandates. The Federal Reserve must conduct monetary policy in a way that encourages both low inflation and high employment. High employment is usually interpreted as a high rate of economic growth.

Despite its clear legal mandate(s), how the Federal Reserve should operate monetary policy is not at all clear. This is because the Federal Reserve has only one instrument, which is the short-term interest rate or the money supply, depending on the analytical perspective chosen. From control theory, it is known that with one instrument, the time path of only one target variable can be controlled if the variables are independent. In other words, the Federal Reserve might not be able to pursue simultaneously the goals of low inflation and high economic growth. Clearly, the conflict between the two mandates might be more or less pronounced at a given time, depending on the economic situation.

The preferences of the Federal Reserve, or which goal it feels is more important, are revealed most clearly when there is a conflict in pursuing the two goals. In a seminal study of monetary policymaking in practice, John Taylor (1993) estimated the response function of the Federal Reserve to deviations of the rates of inflation and real GDP growth from target levels. While Taylor's study was a descriptive analysis, the response function he estimated is often interpreted in a normative way – that is, his empirical model has become 'the Taylor rule.'

As a descriptive rule, it is not surprising to see the Federal Reserve trying to strike a balance between the goals of high employment and low inflation. In the end, the loss function of society is likely to contain terms for both the rate of inflation and the rate of economic growth. On the other hand, when looked at from a normative perspective, it is not clear what we learn from the Taylor rule. First, was the Federal Reserve's past policy necessarily optimal? If the Taylor rule is used for policymaking, this question would have to be answered yes. Second, if Federal Reserve policy was optimal in the past – that is, at a time when the Taylor rule was unknown – why does the Federal Reserve need the Taylor rule today to make optimal policy decisions? At best, the Taylor rule makes explicit something that the Federal Reserve already knows how to do, and has done in the past. One such insight would be that the Federal Reserve has to increase interest rates by more than the increase in the expected rate of inflation. This simply results from the fact that, otherwise, the real rate of interest, which is the nominal rate minus the expected rate of inflation, would decrease despite a fed-funds rate-hike.

Monetary Policy and the Economy

In the following, we focus on the link between the Federal Reserve's operation of monetary policy and the real economy. As noted above, the Federal Reserve's policy instrument is the short-term interest rate or, more specifically, the federal funds rate. Common wisdom states that the Federal Reserve should cut the fed funds rate when trying to stimulate the economy, and raise the rate when it tries to slow the economy.[2]

When the Federal Reserve tries to stimulate or slow economic activity, it aims at economic activity that is sensitive to interest rates. The components of

GDP considered most responsive to interest rate changes are business fixed investment, housing investment, and purchases of consumer durable goods. (Purchases of consumer durable goods might be viewed as household investment decisions similar to business fixed investment or housing.) In the following we consider all forms of investment as similar for analytical purposes.

Conventional wisdom holds that the short-term interest rate itself is a powerful instrument in influencing investment decisions. From a theoretical perspective, however, the link between short-term rates and investment is anything but clear. To appreciate this ambiguity, one must consider the impact of monetary policy actions (rate cuts or hikes) on the term structure of the yield curve (or the term structure of interest rates).[3] For it is the real yield curve – that is, the inflation-expectations adjusted yield curve – that matters for long-lived investment decisions.

First, it is not obvious how monetary policy actions impact the level and slope of the yield curve, save for its certain impact on the short end. Second, it is not all that clear how changes in the level or the slope of the yield curve affect incentives to undertake fixed investment.

Consider the 'simple NPY' (net present value) rule found in any introductory finance textbook. An investment project should be undertaken if and only if the net present value of the project is positive:

$$\text{NPV} = \sum_{t=1}^{T} \frac{CF_t}{(1+R)^t} > 0,$$

where CF is the cash flow and R is the discount rate, both in nominal terms.

The discount rate, R, represents the opportunity cost of capital. An important extension of the Modigliani–Miller theorem states that the discount rate is independent of the company that pursues the project (Bodie and Merton, 2000). Rather, the discount rate is solely determined by the project's beta, that is, the project's contribution to the market risk. The standard textbook decision rule implicitly assumes that the project under consideration does not compete with any other project.

It is now well established in the finance literature that the net present value rule may lead to incorrect decisions if projects can be delayed, that is, if projects 'compete with each other in time'. This is because there might be value of waiting due to uncertainty about the future opportunity cost of capital. Simply put, the value of waiting arises from the possibility that the same project (that is, a project with identical cash flows) might be carried out at a lower opportunity cost of capital some time in the future.

To illustrate the point, compare the following two projects. The projects offer identical cash flows (in 'project time'). The only difference between the projects is the point of time at which each is launched. For the project that is launched today:

$$\text{NPV}_{0,0} = \sum_{t=1}^{T} \frac{CF_t}{(1+R_0)^t} \, ,$$

where the subscripts on NPV refer to today's date and the date of project launch, respectively. Compare $\text{NPV}_{0,0}$ with the NPV of a project that is launched one period later:

$$\text{NPV}_{0,1} = \frac{1}{(1+R_{0,1})} \cdot \sum_{\tau=1}^{T} \frac{CF_\tau}{(1+R_1)^\tau} \, ,$$

where $\tau = 1, \dots T$ indicates project time (rather than calendar time). Project time starts at $\tau = t - 1$, $t = 1$, because the first cash flow does not appear until the end of the first period of operation. The discount rate, $r_{0,1}$, is the one-period risk-free rate of return. The rate R_1, is the opportunity cost of capital as observed at $t = 1$, that is, one period from now.

Assume, for simplicity, that the cash flow stream $CF\tau$, $(\tau = 1, \dots T)$ is independent of whether the project gets started this period (at $t = 0$) or the next period (at $t = 1$). Then the only unknown variable in the decision of when to invest (if at all) is the opportunity cost of capital that will prevail at time $t = 1$, R_1. The uncertainty about the opportunity cost of capital one period from now creates a call option – that is, the option to wait.

Berk (1999) investigated this problem and derived the correct decision rule for 'delayable' projects – a decision rule that incorporates the option of waiting. Berk derived his formula for the special case of a stream of constant periodic cash flows. Berk shows that the correct decision is to invest if and only if

$$\sum_{\tau=1}^{T} \frac{CF_\tau}{\left(1 + \dfrac{r_0^m}{r_0} R_0\right)^\tau} > 0,$$

where r_0^m is the callable risk-free rate with a time to maturity that matches the last cash flow of the project, and r_0 is the duration-matched (non-callable) risk-free rate of return. The callable rate exceeds the non-callable rate because the former includes compensation to the lender for the embedded prepayment call option. Thus the discount factor in the modified formula is always larger – hence the present value is smaller – than in the original NPV formula. The Berk decision rule for projects that can be delayed and have no resolution-of-uncertainty problem with respect to cash flows illustrates the positive value of waiting. Berk's initial assumption about non-stochastic cash flows can be relaxed. Then, the variable R_0 is simply the opportunity cost of capital that would be applied otherwise in the simple NPV decision rule.

Berk points out that the term $(r_0^m/r_0) \times R_0$ is an unambiguous measure of the private sector's incentive to invest. If monetary easing succeeds in lowering this discount rate, then the incentive to invest increases unambiguously. In this case, monetary policy has stimulated investment. Otherwise, the incentive to invest decreases and monetary policy has been contractionary. Clearly, this holds for a fixed set of expected cash flows.

Unfortunately, implementing the formula is not as straightforward as suggested by Berk. This is because the formula rests on real (that is, inflation-adjusted) variables, which means that it holds only in a world of no inflation (and consequently no inflation risk). Suppose we were in such a world and implemented the Berk formula. Then, the variable r_0^m is a callable risk-free rate of return as exemplified by the rate of return on GNMA (Government National Mortgage Association) mortgage-backed securities. GNMA securities are free of default risk (because they are backed by the full faith and credit of the US government) and are callable (because the underlying mortgage borrowers can prepay their mortgages). The variable r_0, on the other hand, is the duration-matched noncallable rate. For instance, for a 30-year project, the GNMA 30-year on-the-run yield can be matched with a ten-year on-the-run Treasury note, which has approximately the same duration.

A somewhat more difficult task is to quantify the opportunity cost of capital, R_0. The opportunity cost of capital consists of the risk-free rate of return and a risk premium that captures the beta of the project's cash flow with respect to the market. The market comprises the population of all projects in the economy, as represented by the population of financial claims. When written in additive form, R_0 equals the sum of the risk-free rate of return, r_0, and a risk premium, ρ – the equity risk premium.

As noted, Berk's decision rule holds only for an economy without inflation or inflation risk. This is because the formula is derived for a time-invariant stream of cash flows, CF_τ ($\tau = 1, \ldots, T$) with $CF_\tau = \overline{CF}$ for any $\tau = 1, \ldots, T$. Clearly, this assumption is adequate only in a world of no inflation. Otherwise, the size of the project would decrease over time if the rate of inflation is positive, and increase if the inflation rate is negative. In other words, it would not be the same project if it were started at a different point in time.

If cash flows are denoted in real terms, so must the opportunity cost of capital. This poses a problem, because there are no inflation-adjusted mortgage-backed securities in the USA. On the other hand, r_0 is observable from Treasury inflation-indexed securities (THS). In the following we derive an approximation of the Berk formula for a world with inflation and inflation risk.

In a world without inflation risk (or, equivalently, diversifiable inflation risk), the link between the nominal interest rate, i, and the real interest rate, τ, is given by the Fisher equation:

$$1 + E[i] = (1 + \tau_0) \cdot (1 + E[\pi]),$$

where π is the rate of inflation and τ is known. The investor demands not only compensation for the expected rate of inflation, but also compensation for the inflation-risk premium.

If we assume that the inflation-risk premium is multiplicative (rather than additive – an assumption immaterial to the following argument), we can write

$$\rho = \frac{i - \pi \cdot (1 + \sigma)}{1 - \pi \cdot (1 + \sigma)},$$

where σ is the inflation-risk premium. If we assume that the inflation-risk premium is identical for the risk-free rate, r, and the callable risk-free rate, r^m, then we can write Berk's investment rule as follows:

$$\sum_{\tau=1}^{T} \frac{CF\tau}{\left(1 + \dfrac{r_0^m - \pi^e \cdot (1 + \sigma)}{r_0 - \pi^e \cdot (1 + \sigma)} (r_0 - \pi^e \cdot [1 + \sigma] + \omega)\right)} > 0,$$

where (ω is the (real) equity risk premium. The opportunity cost of capital equals $r_0 - \pi^e \cdot [1 + \sigma] + \omega$, which is the discount rate that would apply if there were no value of waiting. The value of the call (or value of waiting) is reflected in the term $r_0^m - \pi^e \cdot (1 + \sigma)/r_0 - \pi^e \cdot (1 + \sigma)$. Note that the value of waiting always is greater than one, which does not imply, however, that waiting to invest is the optimal choice at all times (Ingersoll and Ross, 1992).

Clearly, the assumption that the inflation-risk premiums in callable and non-callable default-risk-free rates are identical is somewhat restrictive. One might suspect that the inflation-risk premium is somewhat lower in callable bonds, because the call option insulates the issuer against declines in the expected rate of inflation. (Callable and non-callable bonds are equally affected by increases in the expected rate of inflation.) This means that assuming identical inflation-risk premiums for callable and non-callable rates will underestimate the true discount factor.

We now implement the Berk discount factor,

$$1 + \frac{r_0^m - \pi^e \cdot (1 + \sigma)}{r_0 - \pi^e \cdot (1 + \sigma)} (r_0 - \pi^e \cdot [1 + \sigma] + \omega),$$

under the assumption that the inflation-risk premium in callable rates is identical to the inflation-risk premium in non-callable rates. We choose the following variables:

r_0^m: 30-year current-coupon bond-equivalent GNMA yield
r_0: ten-year constant maturity Treasury yield
$\pi^e \cdot (1 + \sigma)$: ten-year constant-maturity Treasury yield minus ten-year on-the-run Treasury inflation-indexed securities yield
ω: real equity-risk premium (2.4 percent).

The estimate for the real equity-risk premium comes from Arnott and Bernstein (2002), who studied two centuries of US stock market data. (We treat the equity-risk premium as a constant, assuming that the marginal investor is identical at all times, has stable risk preferences, and is not financially constrained.)

Figure 7.2 exhibits the discount rate of the corporate sector taking into account the value of waiting – a discount rate that unambiguously measures the incentive to invest in fixed assets. The figure also displays two of the components of the discount rate: the (nominal) effective federal funds rate and the (nominal) ten-year Treasury yield. Figure 7.3 provides a graph of the value

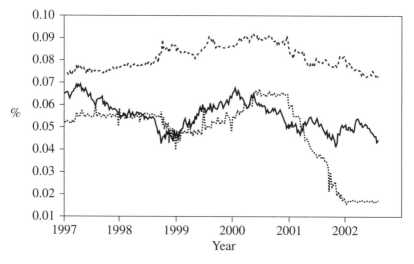

········Fed Funds rate ——— Ten-year treasury-note yield - - - - Discount rate

Note: Weekly observations (Thursday; Fed Funds: weekly median); last observations: 1 August 2002.

Figure 7.2   Berk discount rate

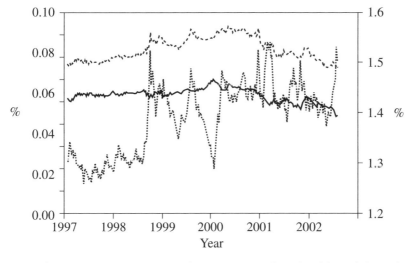

········ Discount rate ——— Opportunity cost ----- Value of waiting (right scale)

Note: Weekly observations (Thursday); last observations: 1 August 2002.

Figure 7.3   Berk discount rate and the value of waiting

of waiting. Figure 7.4 shows an important element of the value of waiting, that is, the uncertainty about the future opportunity cost of capital as expressed by the implied volatility of options written on ten-year Treasury-note futures. Note that the greater the uncertainty about the future opportunity cost of capital, the greater the incentive to delay the project, all else equal.

COST OF CAPITAL FROM AN INTERNATIONAL PERSPECTIVE

From 1982 through March 2000, the USA experienced an unprecedented bull run in the stock market. The realized excess returns on stocks have exceeded the equity-risk premium that reasonably could have been expected (rather than dreamt of) by a wide margin. The run-up in equity prices has wide-ranging implications for the future growth of the US economy.

Arnott and Bernstein (2002) show that the 'reasonable' expected equity risk premium fluctuated in a narrow range around zero between 1982 and 2000. Yet, as measured by the S&P 500, a broad stock market index, the total buy-and-hold realized return on US stocks (assuming all dividends and capital

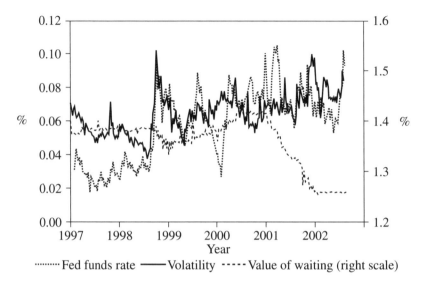

········ Fed funds rate ——— Volatility ·····Value of waiting (right scale)

Note: Weekly observations (Thursday; Fed Funds: weekly median); last observations: 1 August 2002.

Figure 7.4   The value of waiting, cost of carry, and volatility

gains were reinvested) amounted to an annualized 16.9 percent (continuously compounded). American households experienced a windfall gain in equity wealth that some, or perhaps many, perceived to be a permanent addition to their wealth. However, according to analyses such as that of Arnott and Bernstein, the 'fair' or sustainable value of the US stock market (at the time of writing) might amount to only 25 percent of its current market value. The increase in market wealth led to a sharp drop in the saving rate of American households, and to overinvestment in the corporate sector. By reducing the saving rate and increasing the rate of investment (see Emmons and Schmid, 2002), the United States attracted capital from abroad. As a result, the USA today is a highly indebted country *vis-à-vis* the rest of the world. Moreover, both the household and the corporate sectors are highly leveraged.

CONCLUSION

This chapter has analyzed some of the background issues and ongoing implications of the economic and financial boom in the USA during the late 1990s. We discussed resource allocation and social welfare in the USA in the context of the boom. In particular, we focused on issues pertaining to corporate finance, corporate investment, the stock market and monetary policy. Drawing on historical data and cross-country comparisons to evaluate current economic and financial structures in the USA, we concluded that there were several cracks in the façade of the great American boom during the late 1990s. The likelihood that the stock market boom drove businesses and households to make unsustainable spending commitments leaves the future course of the US economy in jeopardy. Federal Reserve monetary policy turned out, by at least one conceptually sound metric, not to have been very stimulative in the wake of the deflating boom. Whether the Fed's unprecedented prestige will survive the aftermath of the boom is highly uncertain.

NOTES

*The views expressed in this chapter are those of the authors and not necessarily those of the Federal Reserve Bank of St Louis or the Federal Reserve System.

1. Part of the material in this section was prepared by one of the authors for William Poole, 'The Role of Finance in the Investment Bust of 2001', delivered to the Annual Southwestern Finance Association Meeting, St Louis, MO, 8 March 2002.
2. Miller et al. (2002) argue that the Fed also reacts to large declines in the stock market. Falling stock prices and potential weakness in economic activity often co-exist, however, so the existence of a 'Greenspan put' (systematic Fed support for stock prices) is difficult to prove.
3. There is a difference between the yield curve and the term structure of interest rates. Yields are actual internal rates of returns (average rates of returns with coupon payments reinvested) observed in practice. The term structure of interest rates refers to the hypothetical rates of return that would be observed on zero-coupon securities traded in frictionless markets.

REFERENCES

Allen, Franklin, and Douglas Gale (1995), 'A welfare comparison of intermediaries and financial markets in Germany and the US', *European Economic Review,* **39**, 179–209.

Allen, Franklin and Douglas Gale (2000), 'Financial markets, intermediaries, and intertemporal smoothing', *Journal of political Economy*, **105**, 523–46.

Amott, Robert D. and Peter L. Bernstein (2002), 'What risk premium is "normal"?', *Financial Analysts Journal*, **58**, 64–85.

Bennett, Deborah L. (1998), *Randomness*, Cambridge, MA: Harvard University Press.

Berk, Jonathan, B. (1999), 'A simple approach for deciding when to invest', *American Economic Review*, **89**, 1319–26.

Bodie, Zvi and Robert C. Merton (2000), *Finance*, Upper Saddle River, NJ: Prentice Hall.

Brealey, Richard A. and Stewart C. Myers (2000), *Principles of Corporate Finance*, 6th edn, New York: McGraw-Hill.

Chan, Louis K.C., Jason Karceski and Josef Lakonishok (2001), 'The level and persistence of growth rates', National Bureau for Economic Research working paper no. 8282, <http://www.nber.org>

Council of Economic Advisors (2002), *Economic Report of the President,* Washington, DC: GPO.

Dimson, Elroy, Paul Marsh and Mike Staunton (2002), *Triumph of the Optimists*, Princeton, NJ: Princeton University Press.

Emmons, William R. and Frank A. Schmid (2003), 'The US policy mix and corporate strategies', in Paul Taylor, Alan Rugman and Gavin Boyd (eds), *Alliance Capitalism for the New American Economy*, Cheltenham, UK and Northampton, USA: Edward Elgar.

Friedman, Milton (1953), 'The case for flexible exchange rates', in *Essays in Positive Economics*, Chicago: University of Chicago Press.

Gordon, Myron J. (1962), *The Investment, Financing and the Valuation of the Corporation*, Homewood, IL: Irwin.

Hart, Oliver (1995), *Firms, Contracts, and Financial Structure*, Oxford, UK: Clarendon Press.

Ibbotson Associates (2002), *Stocks, Bonds, Bills, and Inflation: 2002 Yearbook*, Chicago: Ibbotson Associates.

Ingersoll, Jonathan E. Jr and Stephen A. Ross (1992), 'Waiting to invest: investment and uncertainty', *Journal of Business*, **65**, 1–29.

Keynes, John Maynard (1936), *The General Theory of Employment, Interest, and Money*, New York: Harcourt, Brace & World.

Knight, Frank H. (1921), 'The meaning of risk and uncertainty', in *Risk, Uncertainty, and Profit*, Boston, MA: Houghton Mifflin, Part III, ch. VII, online edition: <http://www.econlib.org/library/Knight/knRUP.html>

La Porta, Rafael, Florencio Lopez-de-Silanes and Andrei Shleifer (1998), 'Law and finance', *Journal of Political Economy*, **106**, 1113–55.

Milgrom, Paul and John Roberts(1992), *Economics, Organization and Management*, Englewood Cliffs, NJ: Prentice-Hall.

Miller, Marcus, Paul Weller and Lei Zhang (2002), 'Moral hazard and the U.S. stock market: analysing the "Greenspan Put"', *Economic Journal*, **112** (478), March, C171–86.

Ritter, Jay (1991), 'The long-run performance of initial public offerings', *Journal of finance*, **46**(1), March, 3–27.

Scholes, Myron, R. (2000), 'Crisis and risk management', *American Economic Review, Papers and Proceedings*, **90**, 17–21.

Shiller, Robert, L. (2002), *Irrational Exuberance*, Princeton, NJ: Princeton University Press.

Shleifer, Andrei (2000), *Inefficient Markets: An Introduction to Behavioral Finance*, Oxford, UK: Oxford University Press.

Taleb, Nassim Nicholas (2001), *Fooled by Randomness: The Hidden Role of Chance in the Markets and in Life,* New York: Texere.

Taylor, John (1993), 'Discretion versus Policy Rules in Practice', *Carnegie-Rochester Conference Series on Public Policy*, **39**, December, 195–214.

8. Industry and finance in the EU: integration, enlargement and economic performance

Paul A. Brenton

EU policymakers have become convinced that the relatively poor economic performance of European economies in relation to that of the USA during the 1990s is a reflection of severe gaps in the completion of the single market in Europe. Enhancing the degree of market integration between European economies is seen as a key element in achieving the rather ambitious objective defined at the Lisbon Summit of making the EU the most competitive and cohesive place in the world to live and to do business by the year 2010. At the forefront of this drive towards competitiveness in Europe will be the increasing integration of financial services and network service industries. The lack of a deep European financial market is perceived, in particular, to have constrained the funding for European high technology companies and new business start-ups in relation to the USA.[1]

Increasing financial integration, while bringing significant economic benefits in its own right, is also seen as important in allowing the benefits of a single European market in goods to be fully attained. But goods markets too are far from perfectly integrated and further economic gains, in terms of higher productivity, greater exploitation of economies of scale and increased consumer choice, are expected from the more effective implementation of EU initiatives that seek to ensure the freedom of movement of goods throughout the EU.

In this chapter we consider the EU approach to the integration of both goods and financial markets, examine the reasons why national markets still remain fragmented and the prospects of the removal of remaining barriers to trade across national borders in Europe. In this context we also consider how the forthcoming enlargement of the EU will influence the ability of the EU to achieve its objectives regarding the creation of a true single market for goods and services in Europe. We consider the implications of further integration for European economic and financial structures, and, in particular, discuss the view that enhanced integration together with important technological changes that are taking place will inevitably push continental EU countries to resemble the economic structures of the USA.

Deeper integration in Europe and enlargement will take place in an external environment dominated by relations with the USA. The USA is the main trading partner for the EU, accounting for 24 percent of total EU external exports and 21 percent of EU imports of goods in 1999. The importance of the USA is even more substantial in overseas direct investment. In 1999, US companies provided 56 percent of the stock of foreign direct investment in the EU, and this comprised more than 45 percent of total US FDI abroad. The EU contributed 61 percent of the stock of FDI in the EU, which was equal to 54 percent of the total stock of EU FDI abroad.[2]

If fundamental changes in European financial structures were to take place, this could have important implications for the nature and structure of European economies. At present continental European financial structures are dominated by banks, in contrast to the bond- and equity-dominated market of the USA. The dominant role of banks in countries such as Germany tends to exert a relatively conservative influence over company activities, which tends to lead to a focus on longer-term horizons in business decision-making. The relatively smaller volumes of shares available for trading dampens the scope for speculation, in contrast to the strong propensity to speculative trading in financial assets in the USA. In the more intensely competitive equity-based system of the USA there is more of an emphasis upon short-term corporate decisionmaking and tendencies toward speculative asset appreciation. In such an economic system innovation will be biased towards the development of new processes and products, with consequent implications for productivity growth, whereas in the more coordinated systems of mainland Europe innovation will tend to be focused more upon incremental improvements to existing processes and products (Hall and Soskice, 2001).

In this chapter we argue that while change in European structures is occurring at a rapid pace, there are a number of policy and 'natural' factors which are likely to constrain such a process and which will ensure that a degree of fragmentation will remain in Europe. This in turn entails that elements of distinct European economic and financial structures will survive. The key feature of integration in Europe has been the success of bringing together different countries with diverse attitudes to public policy interventions. The desire to maintain diversity and the ability to intervene at the national level to protect what is perceived to be the national good ensure that there will be limits to the degree of integration in Europe.

THE SINGLE MARKET AND TRADE IN GOODS

The awareness that differences in national regulations and their application could be an important barrier to economic integration has been an important part of EU policy since the inception of the EEC in the 1950s, with even greater emphasis having been given to this issue under the single market programme. The Treaty of Rome prohibited 'quantitative restrictions on imports and all measures having equivalent effect' (Art. 30 (28)), although, and this is very important, this was qualified to allow exemptions from this obligation for a range of public policy and security issues. We discuss these exemptions in a little more detail below. In practice, one of the key areas of regulation that has affected trade between members states has been rules governing the placing of products on the market, often for health and safety reasons, and the testing of products for conformity with those regulations. Barriers to trade arise when countries regulate for the same risks but in different ways and when products must be tested for conformity with each differing set of national rules.

The basic EU approach to this issue of differences in national regulations is the principle of mutual recognition, which was developed on the basis of European Court of Justice case law, specifically, the Cassis de Dijon and Dassonville judgments. The mutual recognition approach is based on the idea that products manufactured and tested in accordance with a partner country's regulations can offer equivalent levels of protection to those provided by corresponding domestic rules and procedures. Thus, products produced in partner countries can be accepted without the need for further agreement with the presumption that they will not undermine basic regulatory objectives concerning health and safety and so on. Governments maintain substantial freedom to apply their own rules to domestically produced products but have to accept products produced to rules stipulated elsewhere. Hence the application of the mutual recognition principle requires a degree of trust between different countries and regulatory authorities that another country's regulations can offer equivalent levels of protection and that such regulations are effectively implemented, ensuring that products actually conform to the requirements of the regulations. The principle of mutual recognition is the hub of the single market since it provides for the free movement of goods (and services, as we shall discuss later) without the general necessity for regulatory harmonization.

Despite the basic principles of non-discrimination and free circulation of goods, services people and capital, the EU has always permitted what are deemed as legitimate restrictions on trade. Article 36 of the Treaty of Rome provides for restrictions on imports for reasons of 'public policy or public security' and protection of health as long as such restrictions are not a disguised restriction on trade. In such cases the onus is on the importing country to demonstrate that lack of equivalence of regulations is undermining public policies towards, for example, human health. In practice the European Court of Justice has accepted lack of equivalence on many occasions and significantly has not required conclusive proof of a threat to human health or other public policies for the refusal to accept a product legally available elsewhere in the community, accepting in effect that the precautionary principle is sufficient (Holmes and Young, 2001).

A key element in the application of the principle of mutual recognition has been the development of mechanisms at the EU level for disciplining national regulations and interventions into product markets. There are three means by which the EU can affect national regulations (Pelkmans et al., 2000):

1. Infringement procedures whereby the Commission acts to enforce Community law. These are important provisions whose existence can have significant disciplinary effects and where case law can establish clear interpretations of relevant statutes. Nevertheless, such procedures are very time-consuming and costly, have an impact only after the event and are *ad hoc* in nature. As such they are insufficient to prevent the creation of barriers to free movement of goods (Pelkmans et al., 2000).
2. Notification procedures whereby member states are required to notify all draft technical regulations for scrutiny by the 94/34 Committee, whose objective is to prevent new regulatory barriers to trade. In practice all new national regulations of EU member states have to pass an EU test regarding their impact on the free movement of goods.
3. Notification of derogations procedures which require member states to notify cases in which they wish to prevent the sale of goods lawfully produced or marketed in another member state on the grounds of non-conformity and non-equivalence with domestic requirements. This seeks to ensure that any derogations from the principle of mutual recognition are transparent and subject to scrutiny.

Where it is clear that 'equivalence' between levels of regulatory protection embodied in national regulations cannot be assumed, the EU approach to removing technical barriers to trade is for the member states to reach agreement on a common set of legally binding requirements. Subsequently, no further legal impediments can prevent market access of complying products anywhere in the EU market. EU legislation harmonizing technical specifications has involved two distinct approaches, the 'old approach' and the 'new approach'.

The 'old approach' mainly applies to products (chemicals, motor vehicles, pharmaceuticals and foodstuffs) where the nature of the risk requires extensive product-by-product or even component-by-component legislation and was carried out by means of detailed directives. In the main, achieving this type of harmonization was slow, for two reasons. First, the process of harmonization became highly technical, with attention being given to very detailed product categories, including components. This resulted in extensive and drawn-out consultations. Second, the adoption of old-approach directives required unanimity in the Council, which meant that the issuing of directives was a slow process. The limitations of this approach as a broad tool for tackling technical barriers to trade become clearly apparent in the 1970s and early 1980s when new national regulations were proliferating at a much faster rate than the production of European directives harmonizing regulations.

These weaknesses have been addressed through the adoption of the 'new approach' whereby EU directives only indicate the 'essential requirements' that must be satisfied, which leaves greater freedom to manufacturers as to how to satisfy those requirements, dispensing with the 'old' type of exhaustively detailed directives. The new-approach directives also provide for more flexibility than the detailed harmonization directives of the old approach by using the support of the established standardization bodies, CEN, CENELEC and the national standard bodies. New-approach directives are adopted by a qualified majority in the Council.

THE SINGLE MARKET AND TRADE IN SERVICES

Application of the principle of mutual recognition also lies at the heart of attempts to integrate the markets for services in the EU. For certain sectors, such as financial services, negotiated mutual recognition is a better description since integration is based upon a degree of regulatory approximation of national prudential requirements together with mutual recognition of regulatory authority, normally referred to as home-country control. The essence of the system is that the operations of a financial institution throughout the EU, whether provided across borders or through establishment overseas, are regulated by the government of the state in which it has its headquarters. In principle such a system should avoid financial institutions having to satisfy different regulatory requirements in each of the countries in which they operate.

However, as in the case of goods, exceptions are permitted to the general requirement of mutual recognition of services. For example, in the case of financial services, the Second Banking Directive specifies that 'Member States must ensure that there are no obstacles to carrying on activities receiving mutual recognition in the same manner as in the home member state, as long as the latter do not conflict with legal provisions protecting the general good in the host member state' (see CEC, 1997). The Second Banking Directive does not, however, provide a definition of the 'general good' or stipulate limits or conditions under which member states can impose 'general-good' rules on community financial institutions.

Hence in areas without explicit harmonization at the EU level the definition of the general good varies between member states and is influenced by national traditions and national policy objectives. The Court of Justice, through its case law, has specified areas that can be considered to be in the public good. This open-ended list currently comprises: protection of the recipient of services; protection of workers, including social protection; consumer protection; preservation of the good reputation of the national financial sector; prevention of fraud; social order; protection of intellectual property; cultural policy; preservation of national historical and artistic heritage; cohesion of the tax system; road safety; protection of creditors; and protection of the proper administration of justice (CEC, 1997). National rules adopted in these areas can be enforced upon a community company based in another member state provided that the area has not been harmonized at the EU level, that such rules are applied in a non-discriminatory way, that there is an overriding requirement for them in the general interest, and that they are relevant for attaining the objective for which they are imposed and do not go beyond what is necessary to attain that objective.

It is important to note that financial services do not appear to be subject to the same notification requirements as goods, where, as noted above, all new technical regulations and derogations from free movement have to be notified to the Commission. There is no counterpart to the 98/34 Committee for services. Thus the disciplining effect of notification and EU-level scrutiny of new regulations is absent for services. In addition, for financial services, companies are often wary of bringing a problem to the attention of the Commission for fear of undermining their relationship with the regulatory authorities of the country that is constraining trade. This entails that mutual recognition is likely to be less effective in removing barriers to trade in services in the EU.

THE SINGLE MARKET IN PRACTICE

How effectively is the single market working in the current EU of 15 member states? The European Council has identified the single market as being a key element in economic reform and in achieving the Lisbon objectives. In this context substantial problems remain. Again, it is useful to examine the goods and services sectors separately. For goods, the new approach to harmonized standards at the European level has been undermined by the slow development and adoption of European standards implementing the agreed minimum standards under new-approach directives. CEC (2001) reports that CEN (one of the European Standards' Organizations) takes around eight years to draft and obtain consensus on a European standard. As a result, between April 1998 and May 1999 the European standards bodies ratified only 40 percent of the mandated standards and nearly five times as many national standards were adopted (Holmes and Young, 2001).

The Commission also recognizes that there are problems with the application of the principle of mutual recognition (CEC, 2000) and that these difficulties appear particularly in the new-technology sectors and for complex products. Evidence from businesses suggests that many firms will still adapt their products to satisfy different technical specifications in other markets rather than seeking the application of mutual recognition. This reflects, in part, uncertainty about the effectiveness of the available measures in enforcing mutual recognition and expectations about the time taken to change the actions of national administrations either through persuasion or through judicial process. Weak administration and uncertainty by national administrators leads to a very cautious application of the principle of mutual recognition. CEC (1999) reports an average length of procedure for cases of infringement of mutual recognition of 15.5 months for cases initiated between 1996 and 1998. During this period 228 cases were initiated. According to a survey of industry in 1998, some 80 per cent of businesses reported that there were still obstacles preventing the full benefits of the single market from being exploited, with differences in standards and technical regulations being mentioned by 41 percent of respondents and problems with testing, certification and authorization procedures being identified by 34 percent of the sample (CEC, 1999).

The general view seems to be that obstacles to cross-border trade in services in the EU are much more substantial than those in goods. Traditional measures of integration, such as the share of intra-EU trade relative to GDP, provide little clear evidence of an increase in the intensity of cross-border trade and competition in services in recent years (CEC, 2000). Trade in financial services in Europe takes place primarily through physical establishment in another member state. Mergers and takeovers, rather than cross-border supply, have tended to be the main vehicle for change in European financial markets.

EU financial markets are undergoing a period of substantial change following the introduction of the euro, substantial technological change and regulatory initiatives. Whether these will combine to generate a genuine single market in financial services and a large European investment area remains a key issue. A number of important developments have taken place (Danthine et al., 2000; CEC, 2001). A corporate eurobond market has emerged of comparable size to that of the dollar market. European firms are increasingly turning to stock markets for funding via equity issues. EU companies newly admitted to European stock markets raised twice as much capital in 2000 than in 1999. Some researchers detect a fundamental change in the nature of European investment portfolios, with an increasing share of foreign equities (Danthine et al., 2000), whilst others find little evidence that country-specific factors have declined in importance in defining European portfolios (Rouwenhorst, 1998). Heinemann (2002) notes that whilst the market for investment funds in the EU has been growing strongly, national markets remain dominated by domestic fund companies. Wojcik (2001) looks at the extent and nature of cross-border corporate ownership in Europe and concludes that the level of capital market integration in Europe remains low and that 'the contours of national borders on the map of the European capital markets are still very sharp'. These border effects reflect that the conditions of foreign ownership differ between countries, with particular emphasis being placed on the role of corporate governance.

In rather crude terms, the financial structures of continental European economies are markedly different from those of the UK and USA. Figure 8.1 provides some information on the relative importance of bond, equity and bank markets in the eurozone area, the EU-15 and the USA at the end of the 1990s. Traditional bank lending is of much greater importance on the continent, while the English-speaking economies are characterized by the much more widespread sale of securities directly to lenders. Junk bonds and equity issues by small and medium-sized firms in Europe are very rare. Continental banks have a much larger share of intermediated claims than do banks in the USA and the UK. Thus relationship banking dominates on the continent while in the UK and the USA impersonal markets are much more important. To what extent will these differences be eroded and will the continental financial structure come to resemble that of the USA and the UK, or will institutional and

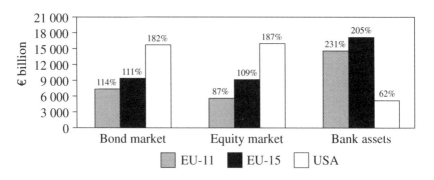

Source: Bank of International Settlements.

Figure 8.1   Equity, bond and bank markets in the EU and the USA (1999, total assets in € billion and as a percentage of GDP)

country-specific factors continue to impede the creation of a truly single market for investment and financial services in the EU? We turn to this issue in more detail below.

ENLARGEMENT AND THE SINGLE MARKET IN EUROPE

Thus there remain substantial problems within the EU, where there is an extensive infrastructure, in completing the single market. Removing remaining constraints upon the free movement of goods, services, capital and labour has been put at the heart of the policy drive to achieve the Lisbon objectives of substantially raising productivity in the EU. Clearly, the efforts of the existing members to effectively implement the single market must increase in the context of enlargement since the accession of between eight and ten new members will substantially increase the pressures on the single market and stretch the abilities of the Commission to monitor and ensure compliance with harmonized directives and the principle of mutual recognition.

The Europe Agreements between the EU and each of the candidate countries in Central and Eastern Europe provide for the widespread approximation of relevant laws in these countries with EU internal market legislation. These provisions have become of particular importance given the subsequent drive towards membership of the EU and the requirement that the applicant countries adopt the legal and institutional framework of the EU. Thus the implementation of EU directives relating to technical regulations has become an essential element of the accession process.

As part of this process the EU has accepted that the Central and Eastern European Countries (CEECs) should be granted sectoral access to the single market before accession if the necessary changes to their domestic legislative systems have been made and implementation of regulations and the EU system of testing and conformity assessment are deemed to be satisfactory. Even when the relevant EU laws relating to technical regulations have been adopted in the CEECs, technical barriers will remain if duplication of conformity assessment procedures persists.

Achieving access to the single market before accession is governed by mutual recognition agreements called the Protocols on European Conformity Assessment (PECAs). Following the satisfactory alignment of laws, individual CEECs can negotiate sectoral access to the single market, subject to the technical competence of conformity assessment bodies being of a level equivalent to that in the EU and the acceptance by both parties of the results from notified conformity assessment bodies.

The European Commission has concluded agreements with Hungary and the Czech Republic, covering machinery, electrical safety, electromagnetic compatibility, gas appliances, hot water boilers and good manufacturing practice for medicinal products. The Hungarian agreement covers in addition good laboratory practice for medicinal products and medical devices, while the agreement with the Czech Republic also includes personal protective equipment and equipment for use in potentially explosive atmospheres. Products from these sectors that satisfy conformity assessment by any notified body in the EU or the CEECs will have freedom of movement in the EU and the country concerned. The EU has also signed a framework agreement covering general principles with Latvia and is negotiating PECAs with Estonia, Lithuania, Slovenia and Slovakia.

The PECAs have primarily been concerned with those sectors where technical regulations have been harmonized in the EU and have concentrated on new-approach sectors. Thus the pre-accession commitments of the CEECs have involved the adoption of EU new-approach directives and the standards issued by CEN, CENELEC and ETSI. Little or no progress has been attempted on non-harmonized sectors, where the principle of mutual recognition operates in the EU. Hence, for certain products, access to the single market will only be delivered, at the earliest, with accession. The basic principle underlying the operation of the single market, that of mutual recognition, will not be applied until after accession, and so there is no clear means of assessing now how effectively mutual recognition will operate after enlargement.

This discussion of the EU approach to technical regulations, which is an essential element in the working of the single market, raises a number of issues regarding the post-enlargement situation and, in particular, the impact that enlargement will have on the single market. Most of the applicant countries have made enormous progress in adopting the relevant EU regulations regarding the placing of products on the market and in upgrading testing and conformity procedures to similar standards in the EU (precise details for four of the applicant countries are available in Brenton and Manzocchi, 2002). This is a key element of the preaccession process. However, as stressed by Pelkmans et al. (2000), the durability of the single market turns on implementation and compliance with single market provisions and the effectiveness of remedies that can be applied in cases of non-compliance.

With regard to the enlargement, we first of all note that the harmonization process will become more difficult and probably slower, since discussions of minimum technical requirements will take place among 23 to 25 members rather than just 15, with a much greater variance in incomes, traditions and national policy objectives. Thus, while there may be greater emphasis on the need for new-approach directives for a broader range of products and issues, the ability of the harmonization procedure and then the standardization process to effectively and quickly deliver the necessary standards is at best uncertain. We still do not have a precise idea of the extent to which the new approach is working and is actually removing technical barriers and stimulating trade between existing member states. Evidence from surveys of businesses suggests that even in the current EU of 15, substantial barriers to cross-border trade remain due to the presence of national technical requirements and their application.

Standardization remains a slow and cumbersome process which, together with the commitment to reduce the regulatory burden on businesses, suggests that increasing emphasis will have to be placed upon application of mutual recognition. On the other hand, the enlargement of the Union to 25 members and the increase in diversity that this implies is likely to make general application of the principle of mutual recognition more difficult and more contested. Administrative capacity is a key element in the application of the principle of mutual recognition. Although it is important to note that mutual recognition is a principle and is not something that can be directly legislated, CEC (2000) states that 'Member States must ensure that appropriate administrative and judicial means exist to enforce Single Market rules properly, including adequately staffed and trained market surveillance and enforcement authorities and that adequate means of redress and appropriate sanctions are available and sufficiently known to economic operators.'

Members require a system that can recognize that equivalent levels of protection are being offered by the regulatory systems of fellow members. How long it takes to establish such a system and the preconditions for its effective operation are unclear. What can be said is that the effective operation of the principle of mutual recognition requires a degree of trust between regulatory authorities and in the testing systems whose role is to ensure conformity with the relevant technical requirements. How long it takes to engender such trust is not clear. Thus it is very difficult objectively to assess to what extent the applicant countries will be ready to implement the principle of mutual recognition.

ENLARGEMENT AND DEEPER INTEGRATION IN EUROPE

The EU is one of the most integrated groupings of countries in the world. From the outset, and recently enhanced by the completion of the single market, the EU has gone beyond the simple removal of commercial policy instruments that constrain trade at the border, such as tariffs and quotas, to address behind-the-border barriers to trade resulting from the application of regulatory policies, such as product regulations, environmental regulations, sanitary and phytosanitary standards, state aids, the protection of intellectual property, and so on. Nevertheless, the EU is far from a perfectly integrated economic area. For both goods and services, and financial flows, trade between European countries is quantitatively small relative to similar exchanges within national boundaries. In highly integrated markets we should not be able to detect any impact from national borders; the propensity to trade internationally with citizens of other countries should be the same as that to trade internally with citizens of the same country of residence. This is the benchmark of perfect integration. However, in practice it appears that borders still loom very large (Brenton, 2002).

The crucial issue emanating from this empirical finding is to identify the factors that lie behind this border effect. In particular, are there impediments which can be broken down, suggesting that there is considerably more, and much more than we have already experienced, globalization to come? Or can we discern whether there are factors that will always constrain and limit the extent of global integration? A second issue is whether the removal of such barriers, if feasible, will lead to the sort of productivity gains that have been achieved from dismantling formal trade barriers, or whether the principal gains from trade have already been reaped. In the context of the future of the EU, this debate revolves around the issue of whether efforts towards further integration can contribute to the Lisbon strategy of raising productivity and competitiveness in Europe.

So what factors could be constraining cross-border integration in Europe? In general, one of the main reasons for the economic impact of the border is that movement across a national frontier, even those in the EU where, with the single market, there are no border formalities and only empty border posts, entails movement into a different legal, regulatory, social and cultural jurisdiction. These borders seperate one geographical area from another, in terms of both consumers' preferences and the legal and institutional environment for doing business.

More specifically, tastes differ across countries. Domestically located firms will tend to have better knowledge of local tastes and more generally firms will tend to locate close to markets to avoid trade costs. This effect will be magnified if intermediate goods producers co-locate with final goods produc- ers (Hillberry and Hummels, 2000). Even if consumers in different countries have identical tastes for products, they may still have different preferences for the way these products are packaged and marketed, which will add to the costs of international trade. Engel and Rogers (1996) suggest that one of the factors behind the border effects in consumer prices that they identify in Europe will be differences in national marketing and distribution systems.

It is also suggested that both consumers and producers tend to have a prefer- ence for purchasing products produced in their own country. Indeed, there is a large literature in the context of marketing that documents the presence and importance of home bias on the basis of consumer surveys (see, for example, Knight, 1999). More generally, systematic evidence on home bias in preferences is sparse. But if home bias in preferences is a genuine phenomenon and reflects actual desires on the part of consumers, then policies that seek to undermine such bias and to promote further trade are unlikely to be welfare improving.

In this context the application of the principle of mutual recognition plays an important role in Europe. CEC (1999) argues that the application of mutual recognition is 'consonant with the idea of a dynamic approach to the application of subsidiarity; by avoiding the systematic creation of detailed rules at Community level, mutual recognition ensures greater observance of local, regional and national traditions and makes it possible to maintain the diversity of products and services which come onto the markets'. In short, mutual recognition preserves the multiformity of tastes and preferences in Europe and allows consumers to affect any bias towards locally produced products. Detailed harmonization and, to a lesser extent, the specification of minimum standards under the new approach, act to undermine nationally disparate preferences by reducing the degree of permissible product differentiation. That is, harmonization acts to suppress diversity.

Thus, although there are clearly additional gains to be had from the more effective implementation of the principle of mutual recognition in Europe, there are limits to the extent to which this process will increase economic integration. Similarly, Holmes and Young (2001) argue that a key feature of the EU's regulatory approach is that progress with market integration has been possible only by allowing members to pursue their own legitimate public policy objectives such that a significant degree of variation in rules between members is permitted. In other words, the principle of mutual recognition is a mechanism of integration that allows, to a certain extent, the accommodation of diversity. Holmes and Young argue that the EU is reaching a 'logical limitation' in that market integration is only possible if some degree of national variation is permitted, but such variation constrains integration. The further that integration progresses, the more intractable will be the national variations that remain. Thus, on the one hand, mutual recognition will play a crucial role in an enlarged EU, allowing the accession of diverse countries to the single market. On the other hand, by increasing diversity in the Union and raising the number of legitimate national public policy objectives, enlargement may constrain the future level of integration in the EU. The immediate priority for the EU after enlargement will be to ensure that there is not a retrenchment from the current level of integration.

CONCLUSIONS

The key mechanism for achieving economic integration between diverse countries, the principle of mutual recognition, has its limits, in terms of the level of integration that it can provide for, which in turn has implications for the future direction of the EU. On the one hand mutual recognition is a powerful tool for undermining barriers to trade in goods and services while avoiding the need for detailed harmonization and extensive EU-level intrusion into national policy-making. On the other hand, mutual recognition preserves a degree of national differentiation and allows national governments to implement specific policies to protect 'the national good'. It is unlikely that the EU could have achieved the level of integration that it has attained today without the use of the principle of mutual recognition as the main tool for undermining national segmentation in Europe.

Now EU policy-makers want to enhance the single market to achieve the bold objectives defined at Lisbon. Clearly, there is scope to make the single market work more effectively. This is particularly true for the service sectors, where enhanced integration will not only generate direct economic benefits, but will also lead to gains in manufacturing and agricultural sectors, where services are a vital input into modern processes. Nevertheless, there are limits to the extent that mutual recognition can integrate the markets of different countries. Whether efforts to increase the effectiveness of mutual recognition will be sufficient, particularly in the light of enlargement, to achieve the Lisbon objectives remains to be seen. What our analysis suggests is that continental European economic structures and finance are unlikely to converge totally towards the US model and that key elements of existing structures, such as the more significant role for traditional bank lending, will remain.

NOTES

1. For example, venture capital funds in the USA mobilized over four times the amount of funding for start-up companies in 1996 than their EU counterparts (CEC, 2000).
2. These data were taken from 'The EU's relations with the United States of America', EU Commission, http://europa.eu.int/comni/external_relationslus/intro/index.htrn

REFERENCES

Brenton, P. (2002), 'The limits to international trade and economic integration', *Journal of World Investment*, **3**, 83–95.
Brenton, P. and S. Manzocchi (eds) (2002), *Enlargement, Trade and Investment: Assessing the Impact of Technical Barriers to Trade*, Cheltenham, UK and Northampton, USA: Edward Elgar.
CEC (1997), 'Freedom to provide services and the interest of the general good in the second banking directive', SEC (97) 1193 final, Brussels.
CEC (1999), 'Mutual recognition in the context of the follow-up to the action plan for the Single Market', communication to the Parliament and the Council.

CEC (2000), *Economic Reform: Report on the Functioning of Community Product and Capital Markets*.

CEC (2001), 'The economic impact of enlargement', enlargement papers no. 4, DG ECFIN.

Danthine, J.-P., F. Giavazzi and E.L. von Thadden (2000), 'European financial markets after EMU: a first assessment', National Bureau for Economic Research working paper 8044.

Engel, C. and J. Rogers (1996), 'How wide is the border?', *American Economic Review*, **86**, 1112–25.

Hall, P.A. and D. Soskice (eds) (2001), *Varieties of Capitalism: Institutional Foundations Of Comparative Advantage*, Oxford: Oxford University Press.

Heinemann, F. (2002), 'The benefits of creating a real EU market for investment funds', working paper, ZEW, Mannheim.

Hillberry, R. and D. Hummels (2000), 'Explaining home bias in consumption: production location, commodity composition and magnification', mimeo, Purdue University.

Holmes, P. and A. Young (2001), 'Emerging regulatory challenges to the EU's external economic relations', working paper 42, Sussex European Institute, University of Sussex.

Knight, G. (1999), 'Consumer preferences for foreign and domestic products', *Journal of Consumer Marketing*, **16**, 151–62. http://www.managementfirst.com/international_marketing/art_Products.htm

Pelkmans, J., E. Vos and L. Di Mauro (2000), 'Reforming product regulation in the EU: a painstaking, iterative two-level game', in G. Galli and J. Plekmans (eds), *Regulatory Reform and Competitiveness in Europe*, vol. 1, Cheltenham, UK and Northampton, USA: Edward Elgar.

Rouwenhorst, K.G. (1998), 'European equity markets and EMU: are the differences between countries slowly disappearing?', mimeo, Yale School of Management, New Haven, CT.

Wojcik, D. (2001), 'Cross-border corporate ownership in Europe is not consistent with an integrated capital market: evidence from portfolio and industrial holdings', WPG 01-06, School of Geography and the Environment, University of Oxford, Oxford.

9. Japanese economic structures and finance: characteristics and causes of the current slowdown

Thomas F. Cargill and Elliott Parker

By the end of the 1980s, the Japanese economy appeared to have reached a 'high plateau of prosperity'. With the exception of a brief period in the early 1970s,[1] Japan's economic stability after 1950 was remarkable, and was matched by political stability with the dominance of the Liberal Democratic Party (LDP). Japan had become the world's second largest economy, the world's largest creditor nation, and the world's most stable industrialized country.

As a result, the 'Japan model' was increasingly being suggested as an alternative to both the market-oriented regimes of Western economies and the socialist-economic planning regimes of the Soviet Union. The World Bank (1993), for example, described the rapid economic growth in Japan and other Asian economies as the 'Asian Miracle', and attributed the economic performance in these countries to government guidance and support in mobilizing their real and financial resources.[2]

Yet in 1990 and 1991, after monetary tightening by the Bank of Japan led to a sudden and dramatic deflation in asset prices (particularly for equity and land), growth in the Japanese economy came to a virtual halt.[3] Financial distress has characterized Japan since 1990, and observers now regard the 1990s as Japan's 'lost decade' of economic and financial development. Real GDP growth during the 1990s averaged only 1.4 percent per year, compared to 4 percent in the previous decade and almost 10 percent per year in the years between the Korean War and the OPEC oil embargo. Despite demand management policies (that is, easy monetary policy and deficit spending) and major restructuring of the financial system (for example, closing the *jusen* industry in 1995, reorganizing deposit insurance in 1995, and the announcement of the Big Bang financial reforms), the economy had not yet recovered by spring 2002. After some signs of a weak recovery in 2000, the Japanese economy declined again in 2001. The level of economic and financial distress is now at its highest level since 1990, and many wonder whether Japan is beginning a second 'lost decade.'

The political stability that characterized much of Japan's postwar period has also eroded. Prime Minister Junichiro Koizumi, who was elected in April 2001, is the eleventh's prime minister in the past decade. Koizumi campaigned as a 'reformist', but Japan's continuing economic malaise has already weakened his once-widespread support. In a recent interview (Brooke, 2002), Koizumi voiced bewilderment at Japan's inability to recover in spite of the many efforts to stimulate and restructure the economy.

This chapter attempts to explain why the Japanese economy has ceased to grow, evaluates the policies adopted by the Japanese government to stimulate and reform the economy, and suggests the most likely course of development during the first decade of the new century. We argue that the design of the Japanese financial system is the primary factor in the Japanese slowdown, just as it was a major factor in the earlier decades of Japanese growth. In addition to the structural problems of the financial system, we argue that the slowdown has been exacerbated by inappropriate monetary policy. We then consider why Japanese policymakers have been unable to address the underlying problems. The answers to this issue are manifold and we consider several contributing explanations related both to Japan's domestic political economy and external international pressures.

THE DESIGN AND STRUCTURE OF THE JAPANESE FINANCIAL SYSTEM

The Japanese financial system is the culmination of an evolutionary process that started with the Meiji Restoration of 1868 and the resulting adoption of policies designed to transform Japan into a modern industrial and military power that could compete with the West. The financial structure that emerged after World War II was a continuation of prewar trends, despite the claim that Japan's financial system was largely influenced by the Allied Occupation of 1945–52.

Japan's financial structure is based on four elements. First, Japan has maintained a high household saving rate despite relatively low returns on financial assets. Japanese households continue to save approximately a fourth of their GDP, one of the highest saving rates in the world, and this high saving rate provides the foundation for a huge financial sector that has traditionally relied almost entirely on domestic sources of funds. Second, the financial sector is designed to transfer the financial resources to the large business firms and other targeted sectors of the economy. Thus the financial system has long been an instrument of industrial policy, and only in the past two decades have consumer and mortgage credit become a significant use of funds. Third, the financial sector is based on intermediation finance, both private and public, and the banking system is the primary private intermediation channel. Fourth, a key characteristic of this financial structure has not been merely to support industrialization by channeling credit to the large business firms, but just as important, to encourage investment by limiting risk and bankruptcy. In this regard, both the private and public channels of finance played a role.

Private and Public Intermediation

The large city banks have long been the center of the Japanese *keiretsu* (lineage) system, in which 40 to 50 groups of firms – some originating from the *zaibatsu*, the huge prewar trusts broken up by the occupation authorities, some vertically integrated – are held together through cross-holdings of equity, reliance on a common group bank and a common trading company, joint subsidiaries, and consultation between firm leaders. This so-called 'main bank system' was credited with reducing individual firm risk in a convoy-system setting, and providing both ready buyers within the group as well as ready access to capital for large, longterm investment projects.[4] The *keiretsu* system was formed with the encouragement of the Japanese government after the Allied Occupation ended. The phrase 'iron triangle' was coined to characterize the supporting relationship between the *keiretsu,* the leaders of the LDP, and government regulatory agencies such as the Ministry of Finance (MOF) and the Ministry of International Trade and Industry (MITI). The *keiretsu* system made bankruptcy relatively rare among Japan's large and most politically connected business firms.

The public intermediation channel consists of the Postal Savings System and the Fiscal Investment and Loan Program (FILP).[5] With two trillion dollars in deposits, the Japanese Postal Savings System is the world's largest financial institution. The FILP, which allocates postal deposits and other sources of funds to eight government banks and other government entities, controls funds equal to about 10 percent of Japan's GDP.

No-failure Policies

Aside from the role of the government in the iron triangle, the government played an independent role in reducing risk and minimizing bankruptcy through financial regulation and supervision. The government adopted a no-failure policy for financial institutions and markets, supported by pervasive deposit guarantees, regulation, non-transparency, and the lender-of-last-resort powers of the Bank of Japan (BOJ). Government financial intermediation also contributed to the objective of lowering risk and minimizing bankruptcy. A significant part of the funds allocated through the FILP was designed to support industries that were no longer competitive or activities that could not obtain funding from the private banks on a rational economic basis.

Events in the 1990s forced Japan to depart from the objective of lowering risk and minimizing bankruptcy. Many small financial institutions (especially the *jusen* banks) failed during the 1991–95 period, but then larger institutions began to fail. Both Hokkaido Takushoka Bank and Yamaichi Securities Company failed in late 1997, and both the Long Term Credit Bank and the Nippon Credit Bank failed in late 1998. Many mergers have occurred since as a way of preventing more bank failures. The Financial Services Agency currently predicts that a large number of small credit cooperatives are likely to fail in the next few years as new regulatory policies come into force. Meanwhile, the number of corporate failures has dramatically increased in the 1990s, averaging about 1500 cases per year since 1996 (Bank of Japan, 2002).

Despite the inability to limit risk and bankruptcy in the 1990s, much of the financial system and much of the government regulation and supervision is wedded to the old financial regime's emphasis on reducing risk and bankruptcy. This is one of several fundamental constraints facing Japan's efforts to recover. It accounts for Japan's willingness to engage in a policy of forgiveness and forbearance in dealing with market-insolvent banks and financial institutions and non-performing loans.

Despite well-publicized corporate restructuring and loan restructuring plans, Japan continues to resist exposing the system to bankruptcy and the increased unemployment that increased bankruptcy would entail, and restructuring plans primarily seem to delay bankruptcy.

A program in 1998 allowed small and medium-sized corporations to borrow up to 50 million yen unconditionally, without screening, and gave them a one-year grace period. Bankruptcies declined in 1998, but increased again after the grace period expired (*Diamond Weekly*, 2000a). In the construction industry, large numbers of firms that received debt forgiveness again at the end of 2001 have since gone bankrupt or forced to sell their firms, once the grace period expired. Tobishima Corp. requested that Fuji Bank make a debt-equity swap of 10 billion yen ($77 million), but this was the second time around; four years ago, Tobishima secured a $5 billion yen debt waiver and a 20-year restructuring plan. The recent debt restructuring plan for a large retailer, Daeei, shows that debt forgiveness without requiring significant structural changes is still the preferred policy. Politicians have brought considerable pressure to continue the policy of delay, forgiveness and forbearance since the country cannot handle a significant increase in unemployment and bankrupt firms.

This attitude has constrained Japan's efforts to adopt deposit insurance. Deposit insurance was established in 1971, but because of its small staff and lack of regulatory authority, it played no role in the deposit safety net system. Several failures of small credit cooperatives and banks in the early 1990s exhausted the reserves of the Deposit Insurance Corporation (DIC). In 1995, the DIC was expanded with the intent of taking over the primary role of providing a safety net for private bank deposits. In order to provide a transition period and given depository institutions more time to improve their balance sheets, the government announced a complete deposit guarantee in late 1995 scheduled to be eliminated on 1 April 2001. It was widely believed at the time that Japan's economic and financial difficulties would be a distant memory by 2001. The elimination of the complete guarantee was extended for one year in late 1999, however, and is to be phased in over a two-year period starting on 1 April 2002. Starting on the date, savings and time deposits are only guaranteed up to a limit of 10 million yen; however, transaction deposits remain subject to the complete guarantee until 1 April 2003. The reduced pace of deposit insurance reform has been influenced by the continuing economic and financial distress and the impact on bankruptcies that removal of the complete guarantee would have on depository institutions.

The emphasis on limiting risk and bankruptcy and the reluctance to adopt a more transparent policy toward troubled financial and non-financial firms can be rationalized by three considerations. First, as Lincoln (2001) argues, there are characteristics of Japanese culture that are more compatible with bank finance and less compatible with a more market-oriented approach to dealing with troubled financial and non-financial firms; the importance of face, non-transparency, informality, façades, and mutual support may bias economic institutions towards limiting risk and bankruptcy. Thus a major difference between the Anglo-American and Japanese societies is the willingness of the Anglo-American system to accept the concept of Schumpeterian 'creative destruction' as a part of the economic development process.

Second, the financial system supported impressive economic performance in Japan for over 120 years. Japan's rapid rise from a feudal–agricultural economy to an industrial power after a mere 30 years of development after the Meiji Restoration was impressive, but even more impressive was Japan's postwar performance. The financial regime thus supported an impressive growth record.

Third, limiting risk and bankruptcy often work for a period. The absence of effective bankruptcy policies can lead to rapid capital formation, and Parker (1995) argued that this could help to explain why Soviet-style economies grew so rapidly in their early years. However, when firms are locked into their past decisions with regard to technology, firm structure and investment, the absence of selection pressures may also lead to slowing growth in the long run as more and more capital gets locked into inefficient technologies. The absence of Schumpeterian creative destruction may help to explain Japan's past growth, especially when combined with its high savings rate and Easterly's (2001) arguments that (a) investments have externally increasing returns, since more new investment increases the return to the accumulation of human capital, which in turn increases the return on investment, and that (b) the technological latecomer has an advantage in applying new technologies, since there are fewer vested interests likely to oppose change.

International Finance

Until the 1990s, international savings inflows played no significant role in Japanese finance, and Japan's interaction with international capital markets was primarily as a source of savings outflows due to its high savings rate and its large current account surpluses, especially with the USA. These surpluses resulted from macroeconomic factors, including Japan's high savings, low interest rates and moderate or low inflation, as well as microeconomic factors such as the *keirestsu*'s tendency to buy from within and the use of regulation to hinder both manufactured imports and inward foreign investment. In a review of the literature, Lincoln (1990, pp. 12–38) notes that Japan's low manufacturing import share could not be explained by its imports of raw materials, per capita income, or other economic factors. He concludes that Japanese implicit protectionism remained high, even though explicit tariffs and quota barriers were largely removed in the 1960s as a result of pressures from GATT and the IMF.

While Japan's trade surpluses with the USA have remained a source of tension, its trade ratio as a share of GDP has decreased over time. In this way too, as Katz (1998, p. 258) notes, Japan appears to be an outlier among developed economies. Even the USA, which accounts for a quarter of the world's GDP and so trades mostly with itself, had a trade ratio that surpassed Japan's by 1990, and Katz argues that this decline in trade has made Japan less competitive overall.

In the 1980s, Japanese exporters began to take better advantage of their foreign currency earnings to significantly increase their outward foreign direct investment (FDI), mostly in North America, Europe and Asia, while their equity investment was primarily targeted just towards the USA. Barrell and Pain (1999) found that FDI in the USA and Europe was significantly determined by the effort to skirt trade barriers, while Mody et al. (1999) found investment in Asia was primarily determined by high costs in Japan and the desire to arrive early in a growing market. As a result, the largest Japanese firms have increasingly become more international in scope and increasingly efficient, with their easy access to foreign management, finance, labor and markets. These multinationals are increasingly independent of administrative guidance from MITI and other government agencies, and this has created somewhat of a legitimacy problem for these bureaucracies. Meanwhile, smaller, domestically contained firms have continued to operate under the old regime, and the productivity gap between them has widened (Porter et al., 2000).

Recently, internationalization has also occurred through foreign investment into Japan, and though the level is still small the rate of change is not. The 'Big Bang' reforms that were implemented in 1998 began to dismantle regulatory barriers that had prevented the entrance of foreign firms into the Japanese market, and also prevented the Japanese from holding offshore accounts. Lower stock prices and land prices have made Japan somewhat more affordable, and FDI into Japan has begun to grow rapidly. Inward FDI, which had accounted for less than 0.5 percent of GDP (compared to ratios of 6 to 30 percent for the G7 countries) and was one-tenth the size of outward FDI, has now been predicted to grow to 4 or 5 percent of GDP by 2003. A third of this new investment is going into the financial sector, where American and European investment firms offered better returns and better cash management services, while the rest is primarily going into the services, machinery and trade sectors. As a result, large Japanese firms are now beginning to use foreign as well as domestic banks for the management of both their yen and foreign currency funds.

Foreign equity investment has also grown dramatically since the Big Bang, though from an even smaller base, and this has prompted some concern from the Japanese. An article in the influential *Diamond Weekly* (2000b) noted that foreign investors were buying up many failing firms in the insurance and financial sectors (for example, Tolio Mutual Life Insurance, Yamaichi Securities and the Long Term Credit Bank of Japan), but also argued that they would soon seek control of Japan's blue chip corporations and force unpleasant changes in their management approach. Masuda (2000) also worried that such foreign investment could further increase Japan's imports. Though some Japanese have argued that foreign equity investment in the stock market would worsen volatility, Hamao and Mei (2001) conclude that foreign investors are instead behaving as long-term contrarian investors and thus so far stabilizing prices.

WHY DID JAPAN STOP GROWING?

Japan's sudden turn of fortune in 1990–91 and its failure to recover after a decade of unprecedented government effort to stimulate the economy can be attributed to the combined impact of seven factors: first, an initial aggressive shift from easy to tight monetary policy that continued to 1994; second, a regulatory response rooted in the old financial regime; third, a bank-finance structure that incorporates a feedback relationship between bank equity, land prices and equity prices; fourth, the culmination of inefficiencies supported by a financial system designed to limit risk and bankruptcy; fifth, fiscal policy contraction in late 1997 and fiscal stimulus packages that were limited and wasteful; sixth, a large and increasing role of government financial intermediation, ensuring that a large part of household savings is channeled into low or negative return projects; and, seventh, ongoing monetary policy that has permitted a slow but definite decline in the price level. We explain these seven reasons in more detail below.

Bank of Japan Policy and the Start of the Decline

Japan's rapid growth in the second half of the *1980s is* now characterized as the 'bubble economy', as equity and land prices started to increase in 1987 to levels that could not be easily rationalized by a reasonable forecast of future economic fundamentals. For example, after rising by an impressive average of 12 percent per year from 1970 to 1985, the Nikkei 500 stock index rose by an average of 28 percent per year from 1985 to 1990, compared to an increase in the consumer price index of only 1.5 percent per year during the same period.

This asset inflation was the joint outcome of an incomplete and flawed financial liberalization process, the adoption of the 1988 BIS capital asset requirements, and easy monetary policy. The absence of any evidence of price inflation for goods and services led the Bank of Japan to conclude that easy monetary policy could limit appreciation of the yen after the Louvre Accord. After a dramatic appreciation in the yen from 1985 to 1987, following the Plaza Accord, money (measured as M2+CD) rose by an average 11 percent per year in the late 1980s, and the yen depreciated somewhat through 1989. The Bank of Japan was in error, however, when they believed they could follow this policy without damaging the domestic economy.

Falling interest rates and rapid growth rates, combined with the common belief that they could be maintained, led to a tripling in prices paid for stocks, real estate and other assets. Excessive liquidity supported the bubble in asset prices because incomplete and flawed financial liberalization allowed banks and other financial institutions to expand, especially into real estate, without adequate oversight and without due regard to the moral hazard of pervasive deposit guarantees. The capital asset requirements set by the Geneva-based Bank for International Settlements (BIS) allowed 'hidden reserves' held by banks (that is, capital gains on equities) to satisfy Tier 2 capital requirements, and increased liquidity by the Bank of Japan combined with rising equity prices thus rapidly increased bank lending, especially into real estate. Rising real-estate prices increased collateral that could be used for further bank lending, as did rising equity prices supported by rising profits of business firms.

In 1989, the Bank of Japan became increasingly concerned about asset inflation and signs that the CPI inflation rate was finally beginning to increase. In May 1989, the Bank of Japan raised the discount rate and for the next several years restricted monetary growth, setting off the burst of the bubble economy. This policy largely remained in place throughout the following decade, with an average annual growth rate in money (M2+CD) of 2.6 percent, even after the economy slumped. Still, Cargill (2001) argues the shift to tight monetary policy was not by itself enough to generate the economic and financial distress that has characterized Japan since the early 1990s; instead, it was the combination of tight monetary policy with an inherently flawed financial and regulatory structure that became the catalyst for the lost decade.

Feedback Relationship Between Bank Lending, Land Prices and Equity Prices

In 1988 Japanese banks were permitted to count up to 45 percent of their 'hidden capital' or 'latent capital' to meeting the BIS Tier 2 capital asset requirements. Hidden or latent capital represented the capital gains on equities held by banks. The gains were significant, since much of the equity held by banks had been purchased many years in the past. This policy, given the large capital gains on equities held by Japanese banks, increased bank capital, and the excessive capital of Japanese banks in the late 1980s was noticed by some writers even before the bubble burst. The BIS capital asset requirements, in the context of the large holdings of equity by Japanese banks, established a feedback relationship between increasing equity prices and bank lending.

Bank lending was dependent on land values because land was frequently used as collateral for bank loans. Land values were likely to increase significantly in the presence of any stimulus because industrial activity in Japan is concentrated in a small number of geographic areas in Tokyo and Osaka, with an inelastic supply of land and extensive regulations over building. Land prices had been slowly increasing throughout most of the postwar period; however, in the 1980s they increased more rapidly as a result of the opening up of the financial system for foreign firms, especially security firms. The resulting increase in demand, in the context of price-inelastic supply, provided the basis for the speculative increases in land prices.

Land prices also increased in response to a shift in lending patterns. Corporations became less dependent on bank credit as a result of liberalization, and banks shifted their uses of funds to real estate, either directly or indirectly through the *jusen* subsidiaries. Thus the role that land played as collateral insured that increasing land values could support increased bank lending. Equity prices responded to higher real GDP growth in 1985 and 1986, increasing business profits, and increasing internationalization of the Japanese economy. Thus, higher equity prices supported higher bank lending through their impact on bank capital.

Regulatory Response Rooted in the Old Financial Regime

As described above, the financial system was designed to limit risk and bankruptcy, and while bankruptcy did sometimes occur in the real sector, the government adopted a 'no-failure' policy for financial markets and institutions. The policy was supported by extensive controls over the flow and cost of funds designed to limit competition, along with pervasive deposit guarantees and central bank 'lender-of-last-resort' services. In those cases where the government had to deal with a troubled financial institution, non-transparency and the mutual support (or convoy) system was the adopted policy.

This approach of forgiveness and forbearance was successful for almost four decades, though in hindsight it is now clear that the success of the Japanese financial system before the 1990s was due to a set of special circumstances that were not sustainable. Still, regulatory authorities had no reason to doubt that the appropriate response to the growing non-performing-loan problem and increasing number of troubled financial institutions was first to deny the problem, and then, when denial was no longer credible, to understate the problem. Even once forced to take action, regulators continued to prefer the policy of forgiveness and forbearance. Thus the failure of regulatory authorities to deal with the pervasive deposit guarantees and growing insolvencies and non-performing loans only postponed the resolution and increased the economic and political cost of the resolution.

Accumulation of Inefficiencies in the Real and Financial Sector

Cargill and Parker (2002) build on Parker (1995) to distinguish between two types of financial regime: market-directed finance that allows bankruptcy, and state-directed finance that restricts bankruptcy. The problem with state-directed finance and limiting bankruptcy comes from the failure to remove inefficient capital, which becomes a deadweight loss of increasing importance over time. This is clearly not true of all firms in Japan since many of the large world-class competitors have been and remain efficient, but these firms are increasingly internationalized in their production, marketing and finance and thus, over time, play a less important role in the domestic economy. Much of the real sector remaining in Japan is inefficient, and as a result generates low rates of return on financial assets. This, in turn, encourages households to allocate their large savings to the Postal Savings System, which has a history of supporting low-return and often negative-return projects through the FILP.

The same situation exists in the financial system. For much of the postwar period, financial institutions were insulated from competition and benefited from both extensive guarantees by the government and the general mutual support system between firms, regulatory authorities and politicians. Japanese financial institutions as a result are among the least efficient among the industrial countries and have been subject to moral hazard incentives for much of the postwar period.

Inappropriate Fiscal Policy

In a detailed review of fiscal stimulus packages through 1998, Posen (1998) concluded that little effort at fiscal stimulus has been attempted despite public announcements to the contrary. The announced fiscal packages before 1998 relied primarily on loan guarantees rather than on direct spending and/or tax reduction. The stimulus packages after 1998, however, were significant in terms of size. Government expenditures rose from 34 percent of GDP in 1997 to over 38 percent in 2000; this increase was financed entirely through increased government debt, as total receipts declined due to the slowing economy. Unfortunately, much of the spending has been allocated to 'pork-barrel' projects, subsidizing public and government enterprises, and in the form of loan guarantees rather than direct spending.

Unfortunately, almost no attention has been given to reforming the Japanese tax code or lowering its high marginal tax rates. While a fiscal stimulus consisting of meaningful tax cuts would likely have had a very positive impact on the economy, the one attempt to change taxes in fact resulted in an increase rather than a decrease in taxes. In 1997, the Hashimoto government, concerned about the increasing size of the central government deficit, raised the consumption tax from 3 to 5 percent. Many regard this restrictive fiscal policy as one of the causes of the sharp decline in real GDP in the fourth quarter of 1997 and in 1998.

Government spending has continued to increase, and the structural deficit has widened significantly since 1997 and government debt as of 2002 represents 130 percent of GDP. Certainly, the monies have been poorly spent and the disincentive effects of taxes have not been addressed, but there may be other reasons why the series of stimulus packages in the 1990s has not been very successful. While Japan's ratio of international trade to GDP is less than that of the USA or the EU, Japan has still long relied on exports as an engine of growth, and since the 1970s has allowed the exchange rate to float freely against the currencies of its major trading partners. In such an environment, international economists would predict that fiscal policy would tend to be ineffective in stimulating demand because it would 'crowd out' exports by increasing the real interest rate and causing real exchange rate appreciation. Furthermore, the dramatic increases in the government debt to GDP ratio may have helped lead Japanese consumers and investors to the conclusion that Ricardian equivalence was real, that current spending would have to be offset by future taxes. Thus the reliance on fiscal policy may have been popular with recipients of increased government spending, but doesn't appear to have been a path back to growth.

Government Financial Intermediation

As described above, households in Japan have one of the highest saving rates in the world and allocate a significant portion to postal deposits which, in turn, provides the major funding source for the FILP. Before 1 April 2001, the FILP budget received funds directly from the Postal Savings System; however, since that date, the Postal Savings System manages its own funds. The Postal Savings System obtains funds from both postal deposits and life insurance sales, and allocates 80 percent of its assets to 'safe' assets such as government bonds. Government entities, including the eight government banks, now obtain their funding from participating in FILP bond issues, which are essentially government debt or agency-type bonds tied to the specific assets and activities of the entity.

To date only 20 entities have issued agency-type bonds and the funds raised represent only a small part of their operating budget. Evidence indicates that the market regards these as government debt. Thus little has actually changed because the Postal Savings System ends up purchasing a major part of the FILP bonds and agency securities. Cargill and Yoshino (forthcoming) present a formal model of the FILP system and show that from an analytical perspective, the old and new FILP system are identical. At the same time, this may be an overly pessimistic view of the 1 April 2001 reforms (Cargill and Yoshino, 2001), but at this point, it is difficult to be optimistic about the outcome of any reform in Japan.

The entities dependent on postal deposits, postal life insurance and other similar sources of funds allocate much of this funding to low-return and, in some cases, negative-return projects like underutilized bridges and other construction projects that are valued more for how they will maintain LDP support throughout Japan than whether they contributed to economic recovery. Postal deposits and postal life insurance during the 1980s and 1990s have increased their market share in terms of total deposits and life insurance, respectively, and the FILP budget has also increased in size relative to GDP.

Aside from the low return on household savings generated by government financial intermediation, there exists a major non-performing-loan and insolvency problem among the government entities dependent on government finance. Among the government banks there is evidence of a non-performing-loan problem. Doi and Hoshi (2002) provide a more comprehensive review of the problem and conclude that the FILP system has a non-performing-loan and insolvency problem of major proportions. Based on a detailed review of balance sheet and other information for FILP entities, Doi and Hoshi conclude that 68 percent of FILP loans are non-performing and expected losses represent about 9 percent of GDP. This is clearly an area that has received almost no attention outside of Japan and suggests that Japan's financial distress in both the private and public financial sectors is much larger than generally accepted.

Monetary Policy Since BOJ Independence

The Bank of Japan Law was revised in June 1997 and became effective in April 1998. In a widely supported institutional redesign, the Bank of Japan became significantly more independent of the Ministry of Finance and the government. With the generally good reputation of the Bank of Japan for following responsible policies through much of the postwar period, one would have anticipated that monetary policy would not become a constraint on economic growth. Unfortunately, Bank of Japan policy has permitted the price level to decline slowly since the mid-1990s. The declining price level increases the real value of the accumulating debt in the economy, makes it difficult to dispose of non-performing loans since the underlying collateral is declining in nominal value, and this discourages spending. Considerable debate has ensued over monetary policy in Japan,[6] with two distinct perspectives. The Bank of Japan argues that it has done all it can to stimulate the economy with its zero-interest-rate policy, and that efforts to engage in more aggressive policy, such as large-scale purchases of government bonds, would be fiscally irresponsible and impose large capital losses on the Bank of Japan's balance sheet. For all practical purposes, the Bank of Japan stands alone on this position. The overwhelming majority of observers, including the Ministry of Finance and a growing number of politicians, argue that Bank of Japan needs to be more aggressive and adopt non-traditional methods to reverse the decline in the price level. There have been increasing calls for the adoption of an inflation rate target framework to guide monetary policy.

AFTER THE SLOWDOWN

In August 1993, the LDP lost its majority in the Lower House or House of Councils, the most powerful of the two legislative parts of the Diet, after almost five decades of dominating the Japanese government. Morihiro Hosukawa formed a coalition government that was able to push a package of political reforms through the Diet in early 1994, but he soon resigned due to the difficulty of carrying out real reforms. Since then, Japan has averaged approximately one new prime minister per year. Hosukawa was followed in swift succession by Tsutomo Hata, Tomichi Murayama, Ryutaro Hashimoto, Keizo Obuchi, Yoshiro Mori and, most recently, Koizumi. Throughout their terms the LDP continued to be the dominant party and return to control the Lower House in 1996; however, the current LDP is more fractionalized than before and holds on to power through a series of unstable coalitions with other parties.

Successive corruption cases and the general perception that the iron triangle controlled the government quickly undermined public support for the Japanese government, even as voters continued to keep the LDP as the dominant political party in the Diet. Koizumi, a dark horse candidate, was able to topple Hashimoto and other LDP-establishment candidates in 2001 with a promise to carry out reform, and with his popularity a reluctant LDP was able to win another election. After the election, the Koizumi administration pledged to eliminate bad debt from the banking sector within two to three years, privatize public enterprises, overhaul the country's social security and taxation systems, and cut public spending, particularly subsidies to local governments, in order to slow the growth of the public debt. Unfortunately, little of this agenda has been enacted. Within a year of taking office, Koizumi's 90 percent approval rating was falling to levels consistent with those of his predecessors; recent polls now find that 72 percent of Japanese voters believe that his administration has made no improvements to government policy, and 50 percent would prefer for him to be replaced within the year (French, 2002).

Delayed Reform Efforts

In spite of the political turmoil that started in 1993, efforts at reform were minimal until 1998, and the policy of denial, understatement, forgiveness and forbearance remained firmly in place. These policies appeared to be successful because Japan had avoided any serious financial collapse or decline in real GDP from 1990 to 1995, and in 1995 and 1996 the economy appeared to be in recovery. By 1996, a sense of optimism spread through government that the worst was over, and Japan had avoided fundamental reform while only having to deal with failures of small cooperatives and banks, the closing of the *jusen* industry, and the restructuring of the Deposit Insurance Corporation.

In November 1996, the LDP's newly elected Prime Minister Hashimoto announced the 'Big Bang' financial reform process. The Big Bang represented a goal statement rather than detailed proposals to restructure the financial system. Subsequent legislation established the Financial Supervisory Agency (now referred to as the Financial Services Agency) to assume much of the responsibility for financial regulation and supervision formerly held by the Ministry of Finance, liberalized the foreign exchange market, and revised the Bank of Japan Law. None of these policy events, however, changed the fundamental nature of the Japanese financial system; nor did they deal with the substantial non-performing-loan problem and weak financial institutions.

The situation changed in late 1997. Financial and economic distress increased significantly with the failures of two large financial institutions and the decline in real GDP following the Asian financial crisis. Japan's economy and its financial system came close to collapse, and starting in 1998 more serious efforts at reform and fiscal stimulus were implemented. At the same time, however, monetary policy became a constraint on reform efforts by allowing the price level to decline. Only recently, under intense pressure both from within and outside of Japan, has the Bank of Japan adopted a more aggressive policy. Since December of 2001, the Bank of Japan has increased the monetary base by 20 percent. The yen has dropped dramatically as a result, and there has been some concern in Japanese circles that a falling yen could be followed by a Chinese devaluation and lead to further devaluations across Asia.[7] However, banks have used this additional liquidity to add to their reserves rather than increase their lending. This suggests to Krugman (1998) and others that Japan is locked in a classical liquidity trap. However, unlike the Keynesian liquidity trap in which monetary policy was impotent, the current theory of the liquidity trap suggests that the economy can be stimulated by monetary policy if the central bank raises inflationary expectations by aggressive increases in liquidity and adoption of an inflation-target framework.

Time is Running Out: The Demographic Factor

The population is projected to decline by the end of the first decade of the new century and some projections indicate a 50 percent decline in Japanese population by 2050. In addition, the dependency ratio, the ratio of the non-working-age population to the working-age population, is increasing more rapidly in Japan than in any other industrial country. Simple national-income arithmetic shows that Japan's standard of living will decline significantly unless Japan can offset these demographic trends (Feldman, 1996).

Japan has a limited ability to offset this projected decline in the standard of living. Japan can increase the working-age population by allowing females greater access to the labor market or by allowing greater immigration of foreign workers. Greater female participation is in progress, but will likely be insufficient to significantly mitigate the effect of the demographic factors on the standard of living. Relaxed immigration could be important, but few expect Japan to open up its country to large increases in foreign workers in the near future. The most important mitigation Japan has available to it is to increase labor productivity, which in turn can only be achieved by generating high returns to investment.

This places a premium on fundamental reforms in the Japanese real and financial sectors to provide opportunities to generate higher rates of return on investment and increase labor productivity. Again, the past focus of the financial system to limit risk and bankruptcy compounds other problems.

WHY SO LITTLE, SO LATE?

Governments are not led by philosopher kings, and there are many reasons why governments may fail to follow policies in the long-term interests of society. As Easterly (2001) recently pointed out, harmful economic policies are not only the result of misinformed or misguided politicians; more often, they are the result of factions seeking their own benefit without regard for society's interests. These policies may even damage the short-run interests of the faction itself if it is engaged in a war of attrition against another group, and reform that would benefit all parties may nonetheless be long delayed (Alesina and Drazen, 1991).

In an examination of the determinants of policy reform in both East Asia and Latin America, Rodrik (1996) points out that reform often requires a precipitating crisis; while this is a simple truism, since a crisis obviously demonstrates that current policies are not working and need to be changed, a deep crisis may also rearrange interest groups and allow reformers a chance to address other long-standing (and sometimes unrelated) problems as part of a package.

Finally, the transition to a financial regime which relies on bankruptcy may precipitate very high costs in the short run, as Cargill and Parker (2002) demonstrate, and politicians may have shorter time horizons and higher discount rates than society overall.

Why has the Japanese government yet to fundamentally change those aspects of its financial structure which have prevented their economy from returning to growth? One reason may be that the Japanese do not really believe that they are in crisis. Despite over a decade of economic and financial distress, Japan remains complacent. Japanese GDP per capita is actually higher in 2002 than in 1999, and while the unemployment rate is historically high, it has not reached levels that threaten the social and political fabric of the country. Japan remains an economically powerful country. Japanese households enjoy a high rate of home ownership and hold substantial amounts of financial assets. Japan has large holdings of international reserve assets and the yen is in no danger of collapse. There is thus no widespread view in Japan that its economy is in a crisis; while the rest of the world keeps referring to Japan in terms of economic malaise and the world's longest crisis, Japan does not see itself in that manner.

In addition to complacency, there are a number of other reasons why Japanese policymakers have failed to adequately address these problems. Some reasons are the result of domestic political forces, especially opposition to serious change from the *keiretsu*, the financial institutions, politicians and households. That is, there is no broad-based support group for departure from the old financial regime. Some reasons are the result of external forces. These will be considered below.

Domestic Politics

Observers of the Japanese economy have long argued that the *zaikai*, the leaders of the four major federations of big businesses, exercise an enormous amount of power over government policy formation, the introduction of legislation in the Diet, and even in the selection of candidates for prime minister (Woronoff, 1986, p. 125). Big business also exercises influence through the practice of *amakudari*, which allows senior bureaucrats to retire into lucrative private sector positions (Gardner, 1998, p. 626). One might argue that the large internationally known Japanese businesses would have an incentive to depart from this system, but as Shoppa (2001) indicates, these entities operate in an international environment and are not adversely impacted by Japan's poor economic performance.

Financial institutions in general are naturally opposed to resolution of non-performing loans and closer regulatory oversight based on 'prompt corrective action' to close institutions rapidly to minimize the impact on taxpayers. Banks that have been allowed to understate their bad debt would have to shut down if they admitted the magnitude of the problem, while others would have to force debtor firms into bankruptcy if they could not keep lending them new funds to cover their repayments. Responsible officials in the Ministry of Finance and other regulating agencies would have their judgment and past actions questioned were they to force transparent accounting, and probably their chances for *amakudari* would be reduced.

The politicians have benefited significantly from the iron triangle of mutual support and are reluctant to change a system that has been so important for maintaining political power. In particular, despite the rational arguments that can be made for privatizing the Postal Savings System and reducing or eliminating government ownership of many financial intermediaries, politicians are reluctant to change a system that provides so much political support at the local level. Koizumi has found it very difficult to reform either the Postal Savings System or the FILP, despite his initially high level of public support.

But why have Japanese voters continued to return the LDP to power, and why have the large firms continued to support policies which seem so contradictory to their own long-term interests? Schoppa (2001) argues that Japan's very wealth makes it possible for many Japanese to now choose to 'opt out', in contrast to times in the past when collective action was necessary and most Japanese were too poor to have alternatives to it. Just as Japanese women, especially mothers, are staying out of the workforce in response to current disincentives for combining work and family, large Japanese firms with access to global capital markets are borrowing abroad, investing abroad, and producing abroad rather than forcing change at home.

As a result of a series of scandals during the 1990s that reinforced past suspicions, the public now regard their politicians as corrupt, and consider themselves excluded from the mutual support system that has characterized Japan's economy. It is difficult for politicians to garner much public support for large-scale taxpayer bailouts of financial institutions because, up until recently, the household sector has been excluded from the financial system as a source of consumer and mortgage credit, and they view the financial problems as the result of corruption. In addition, the public generally support the Postal Savings System and the FILP, and thus perceive little benefit from a reform program that would have to include reform of these two large institutions of the old financial regime.

Thus, there are many interests in Japan that oppose reform of either the real or the financial sector, and it is hard to identify one cohesive group that currently sees reform to be in its interest. When demand is lacking, political institutions are unlikely to supply the reform. This point may also shed some light on the current debate over monetary policy in Japan. Monetary policy has clearly exerted a negative influence on the economy and limited the impact of the reforms that have been enacted; however, the debate over monetary policy reflects a deeper division over reform than merely arguments about independence and inflation targeting. The issue is not simply a central bank pursuing inappropriate policies in isolation from other issues.

The Bank of Japan has historically been an advocate of liberalization while other government agencies resisted reform; when reform was accommodated, however, it was done without any philosophical commitment to more open and competitive markets. The Bank of Japan has long viewed the reform process as too slow, especially in dealing with non-performing loans and troubled financial institutions. On the other hand, the Ministry of Finance and LDP politicians have been less willing to shift to a regime that would require significant numbers of bank and non-financial failures, along with the associated increase in unemployment. Part of the reason the Bank of Japan has resisted more aggressive policy until very recently is its concern that such central bank policy would be used by the iron triangle to delay real reform, in the hope that expansionary monetary policy would allow the economy to recover without it. This war of attrition does not, however, excuse the Bank of Japan from its failure to stabilize the price level, which is required by the Bank of Japan Law, but it does help explain the Bank's resistance to pressures to provide more liquidity.

Finally, politicians may be slow to adapt to changing circumstances, or slow to understand that certain policies may only work in certain circumstances. In a study that addressed Chinese state enterprises, Parker (1995) demonstrates why the no-failure policies of the traditional Japanese financial regime, which led to rapid growth initially, could also cause growth to eventually end. Lincoln (2001, p. 8) cites the continuing Japanese belief in the value of the current system as one of the primary factors inhibiting real reform. In addition, he lists four other factors; the systemic nature of the problem, which makes it difficult to change one piece at a time; vested interests which oppose change; the consistency of the financial system with broader cultural values; and a liberalization process that originates with the bureaucracy rather than the voters.[8] In essence, Japan may be trapped by its own past success into maintaining policies that are no longer appropriate.

External Reasons

International pressures have played an overlooked role as well. First, of course, Japan is very dependent on oil imports and exports to the USA. The effect of the bursting bubble on the Japanese economy was exacerbated by the shock to oil prices that resulted from Iraq's invasion of Kuwait, and the US recession that followed reduced demand for Japanese exports; this in turn helped to pull Japan into its first recession since the 1970s and only its second recession since the Korean War. An unexpected recession, of course, makes it difficult for firms to repay loans. Loans which might have looked good on a balance sheet in a growing economy can become bad debt in a slowing economy, and existing bad debt becomes proportionally less important in a rapidly growing economy. Similarly, the most recent US recession may have hurt the Japanese economy at a critical time.

The Asian financial crisis of 1997–98 did not cause the economic and financial distress in Japan; however, it did adversely affect the Japanese economy, by slowing demand for Japanese exports and increasing concerns about imminent default, thus leading to severe strain in the Japanese financial system. In fact, Japanese monetary policy may have helped to spark that crisis in the first place.[9]

Japan has also found it difficult to increase exports to the USA as a way to return to growth, and Japan's trade ratio has declined significantly in the 1990s. The end of the cold war led to an increased willingness by the Clinton Administration to risk conflict with Japan over rising trade deficits. With the slowing Japanese economy making it difficult for the Japanese to increase imports of US products, and the Clinton Administration willing to block

Japanese exports in an effort to force Japan to open markets, it became even more important to follow US advice to stimulate the Japanese economy with expansionary fiscal policy. This is a textbook example (for example, Krugman and Obstfeld, 2000) of self-interested advice from a major trading partner under floating exchange rates. In contrast to expansionary monetary policy, which would tend to cause depreciation of the yen, expansionary fiscal policy tends to increase the value of the yen and thus make US exports more competitive; as long as increased Japanese government spending is not fully crowded out, US exports would also increase due to rising Japanese incomes.

CONCLUSION

The Japanese economy continues to remain mired in slow growth, and the design and structure of the Japanese financial system is one of the primary causes. Based on a bank-centered web of mutual support between large firms, government regulatory agencies and the LDP, the Japanese financial system continues to operate under policies that minimize failure in both the financial and real sectors. Because there is no selection mechanism that diverts Japanese resources towards more efficient firms, tremendous inefficiencies have built up in the Japanese economy that make the costs of transition ever more intimidating. Because neither banks nor borrowers are forced to admit the true scale of bad debt, a moral hazard has been created that continues to pour good money after bad.

The burst of the bubble economy was precipitated by the Bank of Japan, and Japan's recovery has been hampered by continued tight monetary policy that has created a deflationary environment. But there are a number of other reasons which we have explained in this chapter for Japan's descent into a slow-growth economy. Among these we included an inappropriate regulatory response, an interaction between bank lending and asset prices that turned from a virtuous cycle into a vicious one, inappropriate and ineffective fiscal policy, and a strong government role in financial intermediation.

Why has Japan's government been so ineffective in implementing policies to turn things around, and address the true scope of the financial system? We consider complacency as one reason, and it does appear that the Japanese government believes that it does not have a real crisis on its hands, and that the values embedded in the system of mutual support, forgiveness and forbearance are worth retaining. We considered reasons of domestic politics, and the interests of different groups which lead them to support the current system rather than uncertain changes, and we considered the possibility that the Bank of Japan has, until recently, been engaged in a war of attrition with other government agencies in an effort to force them to enact real reforms by not bailing the economy out with additional liquidity. Finally, we considered external pressures, not only the effects of American recessions and Asian crises, but also the international pressures which came once the cold war ended and which encouraged policies which were not necessarily effective for Japanese recovery.

What does this mean for the current decade? Helweg (2000) argues that Japan has quietly undergone an economic revolution, and is moving away from the corrupt state-dominated system towards a much more market-dominated economy. The small if rising amount of foreign direct and equity investment may indeed be beginning to make Japanese markets more competitive. Though the internationalization of the large Japanese multinationals has reduced their willingness to push for dramatic policy reform, their continued competitive success may eventually filter down to the rest of the economy. There is evidence of a rising high-tech sector that exists out of the traditional *keiretsu* system, and indeed out of the purview of government intervention, and this too may be a sign of a recovery. The *keiretsu* system, along with its attendant lifetime employment system, is being gradually eroded, and the cross-holding of shares by Japanese firms has fallen from 70 percent to less than half of market capitalization. Porter et al. (2000, p. 182) find a number of reasons to be hopeful about Japan's eventual recovery.

While deregulation has begun, and there are signs that the private economy is transforming into a more competitive economy on its own, it is difficult to be as optimistic about imminent and significant changes in government financial policy. In particular, policies protecting inefficient producers from failure continue to be followed. It is still more likely than not that this first decade of the new century will become Japan's second 'lost decade', and it is difficult to isolate a set of policies that would return Japan to stable and sustained growth. What is clear is that Japan's problems are not due to a lack of understanding or a lack of resources, but an unwillingness to shift to a new economic and political regime.

NOTES

1. Cargill et al. (1997 and 2000) provide an overview of macroeconomic performance and policy from the end of World War II to the late 1990s.
2. There have been dissenters from the view that Japan's government direction is responsible for Japan's impressive growth. Porter et al. (2000), for example, argue that Japan's best performance has come in precisely those sectors where government intervention is minimal, and cite a number of examples of failures due to government action.
3. For Americans and other *gaijin*, however, the slowdown of the Japanese economy was initially disguised by a further 30 percent appreciation of the yen from 1990 through 1995, and observers continued to publish articles praising Japanese economic performance.
4. See Aoki and Patrick (1994) for detail on the main bank system in Japan.
5. The Postal Savings System and FILP are discussed in Cargill and Yoshino (2000, 2001, and forthcoming) and the FILP is discussed in Doi and Hoshi (2002).

6. Cargill et al. (2000) and Cargill (2001) provide an overview of the debate as well as references to most of the relevant literature.
7. We think that a devaluation of the yuan is unlikely, however. China held its currency stable during the Asian financial crisis in spite of the effect this had on slowing its exports; it does not compete directly with Japan in most of its exports, and it currently has enormous foreign currency reserves as well as restrictions on capital account transactions. In fact, China's policy makers have recently dismissed suggestions that they were about to revalue the yuan up against the dollar, not down.
8. It has also been suggested that Japan has suffered from a dearth of objective advice, since it lacks an adequate number of active and independent policy research institutes and its leaders also perceive that advice from the USA is excessively self-interested and excessively focused on the bilateral trade balance.
9. In the spring of 1997 the Bank of Japan sent signals that it intended to raise the discount rate, and this expectation (albeit unfulfilled) led to the return of Japanese savings from of many Asian economies; these capital flows were large in relation to the balance of payments for smaller economies like Thailand, and when their central banks attempted to maintain fixed exchange rates in the face of dwindling foreign currency reserves, the stage was set in east Asia for capital flight, speculation, devaluation and crisis. Baily et al. (2000) argue that Japanese bank lending was in fact the primary culprit in setting off the crisis. Though Nagao (2000) defends Japanese banks, arguing that they took heavy losses while the US banks and their hedge funds may have actually profited through currency derivatives, King (2001) concurs with Baily et al. and finds that Japanese banks, weakened by their continuing financial woes, began moving funds out of Asia long before other institutional investors.

REFERENCES

Alesina, A. and A. Drazen (1991), 'Why are stabilizations delayed?', *American Economic Review*, **81**(5), 1170–88.

Aoki, M. and H. Patrick (eds) (1994), *The Japanese Main Banking System*, Oxford: Oxford University Press.

Baily, M.N., D. Farrell and S. Lund (2000), 'The color of hot money', *Foreign Affairs*, **79**(2), 99–108.

Bank of Japan (various dates), *Monthly Report of Recent Economic and Financial Developments*.

Barrell, R. and N. Pain (1999), 'Trade restraints and Japanese direct investment flows', *European Economic Review*, **43**(1), 29–45.

Brooke, J. (2002), 'Japan's premier muses on a recovery-proof economy', *New York Times*, 29 March, p. A:3.

Cargill, T.F. (2001), 'Financial liberalization, asset inflation, and monetary policy in Japan', in G. Kaufman (ed.), *Asset Price Bubbles: Implications for Monetary and Regulatory Policies*, UK: Elsevier Science Ltd.

Cargill, T.F., T. Ito and M. Hutchison (1997), *The Political Economy of Japanese Monetary Policy*, Cambridge, MA: MIT Press.

Cargill, T.F. and E. Parker (2002), 'Asian finance and the role of bankruptcy: a model of the transition costs of financial liberalization', *Journal of Asian Economics*, **13**(3) May–June, 297–318.

Cargill, T.F. and N. Yoshino (2000), 'The postal savings system, fiscal investment and loan program, and modernization of Japan's financial system', in T. Hoshi and H. Patrick (eds), *Crisis and Change in the Japanese Financial System*, London and New York: Kluwer Academic Publishers.

Cargill, T.F. and N. Yoshino (2001), 'Modernising Japan's postal savings system', *The Financial Regulator*, **6**, 42–7.

Cargill, T.F. and N. Yoshino (2002), *The Postal Savings System and Fiscal Investment and Loan Program in Japan: Financial Liberalization, Dilemmas, and Solutions*, Oxford University Press.

Cargill, T.F., T. Ito and M. Hutchison (2000), *Financial Policy and Central Banking in Japan*, Cambridge, MA: MIT Press.

Diamond Weekly (2000a), 'Bankruptcies surge as reckless life-support policies expire' (Narifuri kamawanu enmeisaku mo kokagire de tosan ga kyuzo), 11 November.

Diamond Weekly (2000b), 'Foreign investors have gobbled up Japan' (Gaishi wa Nihon o konnani katta!), 13 May.

Doi, T. and T. Hoshi (2002), 'FILP: How much has been lost? How much more will be lost?', working paper, Graduate School of International Relations and Pacific Basin Studies, University of California, San Diego, February.

Easterly, W. (2001), *The Elusive Quest for Growth: Economists' Adventures and Misadventures in the Tropics*, Cambridge, MA: MIT Press.

Feldman, R.A. (1996), 'The golden goose and the silver fox', *Japanese Economic and Market Analysis*, Tokyo: Salomon Brothers, 12 June.

French, H.M. (2002), 'Japan's bright star is fading fast', *New York Times*, 24 April.

Gardner, H.S. (1998), *Comparative Economic Systems*, 2nd edn, Fort Worth, TX: Dryden Press.

Hamao, Y. and J. Mei (2001), 'Living with the "enemy": an analysis of foreign investment in the Japanese equity market', *Journal of International Money and Finance*, **20**(5), 715–35.

Helweg, M.D. (2000), 'Japan: a rising sun?', *Foreign Affairs*, **79**(4), 26–39.

Katz, R. (1998), *Japan: The System that Soured*, Armonk, NY: M.E. Sharpe.

King, M.R. (2001), 'Who triggered the Asian financial crisis?', *Review of International Political Economy*, **8**(3), 438–66.

Krugman, P.R. (1998), 'It's baaack: Japan's slump and the return of the liquidity trap', *Brookings Papers on Economic Activity*, **2**, 137–87.

Krugman, P.R. and M. Obstfeld (2000), *International Economics: Theory and Policy*, 5th edn, Boston, MA: Addison-Wesley.

Lincoln, E.J. (1990), *Japan's Unequal Trade*, Washington, DC: Brookings Institution Press.

Lincoln, E.J. (2001), *Arthritic Japan: The Slow Pace of Economic Reform*, Washington, DC: Brookings Institution Press.

Masuda, Y. (2000), 'Foreign-owned corporations are not the saviors of the Japanese economy' (Keizai seicho shigeki shirai gaishi kigyo, Nihon keizai no kyuseishu ni arazu), *Diamond Weekly*, 11 November.

McKinnon, R.I. and K. Ohno (2001), 'The foreign exchange origins of Japan's economic slump and low interest liquidity trap', *World Economy*, **24**(3), 279–315.

Mody, A., S. Dasgupta and S. Sinha (1999), 'Japanese multinationals in Asia: drivers and attractors', *Oxford Development Studies*, **27**(2), 149–64.

Nagao, S. (2000), 'A rebuttal to the *Foreign Affairs* article asserting that Japanese banks triggered the Asian currency crisis' (Beishi 'Hogin koso Ajia tsuka kiki no shuhan' setsu ni hanron suru), Japan's *Economist*, 23 May.

Parker, E. (1995), 'Schumpeterian creative destruction and the growth of Chinese enterprises', *China Economic Review*, **6**(2), 201–23.

Porter, M.E., H. Takeuchi and M. Sakakibara (2000), *Can Japan Compete?*, Cambridge, MA: Basic Books/Perseus Pub.

Posen, A.S. (1998), *Restoring Japan's Economic Growth*, Washington, DC: Institute for International Economics.

Rodrik, D. (1996), 'Understanding economic policy reform', *Journal of Economic Literature*, **35**(1), 9–41.

Schoppa, L.J. (2001), 'Japan, the reluctant reformer,' *Foreign Affairs*, **80**(5), 76–90.

World Bank (1993), 'The East Asian Miracle', World Bank policy research report, New York: Oxford University Press.

Woronoff, J. (1986), *The Japan Syndrome*, New Brunswick, NJ: Transaction Books.

10. Real economies and financial sectors in industrializing countries

Gavin Boyd

Most industrializing countries are not coordinated political economies, because of diverse problems of integration and institutional development. Political will for comprehensive and resourceful engagement with the tasks of promoting growth is generally lacking. To the extent that these tasks are taken up, domestic difficulties tend to be made more serious by external factors, in contexts of dependent and therefore vulnerable involvement in the world economy. The most pervasive problem is capital flight to industrialized states, in search of stable and substantial returns: prospects for the home economies are not rated highly, and confidence in their financial systems is not encouraged, as these are weak and poorly regulated. While the financing available for domestically based growth is thus limited, export-led development is hindered by the discriminatory trade policies implemented by industrialized states. These policies restrict opportunities for the export of manufactured products from developing countries: outward-oriented manufacturing at rising technological levels is thus hindered. Low labour costs in these developing countries attract investment by Western and Japanese corporations building international production systems, but with cross-border dispersals of production processes that in effect limit technology transfers. The foreign firms meanwhile gain host-country market strengths and acquire local enterprises, thus indirectly contributing to the capital flight that assists higher industrialization in the West and in Japan.

When industrializing countries do achieve export-led growth, through the efforts of national firms, in cooperation and rivalry with Western and Japanese transnational corporations, they tend to attract portfolio investment from the USA and Europe. This may more than offset their capital flight to industrialized countries. The inflows contribute to currency appreciation, in conjunction with advances that may be made in export promotion, thus hindering further export development. The opportunism of the foreign portfolio investors can then be active in switches to alternative areas for speculation. Meanwhile the outward flight of capital will tend to increase. To cope with a financial crisis a government may seek funding from international lending agencies, but with the disadvantage of a weak bargaining position. Sufficient political will may form to promote more active export-led growth, with capital controls, but bargaining strength in trade negotiations with industrialized states will have been weakened by the financial distress and the increased dependence on international lending agencies.

The foreign portfolio investors are mainly Western financial enterprises, and they make speculative attacks in collusion on currencies affected by balance-of-payments problems (Botman and Jager, 2002). In some perspectives this may be considered a form of market discipline, exerting pressure for sound macromanagement in industrializing countries. The rent-seeking instinct which is evident, however, is also active in speculative operations which affect the real economies of industrialized states. The fortunes of industrializing countries thus become linked with the destructive effects of financial sector opportunism on those real economies. This has been dramatized by the general effects of the recession which ended the speculative boom of the 1990s in the USA.

INVESTOR INTERESTS

The interests of passive investors are more at risk in developing countries than in industrialized states. Very serious uncertainties about political stability, macromanagement performance and economic growth thus motivate individuals to place their savings in safer foreign locations offering substantial rewards. Vicious cycles of capital flight hindering economic development and therefore causing further capital flight tend to persist. Corrupt systems of personal rule prevent the establishment of effective institutions that could aid and regulate growth. Hence local entrepreneurship is discouraged. Investment bidding by the systems of personal rule attracts foreign extractive and manufacturing firms, as well as service enterprises, and their financial resources, organizational strengths and degrees of home-government backing exert pressures for the development of favourable business environments. Opportunities are meanwhile provided for the development of linkages with host-country enterprises, but the incoming firms tend to be increasingly well placed to acquire such enterprises. Investors in the industrializing countries can thus become increasingly inclined to move their savings to more advanced economies.

Well-managed Western and Japanese banks can aid growth by financing national firms in developing countries, and offering investment services for individuals in those countries. It must be reiterated, however, that financial enterprises based in the industrialized states are strongly inclined to exploit opportunities for speculation in world financial markets, especially those provided by underdeveloped and poorly regulated financial systems. Passive investors in one industrializing country can entrust funds to Western and Japanese banks that profit from the exploitation of financial weaknesses in other industrializing countries, and even in their own country. This is a dimension of what has been called the dual-agency problem (Tirole, 2002).

The gains from speculation in world financial markets can be rapid and very substantial, with much tax avoidance, subject to hedging against risks. Enterprises active in these markets tend to be attracted more toward the rent-seeking opportunities than the funding of productive ventures, which offer rewards over longer terms, with tax exposure, that accordingly draw less attention. The clear systemic danger is that productive activity can be significantly under funded because of the diversion of investment into speculation.[1] This danger for the world economy is reflected in dangers for national economies, especially in developing areas, where the financing of operations by producer enterprises is limited by the channelling of investment into rent-seeking.

With the inadequate financing of productive activity, in developing countries especially, and in the world economy, there is a more immediate problem, as the speculation can become destabilizing. There is a history of speculative booms and declines in the USA (Shiller, 2000), which indicates the destructive potential of losses of investor confidence, and the increased gravity of this problem for the world economy because of the expanding dimensions of the USA's structural interdependencies. Japan has a recent history of speculative appreciations and much more serious decline, causing a problem of aggravated duality in the national economy: Japanese transnational enterprises have gained strength while expanding their international production operations, while domestically based growth has been severely affected by a prolonged financial crisis.[2] A problem of structural duality has also become significant in the USA, where recession in the domestic economy after the collapse of a speculative boom has given US manufacturing and non-financial service enterprises stronger incentives to expand their international production activities. Additional strengths have been gained in world markets, risks have been spread more widely, and tax exposures have been reduced. Similar advantages, on a smaller scale, have been gained by the Japanese transnational corporations.

In Europe speculation is on a smaller scale than in the USA, because financial markets are less developed, and financial enterprises are more oriented toward productive funding; problems of structural duality are less serious because European corporations are less engaged in production outside the European Union. Such production, however, is increasing, despite the difficulties of competing against generally more efficient US and Japanese firms, because of high tax burdens and wage costs in the Union.

The gradual development of an integrated financial market in the Union is increasing the availability of funding for European transnational enterprises, and this is contributing to expansions of their production operations in developing countries.[3] Capital flight from those countries, however, is attracted more toward the USA than toward Europe, because of its lower overall growth, and substantial European capital flows are also drawn to the USA.

Altogether, the strong investment-drawing effect of the US economy, together with its vulnerability to speculative destabilization and its problem of structural duality, constitute challenges for industrializing countries and in particular for their investors, governments and emerging producer enterprises. These are very difficult challenges, and resources to cope with them are lacking. Real economies in this pattern are being linked structurally through the building of international production systems by transnational enterprises, in conjunction with the multiplication of financial linkages related both to speculative activities in the USA and to the funding of operations by the transnational enterprises, including their acquisitions of weaker firms in developing countries. Increases in the international market power of the US and other transnational enterprises restrict opportunities for export-led growth by emerging firms in industrializing states, that is in conjunction with US, European and Japanese protectionist trade policies.[4]

Complex coordination problems are evident in the entire pattern. These problems have negative implications for endeavours that might be made to correct internationalized market failures in the pattern, in the interests of balanced, dynamic, interdependent growth. For governments and managements of enterprises in developing countries the most significant coordination problems are those directly related to imperatives for increases in structural competitiveness that can enhance gains from unequal involvement in world trade and investment. The development of linkages with Western and Japanese transnational enterprises is commonly recognized as a developmental requirement, and an especially challenging one because of the widening gaps between the organizational and technological strengths of those enterprises and those of emerging firms striving to grow in Third World environments (UNCTAD, 1999).

THIRD WORLD PERSPECTIVES

Government leaders, technocrats and corporate managements in developing countries are challenged to cope with experiences of cognitive dissonance as they endeavour to absorb economic advice from Western governments, policy institutes and international lending agencies about growth strategies to be implemented in conditions of asymmetric structural interdependence.

Numerous crises in East Asia and Latin America have caused much awareness of the vulnerabilities of real economies in the Third World that are exposed to the exploitation of volatility in financial markets but that are considered to be capable of achieving industrialization through the efficiency effects of economic openness, despite the constraints of inferior competitiveness. The received economic doctrine is recognized to be flawed because of overemphasis on competitive market forces as pressures for higher performance, and also because of the reliance of governments in industrialized states on methods of market restriction and closure that violate the professed economic doctrine but that have had to be accepted because of inequalities in bargaining strengths on issues of trade policy. It is readily understood that interdependent growth on a large scale is made possible through production specializations at rising technological levels when economies become more open to each other, but that this occurs with inequalities in the spread of gains, and with problems of market failure, which advantaged countries do not seek to change (Finger and Nogues, 2002).

Authoritarian guidance and control of private sector industrial development for export-led growth, with substantial protection of the domestic market, tend to be seen as the rational choice in conditions of weak structural competitiveness and exposure to the ruthless competition of large transnational enterprises, as well as to the manipulative practices of dominant firms in world financial markets. Japan's achievements in coordinated export-led growth have much significance as validations of the logic of authoritarian growth strategies, and China's successes in more forceful economic management, with the advantages of bargaining power based on the size of a very large internal market, have indicated that the terms of involvement in world trade and investment can be changed decisively through comprehensive resolute coordination of entrepreneurial ventures under pressure for continued improvements in performance. The faltering of Japan's advanced industrialization, after decades of success, has been recognizable as a serious deficiency in administrative direction of the financial sector (Cargill, 2001).

Numerous cases of large-scale corporate fraud in the USA, during its post-boom recession, have in effect encouraged increased sophistication in Third World perspectives on problems of growth with economic openness, and in particular on problems of managing linkages between emerging host-country firms and transnational enterprises that limit regulatory exposure in their home countries. Increased sophistication in this large area of foreign economic relations has understandably influenced awareness of the darker side of trade policy management in industrialized states, and of the qualifications attached to much rhetoric about the potential benefits of general trade liberalization. Of these qualifications those most evident have been related to the double standards of industrialized states in their anti-dumping policies: these have been biased against producers in developing countries, on the basis of unreal distinctions between foreign and domestic forms of permissible competition, and of protectionist-motivated refusals to recognize the logic of treating foreign and domestic selling practices as matters requiring competition policy cooperation.[5] A major practical effect of the bias against foreign producers has been to enhance the opportunities for importers in industrialized states to source low-cost goods from developing areas, while in effect limiting autonomous export expansion by producers in those areas.

The potential advantages of economic size, in terms of bargaining strengths on issues of trade and investment liberalization, and of the scope for organizing outward-oriented private sector industrial specializations, have been important factors in Third World attempts to form regional systems of economic integration. These have been seen to provide opportunities for collectively self-reliant industrialization, with more equal management of commercial relations with industrialized states. Weaknesses in Asian, Latin American and African regional economic integration ventures, however, have tended to increase policy level and corporate focus on what can be achieved while working within the asymmetries of openness, competitiveness and bargaining strengths in relations with major industrialized states. Macromanagement that can be sufficiently functional to reduce the asymmetries, however, has been difficult because of common problems of political development. In the most numerous cases populist systems of personal rule have operated with very limited policy learning and institutional development, and with instability that has given continual impetus to capital flight. Economic advice from industrialized states and international lending agencies, stressing the potential efficiencies of free market forces, has conveyed little understanding of imperatives to build coordinated market economies.

The intensely competitive dynamics of liberal advanced market economies dominating world commerce has tended to perpetuate the focus of many Third World élites on adaptation to the inequalities of hard competition in the international economy, and to the vulnerabilities of involvement in global financial markets endangered by risky high-volume speculation. International lending agencies and governments in industrialized states have offered guidance on the prevention of financial crises brought on by destabilizing investment inflows after phases of export-led growth, but have opposed capital controls to defeat the strategies of predators in financial markets. For Third World élites, meanwhile, new policy learning has become necessary regarding the dangers of destabilization in world financial markets, as what may be called international market discipline is weakening, and international regulatory discipline is also weakening, that is while these markets are insufficiently oriented toward productive funding, and operate with little regard for the interests of vast numbers of passive investors (Siebert, 2001).

INVESTMENT BIDDING

The attraction of direct investment by Western and Japanese manufacturing firms is a high priority in the adaptive growth strategies of the numerous industrializing states that have been unable to form viable regional economic integration systems and that have had to cope with the disadvantages of small size and of administrative weaknesses that have limited potentials for effective coordination of national entrepreneurial operations. The principal difficulties affecting prospects for dynamic and balanced growth in the real economies, it must be reiterated, are the increasing emphasis of transnational enterprises on spreading manufacturing processes across borders for the building of international production systems, with dispersals of risks, limited technology transfers, and the exploitation of investment bidding rivalries. In prospect is subordinate industrialization, the gradual restriction of opportunities for host-country entrepreneurship, and losses of bargaining strengths (Dunning and Narula, 1997). Competition between incoming transnational enterprises may in effect widen the scope for innovative host-country entrepreneurship, but this can be restricted by alliances between such enterprises, and by their involvement in concentration trends that increase their international market strengths.

Diverse incentives influence the direct investment decisions of Western and Japanese manufacturing firms in developing areas, but a prominent trend is the attraction of production operations to countries which have achieved significant degrees of outward-oriented industrialization with relative political stability and administrative development. In East Asia, South Korea and Malaysia are thus important destinations for US and European manufacturing investment. Interest in hosting this investment have been reflected in policies aimed at raising domestic levels of technological competence. Successes in this regard have depended on political stability, and have tended to make possible concentrations rather than geographic dispersals of industrial operations, with clustering effects. Countries with lower levels of technological competence and less political stability have tended to be locations for widely spread production specializations, less conducive to clustering with innovative potentials.[6]

China has great prominence in the East Asian pattern of incentives for Western and Japanese direct investment, because of the vast size of its market, its controlled economic openness, and the degrees to which the scale and diversity of its guided industrial development encourage concentrations of production processes, with synergies of clustering. This complex significance in the regional pattern has a further attribute of stability because of firm administrative control of the financial sector, which ensures a high degree of protection against foreign speculative manipulation. The regional prominence is assuming larger dimensions because industrializing Southeast Asian countries are being drawn individually into closer structural interdependence with China, in the context of commitments to the formation of a vast free trade area. This trend reflects the failures of the Association of Southeast Asian Nations (ASEAN) to form a viable subregional system of economic integration. Informal ties between Chinese business communities in Southeast Asia, and those in Taiwan and the mainland, facilitate the expansion of trade and investment links. At a later stage increased cooperation in the management of financial sectors may facilitate the development of a very large zone of stability, with considerable protection against the penetration of destabilizing foreign speculation, and substantial restraints on capital flight to areas that might offer higher returns. In such a large area the Southeast Asian trading partners could find their investment-bidding opportunities restricted, indirectly, through the influence of Chinese investment bidding priorities, as well as because of stronger Japanese corporate interest in the expansion of production at Chinese bases.[7]

After East Asia, Latin America ranks next as an area of developing countries attracting Western and Japanese direct investment, achieving degrees of industrialization, and developing structural interdependencies of significance for the productive funding and speculative operations in global financial markets. If a China-centred system of economic cooperation develops in East Asia, the attentions of speculators in large Western and Japanese financial enterprises may well turn more toward Latin America, because of prospects for causing and exploiting volatility. Latin American administrations tend to be influenced by expectations of US-sponsored bailouts if endangered by financial crises, and thus seem to lack awareness of imperatives for sound macromanagement. Investment bidding by Latin American administrations appears to be generally a more dependent process than in East Asia, because Japanese competition against US firms is less active, and outward-oriented industrialization strategies have a more concentrated focus, that is on the US market.[8]

Latin American failures in regional and subregional economic cooperation, through effects on élite perceptions and motivations, contribute to reliance on investment bidding directed at US firms. In this area, then, the structural foundations of international finance are evolving along paths different from those in East Asia. Structural links with the USA are tending to become stronger, relative to other external structural connections, but at a slower overall pace than the expansion of such interdependencies in East Asia, where US and Japanese direct investment develops with more active competition. The growth effects of real investment are weaker in Latin America, and the destabilizing potential of speculative financial investment is tending to become more serious in Latin America than in East Asia.

South Asia, the Middle East and Africa, as secondary areas of real investment and financial investment, with very weak potentials for regional
economic cooperation, lack structural links with other developing areas and
with industrialized states, yet must cope with dangers of capital flight if such
links increase. Opportunism in world financial markets will tend to draw
investment from these very underdeveloped countries to areas promising
higher returns, with greater security, while domestic and foreign funding of
development in the real economies remains inadequate. Structural constraints
on investment bidding must be expected to remain more significant than in
Latin America, and very much more significant than in East Asia.

STRUCTURAL CONFIGURATIONS

Concentration trends, altering economic structures, have stronger effects in
Latin America than in East Asia, especially because of the greater involvement
of US enterprises and the weaknesses of national firms, attributable in a large
measure to histories of dependence on patronage and of excessive diversification. Associated with the concentration trends, and particularly with the prominence of US corporations in those trends, are geographic dispersals of
production processes, reflecting weaker development of industrial clusters
than in East Asia – that is, in a pattern which includes numerous small developing countries which have failed to become substantially open to each other.
Within the pattern, however, there are two large industrializing countries –
Brazil and Argentina – in which degrees of industrial clustering, together with
the size of the internal markets, tend to induce some concentrations of production, notably in Brazil's automobile sector. Also in the pattern is Mexico,
where similar levels of industrial development, and the size of the internal
market, have the same effect of inducing degrees of concentration in production processes, but in a context of high structural interdependence with the
USA; this contrasts with the configurations in Brazil and Argentina, where
structural linkages with Europe roughly balance those with the USA.[9]

Mixes of productive and destabilizing effects associated with real investment and financial investment in East Asia and Latin America have altered
differing paths of development. Industrialization in East Asia has been more
outward-oriented, faster, and more potent in the attraction of real investment,
as well as structurally more capable of recovery after economic crises. In Latin
America growth strategies began with emphasis on import substitution and the
establishment of large state enterprises which were less efficient than the
private sector firms active in East Asia's industrialization. Shifts to outward-
oriented industrialization and to the privatization of state enterprises followed,
but under entrepreneurship generally less vigorous than that in industrializing

East Asia, and under administrations less committed and experienced in the promotion of export-led growth; the attraction of real investment, moreover, was weaker. Financial investment in each region, attracted initially by growth in the real economies, shifted to speculative strategies in response to opportunities for exploitation of balance-of-payments problems caused mainly by currency appreciations following investment inflows and export successes.

Fundamental problems of production coordination and production funding have been evident in East Asia and Latin America, and these difficulties of macromanagement have been reflected in failures of external coordination – the deficiencies of attempts at regional economic integration. Industrializing East Asian states have lacked the social integration and institutional development that could have made possible the formation of coordinated political economies, for higher and more stable growth, with less and less unequal structural interdependencies. Problems of political development, thus hindering economic performance, have severely limited potentials for regional economic cooperation. The East Asian failures have been all the more unfortunate because of the proximity of the Japanese model, visible especially in the construction of an integrated Japanese East Asian production system.[10] The Latin American failures, at greater distances from the Japanese model, have evidenced the effects of cultures with weaker communitarian elements, but with basically similar problems of social integration and institutional development, evident however in contexts of communication flows less challenging and less conducive to policy learning than those in East Asia.

Prospects for stable growth in East Asia and Latin America depend very much on external factors: financial crises in these areas have severely discouraged hopes of sustained performance in the countries emerging from distress. The formation of viable systems of subregional and regional economic cooperation is not anticipated, and governments with increased awareness of requirements for self-reliant growth strategies have been obliged to look more toward opportunities for increased commerce with large advanced states outside their areas. Latin American administrations have been seeking individual rather than collective arrangements for improved access to the US market, while in East Asia similar uncoordinated quests have sought preferential trade agreements with the USA but also with Japan, China and the European Union. The scope for bargaining with large external states has been restricted for Latin American countries, compared with those in East Asia, because of more concentrated trade and investment dependencies, and lags in the development of outward oriented-industrialization.

Patterns of productive and speculative investment may well be less favourable for growth in Latin America than in East Asia. Latin American countries are more vulnerable to external pressures for trade and investment liberalization, and, with greater and more.concentrated external investment dependence, can attract more attention from US financial enterprises focused on opportunities in global currency markets. Challenges for Latin American governments to strengthen and improve the regulation of domestic financial sectors appear to be less potent than those obligating improved performance in industrializing East Asian countries, because of the greater diversity and strength of external pressures. Governments and corporate managements in industrializing East Asia have to respond to policy and entrepreneurial initiatives from Japan, China and the European Union as well as the USA.

Brazil, as the largest and most industrialized Latin American country, has special interests in drawing its neighbours into a Southern regional economic system, for collectively more self-reliant industrialization and more equal bargaining with the USA on hemispheric trade and investment liberalization. In addition to losses of status due to financial crises and the weaknesses of MERCOSUR, however, Brazil has to contend with the efforts of numerous smaller Latin American countries to seek special economic ties with the USA for their own economies, in rivalries which are advantageous for the USA. The prospective benefits of expanded commerce with the USA have more significance than the possible advantages of involvement in a Southern regional economic system, which have to be assessed with reference to its uncertain viability and to the chances that its negotiations with the USA might yield fewer benefits, especially in terms of market access, than those attainable by a few Latin American countries open to US proposals for privileged trading status.[11]

CRISIS PREVENTION AND ADJUSTMENT ASSISTANCE

The severity and frequency of financial crises in Latin America and East Asia have motivated endeavours by international lending agencies and Western governments to establish warning systems and arrangements for the prevention of serious distress in Third World financial systems. Alerting governments in developing areas to problems of trade, monetary and financial management that invite speculative attacks has become well recognized as an imperative for stability in world finance. On the specification of remedies and preventive measures, however, there is ambivalence due to differing degrees of emphasis on the utility of market discipline as a force obliging sound macromanagement. The concept of market discipline has ambiguities because it can refer to the stimulus for performance caused by the virtually preferential funding of the most productive enterprises, or to the capacities of international financial enterprises to engage in speculative exploitation of the difficulties of firms and national economies in distress. While such distress may be due to faulty administration, it may also be caused by other problems for which policy-makers and managements cannot be held accountable, and in these cases the concept has to be used with clear recognition that it refers to the operations of financial predators with interests in causing and exploiting volatility.

Surveillance of economic policy management by governments in developing countries is difficult for international organizations, and surveillance of corporate performance in those countries is even more difficult. Understanding and assessment of the pressures of differing forms of productive and speculative market discipline is thus inevitably quite incomplete at times when it can be considered most necessary because of indicators of impending strain. Speculative market discipline can be especially destructive, despite sound fundamentals, because market manipulation can be intended to have herd effects which open the way for further exploitation of the distress that has been caused. The significance of what may be called productive market discipline greatly diminishes as the distress becomes more serious because of general declines of confidence.[12]

Surveillance of Third World macromanagement has to be combined, more and more, with surveillance of transnational enterprises producing in and moving production between developing countries, as the interacting growth and employment effects of these corporations have consequences for balances of payments, investment inflows and outflows, inflation levels, and monetary as well as fiscal policies, and the health of financial systems. Sound macro-management in a developing country can be severely affected by changes in the fortunes of transnational enterprises because of events in major industrialized states, especially during an economic decline in the USA. Estimates of the health of such multinationals, moreover, may be flawed because of their use of opaque financial instruments for spreading risks, and may be challenged by unanticipated shifts in their production and marketing strategies.[13]

A common theme in economic advice directed at developing countries by international lending agencies and governments in industrialized states is the importance of economic openness, allowing free market forces to drive efficiencies, thus imposing productive market discipline (Tirole, 2002). Yet it is well understood that large corporations, especially transnational enterprises, set up and maintain barriers to entry that shelter their expanding market positions, and that this kind of corporate protectionism can hinder domestically based growth in a country that has accepted strong multinational penetration. Openness to entries by financial enterprises from industrialized states is urged because of the contributions which these can make to the development of financial markets in host countries, but, as entities in large international financial corporations, the incoming enterprises can be very active in the imposition of speculative as well as productive market discipline.[14] The monitoring capacities of the foreign as well as domestic financial enterprises, moreover, that may be significant for their exercises of speculative or productive market discipline, can be inadequate for tracking changes in the operations of multinational producer enterprises that affect growth in host countries and their balances of payments.

Problems of coordination and declining economic sovereignty in developing countries have to be recognized in evaluating the external advice received by their governments, especially any communications intended to help them cope with impending financial crises. While the commercial intelligence at the basis of the foreign advice may be inaccurate, it may reflect ignorance of deficiencies in macromanagement capabilities. Investigations of these, in the interests of the developing countries, have to take into account complex structural problems which are not addressed in the external advice for crisis avoidance and the management of stable growth. When these problems are considered they indicate requirements for structural policy cooperation between advanced and developing countries, with the collaboration of multinational corporations, and with the support of domestic systems of coordination in the industrializing states.[15]

Continuing losses of economic sovereignty are experienced by industrializing countries as transnational producer enterprises and financial corporations extend their Third World operations, with increasing effects on national economic structures and structural interdependencies that can be altered as the multinationals become more active in rivalries and alliances and reorganize their international activities. The promotion of linkages between host-country firms and the transnational enterprises assists diversified interdependent growth, but with vulnerabilities because of the scope for independent structural initiatives by the international corporations, and because industrial policy measures to aid growth by host-country firms can risk outright or indirect opposition from the international corporations. The vulnerabilities increase if there is a financial crisis, and one of its principal effects will be to increase opportunities for multinational acquisitions of host-country firms.[16]

The formation of domestic systems of intercorporate coordination is a structural imperative in industrializing states, to improve prospects for self-reliant progress toward more balanced, more dynamic, and less vulnerable involvement in the world economy, with less exposure to speculative external market discipline. Policies and corporate endeavours to achieve the necessary coordination can provoke opposition from transnational enterprises, and criticism from international lending agencies, and accordingly are likely to require strong political will. If groups of developing countries can form very active subregional or regional systems of economic integration, their efforts to develop intercorporate coordination will be aided by the advantages gained in bargaining with the multinationals. More equal bargaining on trade and investment issues with large industrialized states will then be possible.

The manifest requirements for internal and external coordination, however, are difficult to meet, while the internalization logic driving expansion by transnational producer enterprises tends to become stronger, in response to global market opportunities, and while international financial corporations gain strength through exerting speculative as well as productive market discipline. This is the context in which constructive and preventive macromanagement advice is directed at governments in developing countries, with cautions about attempting to impose capital controls and endeavouring to aid the development of national enterprises. Adjustment assistance is typically offered on conditions obliging freedom for the operation of market forces, without recognition of the kinds of internationalized market failures that affect prospects for asymmetrically interdependent growth. The structurally most significant forms of market failure result from concentration trends and their associated externalities: issues of international competition policy result, but are not taken up, because of deficiencies in the global system of economic institutions. The World Trade Organization has no responsibility in this area of policy, and significant cooperation has developed only between the USA and the European Union, with restraints on each side against working for multilateral collaboration.[17]

Advice and assistance from international lending agencies and Western administrations, being directed at governments, not corporations, and emphasizing the efficiencies of free market forces, diverts attention from structural policy challenges. Fundamental considerations in the advice are that financial development in Third World countries facilitates economic growth by funding domestic producer enterprises, and by attracting external investment into such funding, as well as by drawing foreign direct investment, but it is well understood that outward investment flows are also facilitated. These can be attracted very strongly to an industrialized state experiencing a speculative boom. It is also well understood that developing countries offering higher returns and lower tax treatment than other developing countries tend to draw above-average flows of direct and portfolio investment, but that the patterns are not stable. A country that has achieved significant export-led growth, it must be reiterated, can attract investment that causes its currency to appreciate, thus reducing its exports, and transnational enterprises which it is hosting can switch production processes to less developed countries with lower labour costs. Meanwhile a regional venture in economic integration which has aided export expansion may be disrupted by conflicts of interest and changes of government (Telo, 2001).

The structural policy challenges which demand attention for comprehensive macromanagement in developing countries require solutions through internal and external coordination. The internal coordination has to be directed toward the concerting of entrepreneurship for the multiplication of productive complementarities by national firms, with constructive participation by incoming transnational enterprises. Relational rather than instrumental cooperation between national firms, inviting collaboration by the multinationals which are hosted, can promise orderly interdependent growth, if there is substantial external coordination, for which active cooperation by other developing and advanced states has to be sought. Efforts to meet these imperatives cannot be mandated by international lending agencies, and are not normally encouraged by governments in industrialized countries, but enlightened external advice can increase understanding of the requirements that have to be met for stable balanced growth. The key insight to be conveyed is that disruptions of the real economies in industrializing countries through changes in transnational production and through speculative manipulation by international financial enterprises have to be prevented by building more integrated economic structures, in effect applying internalization logic above the corporate level, for the formation of solidarity-based national intercorporate systems, capable of collective engagement with issues of cooperation with incoming transnational enterprises.

A counter-argument can be that the international community as a whole will benefit if market forces are allowed free play, allowing the most efficient and most substantially funded enterprises to profit, expand and absorb weaker firms, thus causing structural changes, with increasing efficiencies, across national borders. Since international competition policy cooperation sensitive to Third World interests is not to be anticipated, however, governments in developing countries have to act on behalf of their populations and their disadvantaged firms. They will be aided if governments in advanced countries and transnational enterprises based on those countries work for the development of collegial forms of capitalism, open to relational cooperation with Third World governments and firms. For industrialized states, management of their interdependent knowledge-based political economies requires collaborative coordination tasks on a vast scale, and for these a spirit of collegial capitalism is becoming more and more necessary, for general efficiency and equity.[18]

INSTITUTIONAL POLITICAL ECONOMY

Dynamic, diversified and balanced growth requires widely coordinated production specializations. The logic of coordination is well recognized in the internal organization of functions within a producer enterprise, and in the development of alliances and other forms of cooperation between such enterprises. Basic motivational contrasts, however, assume much significance in the coordination processes. Relational coordination, based on unqualified goodwill and trust, is innovative in the service of organizational and alliance objectives, and thus builds solidarity while ensuring effective performance. Instrumental coordination, the activity of exclusively self-interested opportunists, develops with multiple uncertainties, low levels of trust, and limited knowledge-sharing, with efforts to set precise contractual obligations. The larger context is set by struggles for corporate control, in which general uncertainties motivate continuing opportunism.

The contrasting effects in intercorporate systems are indicated with reference to overall balances between cooperation and competition that affect market efficiencies and failures. Associated with these differences a further contrast that has to be recognized is that between orientations toward productive ventures and tendencies to seek speculative gains, in which motivations can be increasingly open to the acceptance of high risks. The speculative tendencies can become strong because of higher and faster prospective rewards, for example through acquisitions and subsequent asset stripping, and because of high-volume funding for anticipated successes from financial enterprises operating with similar opportunism.[19]

Third World governments and enterprises have to reckon with different balances between corporate cooperation and competition, and policy-level cooperation and competition, in the structurally more prominent areas of the world economy, and between the productive and speculative propensities of firms active in those areas, as well as with the involvement of major financial enterprises in proximate parts of the entire pattern. Institutional political-economy concerns thus demand attention. Possibilities for regulatory responses are immediately evident, especially for the protection of internal markets, but there are clear imperatives to find structural policy solutions for the problems of vulnerability in dependent growth.

The coordinating and synergistic potentials of institutions, and therefore of institution-building, thus become very significant for Third World governments and enterprises. Relational intercorporate coordination under dedicated administrative guidance can be seen as the necessary response to the dangers of inferior but necessary involvement in world trade and investment. The asymmetries in organizational capabilities confronting national firms in external commerce clearly have to be reduced through collegial entrepreneurship, supported by concerted innovations, and concerted responses to the tacitly anti-competitive operations of well-positioned transnational enterprises. Meeting these imperatives is difficult for the diverse systems of personal rule operating with various authoritarian methods in many developing countries, but the logic of institutionalized coordination tends to become more persuasive as asymmetries in structural interdependence increase with economic openness: the organizational strengths of transnational enterprises, it must be repeated, have to be balanced, for fully productive linkages, by systems of sustained cooperation between national firms in host countries.

Institutional economics has been developing with tendencies to avoid problems posed by asymmetries in structural interdependence, despite the efficiencies achieved by systems of coordinated entrepreneurship in South Korea and Taiwan, and in Japan until its financial crisis developed during the 1990s. The evolution of national systems of capitalism, with distinctive cultures and institutions influencing degrees of integration or independent corporate activity, has been studied without sufficient regard for the structural significance of transnational corporations in the shaping of cross-border production linkages and challenging the generally weak enterprises of developing countries. Relatively integrated national political economies become less coordinated as their firms become more active in transnational production, and such production, as it extends into developing countries, weakens whatever coordinating institutions they may have, unless there are concerted efforts to strengthen or replace those institutions.[20]

Developing countries are tending to become more dependent in their efforts to industrialise, as the world economy is becoming more oligarchical with the expansion of operations by transnational corporations and the evolution of concentration trends which results from their rivalries. With this dependence, capital flight to higher-growth areas tends to increase, because of the persistence of developmental problems and the attractions of areas where speculation causes asset appreciations. Meanwhile vulnerabilities to recessions in those areas, after asset appreciations, tend to become more serious. In a large part of the world, then, the structural foundations of international finance are at risk, (Tirole, 2002; Dobson and Hufbauer, 2001).

Transnational enterprises are emerging in developing countries – in Southeast Asia with the aid of cross-border links between Chinese business communities. Overall prospects for these transnationals are not favourable, because of the strengths of US, Japanese and European multinationals, and their tendencies to seek collaboration in alliances mainly in order to prepare the way for acquisitions. The industrializing economies in which the emerging multinationals are based provide generally weak support for their expansion, and in most cases the small or moderate size of those economies hinders effective bargaining with industrialized states on issues of market access. International expansion by the Third World transnational enterprises, moreover, is often not matched by structural achievements through industrial coordination in their home economies: these can be disrupted by political stresses and destabilizing speculation in their financial sectors, as has been indicated by the recent history of South Korea.[21]

Imperatives for highly dedicated management of structural policies in developing countries are thus becoming stronger while international oligopolistic trends are becoming more adverse, and the necessary statecraft is becoming more dependent on active cooperation by national firms, in coordinated innovative entrepreneurship. Governments and corporate managements in industrialized states can assist Third World growth by cultivating a spirit of collegial capitalism, based on concepts of social solidarity and obligations. The gross moral failings dramatized by large scale fraud-related bankruptcies in the USA during its post-1990s recession have not encouraged hopes of change, especially because the frauds have exposed the influence of moral relativism in industrialized states. Deepening awareness of issues of international social justice, however, and of links between these and issues of efficiency and stability in the world economy, is becoming possible for future policymakers and managements emerging from Western institutes of higher learning.[22] The macromanagement endeavours of governments in industrialized states are obligating efforts to secure the cooperation of transnational enterprises, for the development of more coordinated market economies. Quests for instrumental cooperation can have some utility, but the interdependencies to be managed really require relational cooperation, with solidarity-based collegiality. Many market failures and government failures have to be overcome: a great transformation is necessary, and it will require magnanimous efforts, with civic virtues active across borders.

NOTES

1. See symposium on financial instability, *Oxford Review of Economic Policy*, **15**(3), Autumn 1999 and symposium on savings. *Oxford Review of Economic Policy*, **17**(1), Spring 2001.
2. See Chapter 9, this volume.
3. See UNCTAD, *World Investment Report 2000* and *World Investment Report 2001*, and Thomas L. Brewer, Paul A. Brenton and Gavin Boyd (eds) (2002), *Globalizing Europe*, Cheltenham, UK and Northampton, USA: Edward Elgar, chapter 7.
4. On the protectionist trade policies see Finger and Nogues (2002).
5. See references to anti-dumping in Thomas L. Brewer and Gavin Boyd (eds) (2002), *Globalizing America*, Cheltenham, UK and Northampton, USA: Edward Elgar, 3, chapters 4 and 12.
6. Geographic factors, transport costs and levels of infrastructure development, as influences on trade, have also been important. See Nuno Limao and Anthony J. Venables (2001), 'Infrastructure, geographic disadvantage, transport costs, and trade', *The World Bank Economic Review*, **15**(3), 451–80.
7. See symposium on the Chinese economics, *The World Economy*, **25**(8), August 2002, and Nicholas R. Lardy (2003), *Integrating China into the Global Economy*, Washington, DC: Brookings Institution.
8. See coverage of trade and investment flows in Jose M. Salazar-Xirinachs and Maryse Robert (eds) (2001), *Toward Free Trade in the Americas*, Washington, DC: Brookings Institution, and reviews of Latin America in *72nd Annual Report*, Bank for International Settlements, Basel, 8 July 2002, pp. 47–48 and in IMF (2002), *World Economic Outlook*, April, pp. 26–30, 61–73.
9. See Salazar-Zirinachs and Robert, *Toward Free Trade in the Americas*, cited in note 8, and Jeffrey J. Schott, *Prospects for Free Trade in the Americas*, Washington: Institute for International Economics.
10. See Alan M. Rugman and Gavin Boyd (eds) (1999), *Deepening Integration in the Pacific Economies*, Cheltenham, UK and Northampton, USA: Edward Elgar, chapter 3.
11. The USA has scope for a 'hub-and-spoke' strategy; see Ronald J. Wonnacott, 'Regional Trade Agreements', chapter 10 in Brewer and Boyd, *Globalizing America*, cited in note 5.
12. Herd behavior is made all the more serious by coordinated speculative attacks – see Botman and Jager (2002).

13. On the use of opaque financial instruments, see comments by David Folkerts-Landau and Peter M. Garber in Charles Enoch and John H. Green (eds) (1997), *Banking Soundness and Monetary Policy*, Washington, DC: International Monetary Fund, chapter 13.
14. The speculative discipline is associated with capacities for reversals of investment flows, which may evidence herd behavior. On the capacities of large international financial enterprises to switch investments see Wendy Dobson and Gary Clyde Hufbauer (2001), *World Capital Markets*, Washington, DC: Institute for International Economics.
15. The basic logic of institutionalized corporate cooperation is demonstrated in Peter A. Hall and David Soskice (eds) (2001) *Varieties of Capitalism*, Oxford, Oxford University Press, chapter 1.
16. On overall trends see UNCTAD, *World Investment Report 2000*, cited in note 3.
17. See P.J. Lloyd and Kerrin M. Vautier (1999), *Promoting Competition in Global Markets*, Cheltenham, UK and Northampton, USA: Edward Elgar.
18. On the logic of intercorporate cooperation see Hall and Soskice, *Varieties of Capitalism*, cited in note 15.
19. See references to the importance of funds available for speculation in *Oxford Review of Economic Policy*, **15**(3), autumn 1999.
20. Developing countries hosting transnational enterprises have relatively weak capacities to influence the evolution of international production systems by those enterprises: see discussions of their interests in promoting linkages with such incoming firms in UNCTAD, *World Investment Report 2001*, cited in note 3.
21. See comments in Arvid John Lukauskas and Francisco L. Rivera-Batiz (eds) (2001), *The Political Economy of the East Asian Crisis and its Aftermath*, Cheltenham, UK and Northampton, USA: Edward Elgar.
22. An important contribution has been the symposium on economic efficiency and social justice in the *Cambridge Journal of Economics*, **24**(6), November 2000.

REFERENCES

Botman, Dennis P.J. and Henk Jager (2002), 'Coordination of speculation', *Journal of International Economics*, **58**(1), October, 159–75.

Cargill, Thomas F. (2001), 'Central banking, financial and regulatory change in Japan', in Magnus Blomstrom, Byron Gangnes and Sumner L. Croix (eds), *Japan's New Economy*, Oxford: Oxford University Press.

Dobson, Wendy and Gary Clyde Hufbauer (2001), *World Capital Markets*, Washington, DC: Institute for International Economics.

Dunning, John H. and Rajneesh Narula (1997), 'Developing countries versus multinationals in a globalizing world: the dangers of falling behind', Department of Economics discussion paper 226, February, University of Reading.

Finger, J. Michael and Julio J. Nogues, 'The unbalanced Uruguay Round outcome: the new areas in future WTO negotiations', *The World Economy*, **25**(3), March, 321–40.

Shiller, Robert J. (2000), *Irrational Exuberance*, Princeton, NJ: Princeton University Press.

Siebert, Horst (ed.), *The World's New Financial Landscape: Challenges for Economic Policy*, Berlin: Springer.

Telò, Mario (ed.) (2001), *European Union and New Regionalism*, Aldershot, UK: Ashgate.

Tirole, Jean (2002), *Financial Crises, Liquidity, and the International Monetary System*, Princeton, NJ: Princeton University Press.

World Investment Report (1999): Foreign Direct Investment and the Challenge of Development, New York and Geneva: United Nations Conference on Trade and Development (1999).

11. International structural cooperation and financial architecture

Gavin Boyd

The international financial system is evolving with virtually priority funding for more competitive manufacturing and non-financial service firms demonstrating high short-term returns; their strong drawing effects enable them to assume greater prominence in concentration trends, and they are increasingly significant challenges for less advantaged enterprises. With the concentration of trends, large-scale structural change is under way, and the USA is at the centre of this process, attracting investment from Europe and other areas experiencing slower growth. Efficiencies are evident in the financing of the more competitive firms and in the direction of capital flows from less developed areas, but there is a perverse destabilizing dynamic: very active large-scale speculation by financial enterprises in the USA tends to bid up the stocks of the more successful manufacturing and non-financial service firms to unsustainable levels, at which losses of investor confidence cause recession that destroys much growth. This has to be regarded as a problem of market failure, and associated with it is a type of market failure that results from diversions of investment into the speculative operations, that is, away from productive use. These diversions occur because of opportunities for high profits, with reduced tax exposure. The funding of growth in real economies tends to be below potential, imbalanced and unstable; managements of productive enterprises, moreover, can be attracted by the potentially high rewards of speculative expansion that can involve risky mergers and acquisitions.

The deficiencies in financial markets have effects in a larger context in which potentials for productive balance between competitive and cooperative corporate activities that shape structural interdependencies tend to be altered by increasingly hard competition, evident especially in the concentration trends. Associated with these very prominent examples of internationalized market failure are corporate failures to seize opportunities for complementary forms of entrepreneurship that can enhance overall growth: coordination functions necessary for dynamic efficiencies are not performed, due to the hard

227

competition. This problem is especially evident in the USA, and is all the more serious because of vulnerabilities to speculation-led destabilization, as well as because of uncertainties that persist because of the intensely competitive business culture. In Europe there is less vulnerability to speculation-led destabilization, as there is much less trading of stocks, and considerable intercorporate cooperation, supported by more active consultative links with policy levels.

The increasing scale and complexity of structural interdependencies between the major industrialized states, and especially between the USA and the European Union, is making comprehensive structural policy cooperation imperative, in the common interest, and is also making fundamental reform more and more necessary in financial markets, that is, for stable and balanced growth in the real economies. To meet these challenges policy-level and corporate responses must be combined, with emphasis on entrepreneurial coordination. For the necessary efforts to build consensus the initiatives that it is hoped will be taken by policy communities and corporate associations will have to stress the public goods requirements that become more demanding when knowledge-based economies become more closely linked, through transnational production, trade and financial flows.

INTERNATIONAL FINANCIAL MARKETS

Financial enterprises compete for returns from speculative and productive investment, under supervision and varying degrees of regulation by national authorities. The two types of investment evolve in changing mixes, mainly in the course of portfolio switching, which in effect pressures producer enterprises to demonstrate rising returns. The leading international financial firms are American, and are increasing their global market strengths, especially in Europe, where they are advantaged by superior resources and by the interests of European investors in the USA as a higher-growth economy.

A large Atlantic financial market is evolving, as a central pattern in the world economy, but without substantial collaborative bonds between managements of US and European financial enterprises that could generate spontaneous collective regulation, and consultative links between governments on each side are not sufficiently active for effective policy-level surveillance and controls. National administrations compete to provide liberal business environments, and official attitudes can reflect optimism that market discipline will punish imprudent borrowing and lending.[1] Intensifying competition, in the Atlantic context and globally, tends to result in increasing quests for gains through speculation – often with high risks – a trend associated with ongoing concentration in financial sectors. The attractions are potentially high profitability with much tax avoidance, and with risk-shifting through the use of very sophisticated financial instruments outside regulatory surveillance.[2] In prospect, then, is a weakening of the moderate degree of overall market discipline, yet this is not likely to alter policy-level reluctance to institute stronger regulatory functions. In the USA the liberal business culture remains very influential;[3] in Europe policymakers are more willing to recognize regulatory imperatives, but member governments, unwilling to lose their own regulatory powers, tend to prevent the development of a Union-level pattern of regulation.[4]

Over the past decade conferences sponsored by international organizations, including the International Monetary Fund and the Organization for Economic Cooperation and Development, have failed to build consensus for comprehensive regulation of world financial markets, despite destabilizing events that have revealed serious deficiencies in surveillance and control.[5] These events have included the failure of very high-risk speculative operations by Long Term Capital Management and the bankruptcy of Enron, the large US energy firm. Before these extremely disruptive failures the destabilizing potential of very risky unsupervised speculation, especially with the high-volume use of derivatives, was known to be making financial institutions and systems extremely vulnerable.[6]

Concentration trends in financial markets have been making issues of stability more serious, but international competition policy cooperation, which in the Atlantic context has focused on major changes of market strengths in manufacturing and non-financial service sectors, has rather avoided engagement with the effects of increases in the international market strengths of major financial enterprises. A problem resulting from the expansion of these firms is that, while their speculative operations evidently tend to increase relative to their productive funding, their risk-taking can be encouraged by expectations of bailouts, in the event of distress, because of the scale of likely adverse effects.[7]

Problems relating to the stability of individual financial enterprises are linked with problems of overall stability in the boom and decline cycles associated with speculative stock appreciations. In a decline, the dangers of failure by a major financial enterprise become greater, depending on the scale of its high-risk speculation. With a decline, moreover, it must be stressed, speculative propensities remain active, as the US experience has indicated, thus in effect limiting productive investment for recovery. In the USA this negative consequence is offset to degrees by investment inflows from low-growth areas, depending on the operative strategies, but the expanding market activities of major financial enterprises result in increasing capacities to guide and influence the direction of incoming capital. Monetary loosening, meanwhile, can provide less stimulus than intended, because of incentives for investors to borrow at low cost for speculative rather than productive ventures.[8]

Altogether, the independent activities of financial enterprises, advancing their own perceived interests in world markets, and especially in the Atlantic setting, are presenting very difficult challenges for macromanagement in the USA and Europe. Orderly interdependent growth in the real economies that are becoming more knowledge-based, and more in need of pervasive entrepreneurial cooperation, is not being sufficiently promoted, guided and supported through collective endeavours. Productive functions are being subjected to the pressures of portfolio switching for the bidding up of stock prices, in sequences of destabilizing business cycles; productive funding, with virtual priority for large firms demonstrating high short-term profitability, is suboptimal because of drifts of investment into the speculation by major financial enterprises. Strains are thus imposed on structural policies, which have to cope at the same time with the degrees of deindustrialization associated with the development of transnational production systems.[9] Producer enterprises, meanwhile, while coping with longer-term funding problems, and responding to transnational production opportunities, have to reckon with coordination problems that tend to be all the more serious because of the divisive and trust-lowering effects of the opportunism in financial sectors.[10]

STRUCTURAL INTERDEPENDENCIES AND INTERNATIONAL FINANCE

Structural interdependencies in the world economy, and especially in Atlantic relations, are evolving mainly through the development of international production systems, principally by US manufacturing and non-financial enterprises that are leaders in global concentration trends. As the market linking through these production systems and through smaller-volume arm's-length trade continues, the dominant firms have much scope to discriminate between markets and to choose between production locations, while dispersing production functions. In the emerging transregional Atlantic economy the structural interdependencies exhibit marked asymmetries, due to the superior competitive strengths of US firms, generally advantaged by higher-level funding from financial sectors.[11]

At the centre of asymmetries in Atlantic structural interdependence are the effects of a gap between domestic demand and output in the USA. This is related to the US corporate emphasis on serving foreign markets through international production, and to the demand-side effects of capital inflows. The international production preference of US firms is attributable to the higher profitability and lower tax exposure of foreign operations, and to continuing increases in the opportunities for such operations, due to the weaker competitiveness of European firms and to the prolonged financial crisis in Japan.

The US international production, which also reflects the export-inhibiting effects of degrees of currency appreciation caused in part by capital inflows, is shaping major trends in structural interdependence while very large American trade deficits continue to rise above sustainable levels. Capital inflows offset the current account deficits, and have been doing so even while the US economy has been in a post-boom decline, but may well decrease if there is a further decline. The danger of such a decline, and of adverse shifts in exchange rates, are factors likely to influence the operations of US and other financial enterprises as they seek to exploit volatility in stock prices and foreign exchange markets.[12]

The large trade deficits indicate requirements for structural balance, that is, for the US economy and for the world economy, especially its Atlantic component. The liberal US political tradition tends to exclude governmental consideration of structural policy issues, but this can be forced by domestic pressures for trade policy activism, notably from the steel industry, or by broad sectoral concerns about losses of competitiveness in high-technological areas. The dynamics of trade policy processes tend to limit the focus and duration of any structural measures, and corporate demands for trade policy activism do not alter the liberal orientation of US economic policy, or affect long-standing corporate distrust of, and opposition to, governmental involvement in the economy, but problems of balance in the USA's structural interdependencies are becoming more challenging. Policy-level and corporate responses may not occur until there is a crisis, and this is a danger that deserves emphasis in domestic and foreign advice to US decision-makers.

Because of its size, resources and industrial development, the US economy has great potential for domestically based growth, but intense competition, under financial sector pressures for high returns, is obliging national firms to venture more into international production, for the home and foreign markets. Neglect of the external opportunities risks declines, that is as concentration trends continue: firms with smaller international production systems become vulnerable to the merger and acquisition strategies of larger multinationals.[13] A general effect is that the USA's structural interdependencies expand with degrees of deindustrialization at home, and in a somewhat fragmented pattern because of the independent strategic choices of competing firms, but with changes in that pattern as concentration trends continue. With these concentration trends the more successful firms are able to bargain more effectively with foreign governments and the home administration over issues of taxation, trade and location. Meanwhile problems of balance in the European Union's structural interdependencies tend to assume larger dimensions, yet the development of a common Union structural policy remains difficult, and may well become even more difficult as the Union enlarges.[14]

The asymmetries in Atlantic structural linkages are extending into other areas of the global economy, while associated market failures are assuming larger international dimensions, especially because of the oligarchical configuration that is resulting from concentration trends. The international public goods issue that is becoming more visible is a failure to promote the development of dynamic balanced structural interdependencies. Market opportunities are not motivating patterns of entrepreneurship along complementary lines that would introduce more balance and greater efficiencies into those interdependencies, and this is an especially serious deficiency in the Atlantic pattern. Recognizing this problem requires some rethinking about problems of market failure: systemic development of a market, as it becomes more international, requires entrepreneurial coordination for the full development of productive potentials. That requires pervasive cooperation, widening areas of complementary innovations, with collegial competition, restrained in the common interest, that is, in recognition of possibilities for enhancement of the production capabilities of firms that are less dynamic but that may be energized through collaboration and through initiatives responding to new technologies. Intense competition that can force such firms into declines tends to lead to forms of market dominance that are exploited to maximize returns, and this problem becomes more serious as concentration trends continue.[15]

Dynamic efficiencies are negatively affected by hard competition, and more so as this activates concentration trends, and these trends adversely affect allocative efficiencies. Hard competition, it must be stressed, restricts interactive exploration of opportunities for innovative complementary commercial applications of new technologies, and thus can be seen to have increasing costs as widening advances are made in frontier research. It can be argued that competitive pressures tend to drive highly innovative uses of new technologies by firms acting alone, but this will depend on the learning capacities of managements endeavouring to be highly self-reliant, on the basis of assessments of advanced research that are necessarily provisional, and that must be sensitive to uncertainties which rival managements might be able to resolve.

The functional logic of entrepreneurial collaboration in the development of complementarities, thus enhancing dynamic efficiencies, becomes more significant if the scope for productive technocratic involvement is recognized. Technocratic participation in corporate consultations on potential complementarities can expand and deepen the range of discussions, while motivating stronger shared concerns with the common interest. Such concerns can be focused more and more on requirements to promote the development of dynamic balanced structural interdependencies. If these requirements can be met, greater allocative efficiencies will tend to result.

For Atlantic relations the challenges to work for more dynamic efficiencies in structural interdependence are clearly of vital importance, and the degrees of balance that may be achieved demand earnest consideration especially in

Europe, because of the prospect of increasing disparities in gains from Atlantic commerce, but also because of the potentially destabilizing effects of the USA's large trade deficits.[16] Advice to policymakers and corporate managements for the promotion of dynamic efficiencies in Atlantic structural interdependencies is needed, and clearly its theoretical basis will have to be an enlargement of insights drawn from institutional economics, relating to the internationalization of market failures and policy failures. New institutions for comprehensive coordination tasks have to facilitate the development of entrepreneurial complementarities, and greater harmony in the management of US and European-policy mixes.

The rationale for promoting dynamic efficiencies through institutional development has to affirm urgent imperatives for structural balance in Atlantic relations, which it is hoped will be sustained through the coordinating functions of networks of corporate associations, activating complementary strategies and contributing to cooperation between policy levels. With the thrust toward greater collaboration in the development of increasingly interdependent real economies, moreover, more functional service of those economies by financial sectors will have to be made possible. The cumulative effects of distinctive failures in financial markets will have to be stressed to give motivational force to the rationale for structural cooperation: stable relational funding of industry will be necessary for that cooperation.

MACROMANAGEMENT CAPABILITIES

For structural cooperation across the Atlantic, and its expansion in the world economy, adaptation and development in US and European macromanagement capabilities will be necessary, in line with requirements for advanced interdependent political development. Macromanagement tasks responding to domestic demands can distract attention from cooperation required by external structural linkages, and the domestic pressures can hinder effective decisionmaking. Macromanagement capacities, meanwhile, can be weakened as firms extend their international operations, linking and altering structures and markets.

Macromanagement capabilities in the USA have vital significance in the evolution of Atlantic structural interdependencies. Overall, the liberal economic policy orientation and the tax treatment of foreign production operations add to the incentives for US firms to produce abroad in lower-cost areas and compete more directly with generally weaker host-country enterprises.[17] Meanwhile the toleration of very active speculation in financial markets draws inward investment that contributes to currency appreciation, hindering export expansion. Aggressive individualism in the business culture generates hard competition, to which shareholder pressures contribute. Accordingly coordination problems result, with failures in the use of productive capabilities, and these persist because of the lack of a structural policy capability that could promote entrepreneurial cooperation. Degrees of deindustrialization are associated with this problem, that is, together with considerable insecurity for workers, and downward pressures on wages.

The hard competition for market shares is reflected in hard political competition, with much trading of political favours in legislative processes that impart an expansionary bias in fiscal policy, while causing much corporate opposition to government involvement in the economy. A major source of pressure for fiscal expansion comes from the Democratic Party, as a distributional coalition drawing support especially from workers adversely affected or threatened by the expansion of production at foreign locations, and by corporate restructuring after mergers and acquisitions. Reduced tax exposure thus tends to become a more important factor in the incentives for firms to expand international production.[18] Included in these incentives, moreover, are considerations relating to stability in the national economy, in view of the dangers of unsustainable stock appreciations and of a crisis brought on by the large trade deficits.

The increases in structural interdependence which challenge the USA to develop more effective macromanagement capabilities – for more balanced and more soundly based dynamism in domestic and external linkages – are not evoking significant policy-level or corporate responses. Any efforts to promote a broad policy consensus are discouraged by the hard political competition.[19] The logic of working for wide-ranging public-spirited cooperation, however, may inspire new forms of political entrepreneurship. These could develop in conjunction with, and be challenged by, European initiatives.

Macromanagement capabilities in the European Union constitute a pattern of weak federalism, in which member governments endeavour in various ways to enhance the structural competitiveness of their own economies as regional market integration continues, with the evolution of complex Union structural interdependencies. Germany is the central economy in this process, but its coordinated entrepreneurial system is not providing leadership for the development of a Union structural policy, and the collective decision problems that would have to be overcome for such a policy will be increased as the Union admits new members. The German coordinated system is expanding through investment in other member countries, but with continued preferences for serving their markets through exports.

The macromanagement problem for the Union is the persistence of slow growth with high unemployment and large capital flows to the USA – in conjunction with expansion of a strong US corporate presence that tends to push European firms into declines. Regionally based growth could be increased if the capital outflows were reduced, but they are encouraged by perceptions of superior prospects in the US economy. There is gradually increasing vulnerability to downturns in the USA, but the development of Union financial sectors, while assisting productive investment in Europe, is also facilitating increases in the outflows to the USA.

Structural interdependencies with the USA are thus being changed, with imbalances that are having cumulative effects. These consequences are not evoking a regional consensus for more effective macromanagement, and the need for such a consensus is being partly obscured by official affirmations that growth has to be achieved through more active competition that will lead to the emergence of larger and more efficient Union firms. Intra-Union mergers and acquisitions encourage such confidence, but the development of links with US enterprises has strong attractions, and the investment outflows to the USA remain very substantial.

The European vulnerability in interdependence with the USA is an especially difficult problem because of the gravity of the risks and an incapacity to press for strong restraint on the speculation in the US financial sector and for drastic reductions of the US trade deficits. Concentration trends in the US financial sectors are increasing the danger of excessive risk-taking by the more powerful firms that are emerging: they are competing more intensely against national and foreign rivals, and their sizes tend to encourage expectations of bailouts if necessary; further, their risk-taking may well be insufficiently sensitive to overall problems of stability in the US economy. The entire sector, moreover, because of information problems and investor irrationality, may become fragile because of herd behaviour triggered by speculative attacks on the dollar related to the large current account deficits, the high levels of personal and national debt, or to contractions of lending by overextended financial enterprises.[20]

FINANCIAL COOPERATION FOR PRODUCTIVE FUNDING

Much literature on financial cooperation focuses on the responsibilities of central banks and regulatory authorities to prevent and cope with crises. These are seen to result from speculative credit expansion which contributes to asset appreciation, with risks that tend to escape notice but which lead to losses of investor optimism, with delayed awareness of system-wide risks. For crisis prevention there are prescriptions to restrain credit expansion during booms, in view of dangers that asset prices will rise faster than increases in output. Affirmation of this requirement typically reflects awareness that considerable investment is flowing into speculative rather than productive financing, but that is seen simply as a threat to stability, to be moderated through monetary restraint and prudential regulation.

The public goods imperative that demands recognition is that financial systems must be oriented toward funding producer enterprises, for growth in real economies, rather than toward speculation that can severely disrupt those economies. This imperative has to be affirmed as a basis for policy because the drift of investment into speculation tends to increase, relative to productive funding, because of prospects of higher returns, with reduced taxes, in the trading of financial assets, and because failures to coordinate production and distribution activities, especially in industrialized states, provide opportunities for lending to firms advantaged or disadvantaged in intense rivalries for market shares.

The experience of coordinated market economies suggests that the necessary reorientation of financial enterprises toward productive funding has to result from the socializing and disciplining influence of comprehensive business associations and networks, operating in collaboration with national administrations.[21] The principal model to consider is Germany, and the challenge for political entrepreneurship is to draw lessons from this for the reform of international financial markets. One lesson is that stakeholder systems of corporate governance can contribute to the development of business community solidarity. Another lesson is that relational bank financing and monitoring helps to ensure stability for long-range corporate planning. Further, the German system has demonstrated that cross holdings can help to sustain business community solidarity.

Critics have argued that the German stability and order comes at the price of slow growth and facilitates only incremental rather than radical innovations. Technological progress and overall growth do tend to be below potential because of pressures from organized labour exerted through co-determination arrangements, but these features of the system of stakeholder corporate governance can be made more functional through managerial and union initiatives. The stability of the system, moreover, has to be evaluated in comparisons with the sequences of booms and declines that tend to result from speculation in a liberal market economy, and the efficiencies and social justice aspects of the booms and declines have to be assessed not only with reference to the costs, in terms of human capital, but also with reference to the probability that strong speculative propensities will lead, through risk concealment, to fraudulent practices.

The key consideration, in discussions of efficiencies in financial markets, is the availability of credit for speculation.[22] With the internationalization of those markets much credit is provided from external sources, and as concentration trends continue, the leading financial enterprises have wide scope for use of this credit. International regulatory discipline lags, because of information problems resulting from the use of sophisticated financial instruments, and because of competition between governments to enhance the attractions of their financial centres. International market discipline, meanwhile, tends to diminish with the concentration trends, because of the opportunities for oligarchical collusion in the spreading of risks.

The international speculation disrupts and endangers growth in real economies, and is thus a challenge for strong policy-level resolve to promote reform, in response to the prospect of increasing systemic risk, and to the problem that this risk tends to be less recognized during booms, when it is most serious. Monetary tightening, as noted, can dampen the speculation, but monetary sovereignty is declining, and political will for international monetary cooperation is lacking. Monetary authorities, however, have to provide leadership for international financial market reform, to promote stable growth with low inflation. Here the basic requirement to be recognized is the need to give impetus to the development of increasingly innovative forms of complementary entrepreneurship – an imperative that tends to be obscured by fixation on unemployment as a necessary restraint on inflation,[23] rather than as a problem of market failure, a fixation that has become all the more unrealistic with the increased linking of markets through transnational production and trade.

Innovative forms of complementary entrepreneurship are needed for the development of dynamic balanced structural interdependencies: efforts to reform financial markets must have this perspective. The growth effects of a reorientation of financial markets toward productive funding will be greater if impetus is given to complementary entrepreneurial endeavours, and these will be conducive to the evolution of dynamic efficiencies in the linking of markets across borders. The collaborative spirit thus given expression, moreover, will tend to introduce balance into the expanding interdependencies.

The reciprocal causality that has to be activated must be operative with extensive international corporate cooperation. Collaboration between governments cannot be sufficient for the management of structural interdependencies. This tends to be overlooked in literature on international economic cooperation. The collaboration of producer enterprises, in public-spirited coordinated entrepreneurship, will be essential for the resolution of internationalized market failures in the development of dynamic structural interdependencies; and the collaboration of financial enterprises in the service of this interdependent growth will have to be secured mainly through concerted efforts by the producer enterprises, with policy-level support. Governments, concerned with the common good, clearly have to assume educational and motivational functions for the promotion of solidarity and entrepreneurial complementarities between producer enterprises.

A strand of international relations theory asserts that there must be a dominant provider of benefits for the success of collaborative ventures between governments at the regional or global level: the prospect of gains dependent on agreement between an assortment of parties without a hegemon is considered to be unfavourable.[24] This, however, assumes that integrative cooperation between unequal states under highly motivated leadership is not possible. What has to be considered for the development of financial market reform and extensive complementary entrepreneurship is the diffusion of economic power among transnational enterprises, which challenges governments to be more responsive to international public goods imperatives through advisory interactions with international managements.[25] The benefits of economic cooperation between governments depend more on the generally independent decisions of transnational enterprises to build international production systems than on bargained outcomes of trade negotiations that facilitate arm's-length commerce.

In the Atlantic context, where the potential for structural cooperation through complementary entrepreneurship is most significant, US trade policy activism has been the main source of pressure for economic openness, but the benefits for the US economy, once thought of as trade surpluses resulting from the competitiveness of US firms, now have to be assessed with reference to the results of foreign production by such enterprises for Europe, which greatly exceeds US exports, and also with reference to America's large trade deficits.

For the Europeans, proposals to work toward more balanced Atlantic structural interdependencies through sponsorship of entrepreneurial complementarities certainly can be interpreted as designs for superior US corporate benefits, attainable because of greater competitiveness. Because of the weaknesses of European enterprises, however, there is sound logic behind the proposal for consultations aimed at the development of those complementarities. In interactions on the reform of financial markets, moreover, European policymakers and management élites would be advantaged by the unifying effects of common concerns about vulnerability to financial instability in the USA; further, this could assist understanding that collaboration between European producer enterprises, with policy-level encouragement, could make for relatively equal interactions with US enterprises in discussions of opportunities for complementary entrepreneurship.

Financial cooperation within Europe, for productive funding in the Union, it must be stressed, is an urgent imperative demanding clear recognition, based on understanding of the importance of maintaining stakeholder systems of corporate governance and limiting speculative trade in financial assets.[26] Here a vital public good is a matter of investor protection, in the context of uncertainties dramatized by the Enron failure in the USA. Another vital public good is a matter of systemic stability and development: this can be imperilled by manipulative appreciation of stocks to unsustainable levels.

SUSTAINING STRUCTURAL AND FINANCIAL COOPERATION

Systems of government and corporate cooperation for governance of structural interdependencies through entrepreneurial complementarities will have to be planned for self-sustaining growth. An endeavour proposed for the Atlantic can be dedicated to the formation of a supraregional coordinated market economy, with potentials for spontaneously organized complementary corporate specializations, aided by technocratic advising. An international management culture of collegial capitalism could well be promoted, especially in business schools. Policy communities and corporate associations could seek to institutionalize arrangements for consultative explorations of opportunities for matching and mutually reinforcing forms of innovative entrepreneurship.

The European Union's decisional problems and structural weaknesses discourage promotional initiatives, but the European Central Bank is well placed to sponsor an authoritative study that would present a comprehensive rationale for such initiatives. Preparation of this study could be aided by the European Round Table, comprising Union industrial leaders, and by the European Commission, for which this would be a challenge for higher achievement. There would be a need for strong leadership, of the kind that might be provided by another Jacques Delors.

The European Central Bank's initiative could invite positive responses from the US Federal Reserve. Its research capabilities and consultative links with national industry and finance could enable it to collaborate for further development of a design for Atlantic entrepreneurial partnering. Acceptance of this role would be possible in part because of the problems which Atlantic trade frictions pose for monetary policy concerns with growth, stability, exchange rates and broad measures of inflation, including shifts in asset prices. The proposed entrepreneurial collaboration would promise greater stability in the USA and in Europe, with increased security against risk-taking by financial enterprises, through stronger market discipline. The dangers of such risk-taking have been recognized in Federal Reserve statements opposing increases in Federal Deposit Insurance levels on the ground that this would encourage banks to take on more risk.

Heavy corporate reliance on shareholder financing and very high-volume trading in stocks are sources of systemic risk in the USA which could be moderated by the degrees of stability which could result from a substantial pattern of Atlantic entrepreneurial collaboration. This could be made explicit in the stance of the Federal Reserve, with emphasis on the prospect that the order introduced into the USA's structural interdependencies would provide increased market discipline on the trading in stocks, while contributing to shifts to stakeholder corporate governance. Federal Reserve affirmations in this context could be made with reference to the tightening of functional linkages between monetary, structural and trade policies in interdependent knowledge-based economies, and to the vital importance of coordinated corporate production activities in interactive alignment with the linked policy processes.

The danger of increased exchange rate volatility could be emphasized in the US Federal Reserve's endorsement of the concept of Atlantic entrepreneurial cooperation. The increasingly dominant financial sector firms emerging in concentration trends acquire wider scope for speculation in foreign exchange markets and can be inclined to greater risk-taking because of the investment which they draw and the wide dispersal of their holdings. The central issue in their calculations, which is the stability of the dollar in relation to the euro, as affected by increases in the current account deficit, capital flows to the USA, and changes in the US political business cycle, can demand difficult Federal Reserve decisions in quick succession, with alertness to possibilities for speculative attacks on the dollar that could precipitate herd behaviour.[27] Uncertainties about Japanese and European use of dollar reserves are factors in this context. The magnitude of the dangers associated with the current account deficit would deserve great stress in the affirmation of policy linkages tied with the promotion of entrepreneurial complementarities.

One consequence of the expansion of the Federal Reserve's role would be an increase in status as an independent source of guidance for macromanagement. This would help to correct the dysfunctional consequences of political trading in economic policy: a difficult problem of advanced political development could become less serious because of the comprehensive impartial assessments of policy options and processes. This enhanced role, moreover, would develop in productive interaction with the matching role assumed by the European Central Bank – a role which, as noted, would be a beneficial challenge for the European Commission.

What can be projected from current trends, to strengthen the logic of promoting Atlantic entrepreneurial cooperation, is increased strain in competition and trade policy interactions between the USA and the European Union. Continuing global concentration trends and the strengthening of the US corporate presence in Europe are to be expected, while the USA's current account deficit will motivate stronger trade policy activism. The uncertainties to be anticipated in product markets, stock prices and exchange rates will tend to attract further investment into speculative operations that will contribute to greater volatility.

ECONOMIC ADVICE AND POLITICAL WILL

Large flows of economic advice to governments, from US and European research institutes, identify potential benefits attainable through macroeconomic policy cooperation and openness to trade and investment. Free market forces are expected to generate increasing efficiencies, while rationales for collaborative or competitive structural policies are largely ignored. International financial markets are seen to be serving productive activities in real economies with performance-based discrimination, thus forcing continual improvements. Stability problems in financial markets are viewed with guarded optimism about the combined benefits from prudential regulation and competitive pressures for achievement.

Much of the economic advice is relativized by pressures of information overload and by calculations of comparative political advantage in the trading of political favours. Little constructive motivational resolve is communicated, except on the importance of allowing free market forces to operate, but disparities in gains from trade and investment cause willingness to resort to interventionist measures. Direct and indirect aids to industry tend to be considered justified because of tacit qualifications attached to affirmations about market efficiencies, and because of implicit concerns about enhancing structural competitiveness.

What has now become imperative, in the flows of economic advice, is emphasis on the problems of imbalance in structural interdependence, and on imperatives to overcome these by promoting more collegial capitalism, with technocratic cooperation, while inducing stronger orientations toward productive funding in financial markets. Warnings are necessary about detached surveillance that entails virtual toleration of disruptive stresses in structural interdependence, especially because these strains invite speculative manipulation. The status of monetary authorities, moreover, as institutions with the broadest macromanagement functions, and with highly specialized expertise resistant to political pressures, must also be emphasized, to open the way for leadership to guide structural policy initiatives.

Clearly the required advice must be highly constructive, responding to fundamental change that has raised levels of structural interdependence, unevenly, without adequate cross-border linkages of the national cultures and institutions studied in institutional economics. There is an internationalized public goods issue related to an international agency problem. Citizens in the advanced market economies have to entrust to national authorities responsibilities for interdependent macromanagement tasks that can be assessed only by institutions with exceptional expertise and dedication and that require entrepreneurial cooperation on a vast scale. The policy achievements and failures and the market efficiencies and failures affect large populations, with increasing dangers because coordination deficiencies in the real economies are open to exploitation by speculative operations in financial markets, and these may well draw increased investment away from productive use.

The generation of élite political will, for highly dedicated comprehensive macromanagement, must be recognized as a vital task for corporate associations, policy networks and institutes of advanced study. Degrees of validity in public choice studies of the economic motivations of policymakers must serve as warnings, but not sources of discouragement: the public choice perspective is a mean-spirited refusal to recognize idealism, and its influence, in conjunction with theorizing about the pervasive effects of quests for economic advantage, can result in policymaking guided only by the motivational strengths of incentives. The vital importance of public-spirited endeavours can thus be overlooked.[28]

The institutional innovation that has become necessary for interdependent macromanagement, however, does not have to serve regulatory or allocative functions. These remain necessary, and can be performed by established organizations. The new function that has to be served is consultative, for concerting entrepreneurship through interactive learning. This is a public goods requirement, to be supported by the development of internationally linked comprehensive corporate associations. The main area of endeavour must be the Atlantic, because of the scale of structural interdependencies between the USA and Europe: the objective must be a coordinated supraregional market economy, with financial sectors reformed for their proper functions, and with pervasive relational cooperation based on fundamental values rather than particularistic attachments and loyalties. This could become a model for collaborative macromanagement in the rest of the world economy.

Monetary cooperation between the US Federal Reserve and the European Central Bank, it is well recognized, has become essential for exchange rate stability, which will help to smooth the evolution of Atlantic structural interdependencies, although without altering their imbalances. The capacities of the two central banks to influence exchange rates however are weakening, because of the vast dimensions of independent speculative flows in financial markets. Moreover, the significance of exchange rates in multinational financing of production and intrafirm as well as intra-alliance commerce is diminishing as internal financing capacities increase with concentration trends, which continue in producer sectors and are aided by such trends in financial sectors. The evolution of structural linkages between real economies becomes more dependent on the competitive and cooperative production and marketing activities of transnational enterprises than on exchange rate shifts that may occur with or without monetary interventions. The structural linkages and related growth processes, however, are vulnerable to the effects of speculation in financial markets – causing and exploiting volatility while drawing investment away from productive use. The public goods imperatives which thus must be affirmed emphatically are the promotion of entrepreneurial complementarities on a large scale between producer enterprises, and their assertion of collective influence on the operations of financial firms, for greater service of growth in the real economies. Central bank initiatives could begin to respond to these imperatives. This has to be said with a sense of urgency because of the danger of a financial crisis in the USA.

NOTE

1. For observations on discussions of regulatory issues see Bank for International Settlements, *71st Annual Report*, Basel, 11 June 2001.
2. See Garry J. Schinasi, R. Sean Craig, Burkhard Drees and Charles Kramer (2000), *Modern Banking and OTC Derivatives Markets*, Washington, DC: International Monetary Fund; Wendy Dobson and Gary Clyde Hufbauer (2001), *World Capital Markets*, Washington, DC: Institute for International Economics; and *Financial Market Trends*, **75**, Paris, Organisation for Economic Co-operation and Development, March 2000.
3. On the volume of speculative trading in financial assets, see comments by Peter Martin, 'Trading on dangerous ground', *Financial Times*, 12 February 2002.
4. Hans Eichel, German Finance Minister, citing the dangers posed by hedge funds, indicated that his administration was seeking to improve German financial market regulation – *Financial Times*, 7 February 2002. Cases of fraud in the hedge fund industry were reviewed by Robert Clow in the same issue.
5. See comments on outstanding regulatory issues in Bank for International Settlements, *71st Annual Report*, cited in note 1.
6. See comments by David Folkerts-Landau and Peter M. Garber in Charles Enoch and John H. Green (eds) (1997) *Banking Soundness and Monetary Policy*, Washington, DC: International Monetary Fund, chapter 13.
7. The Federal Reserve intervened after the failure of the US hedge fund Long Term Capital Management, which threatened to have severe effects on the financial sector.
8. Hedge funds continued to attract high-volume investment during the US recession. Flows of investment into these funds were reported in numerous issues of the *Financial Times* during the first two quarters of 2002.
9. On the development of these systems see UNCTAD (1993), *World Investment Report*, New York: United Nations Conference on Trade and Development.
10. See discussions of financial markets in *Oxford Review of Economic Policy*, **17**(4), Winter 2001, symposium on finance, law and economic growth.
11. See references to slow growth in Europe in Thomas Brewer, Paul A. Brenton and Gavin Boyd (eds) (2002), *Globalizing Europe*, Cheltenham, UK and Northampton, USA: Edward Elgar.
12. On the dangers for the US economy see John Plender's report on an assessment by Henry Kaufman, citing high levels of corporate debt, *Financial Times*, 17 April 2002, and David Hale, 'A fragile recovery', *Financial Times*, 26 April 2002.
13. The larger multinationals are better placed to secure financing for expansion. On the trend in corporate expansion see UNCTAD (2002), *World Investment Report*, New York: United Nations Conference on Trade and Development, chapter 1.
14. See references to decisional problems in Brewer et al., *Globalizing Europe*, cited in note 11.
15. On the dynamics of corporate decisionmaking see Mary O'Sullivan (2000), 'Corporate governance and globalization', *Annals of the American Academy of Political and Social Science*, July, 153–72, and 'The innovative enterprise and corporate governance', *Cambridge Journal of Economics*, **24**(4), July, 393–416.
16. See Hale 'A fragile recovery', cited in note 12.
17. See James R. Hines (2000), 'International taxation', *National Bureau of Economic Research Reporter*, Spring, 10–14.
18. On the significance of reduced tax exposure, see also Dani Rodrik (1997), *Has Globalization Gone Too Far?* Washington, DC: Institute for International Economics.
19. A major consequence is continued failure to adopt measures for reduction of the large trade deficits, despite warnings by numerous commentators, including Hale, 'A fragile recovery'

The structural foundations of international finance

cited in note 12. See references to US trade policy in John H. Dunning and Gavin Boyd (eds) (2003), *Alliance Capitalism and Corporate Management*, Cheltenham, UK, and Northampton, USA: Edward Elgar.

20. See Hale and Kaufman, cited in note 12; and on problems in recognizing systemic risk see Andrew Crockett (2001), 'Monetary Policy and Financial Stability', speech at Financial Stability Forum, Hong Kong, 13 February.

21. See observations on coordinated market economies in Peter A. Hall and David Soskice (eds) (2001), *Varieties of Capitalism*, Oxford: Oxford University Press, chapter 1.

22. See symposium on financial instability, *Oxford Review of Economic Policy*, **15**(3), 1999.

23. On this fixation see Frank Wilkinson (2000), 'Inflation and employment: is there a third way?', *Cambridge Journal of Economics*, **24**(6), November, 643–70.

24. See Michele Fratianni and John Pattison (2001), 'International organizations in a world of regional trade agreements: lessons from club theory', *The World Economy*, **24**(3), March, 333–58.

25. For a general discussion of governmental capacities for productive interaction with private actors in the provision of public goods, see Christoph Knill and Dirk Lehmkuhl (2002), 'Private actors and the state: internationalization and changing patterns of governance', *Governance: an International Journal of Policy, Administration, and Institutions*, **15**(1), January, 41–63. In the US context see also references to requirements for technocratic relationships with the venture capital industry in Josh Lerner (2002), 'When bureaucrats meet entrepreneurs: the design of effective "public venture capital" programmes', *The Economic Journal*, **112**, February, 73–84.

26. See references to European systems in Stephen S. Cohen and Gavin Boyd (eds) (2002), *Corporate Governance and Globalization*, Cheltenham, UK and Northampton, USA: Edward Elgar.

27. On the role of the euro, see discussions in Pier Carlo Padoan (ed.) (2001) *Monetary Union, Employment, and Growth*, Cheltenham, UK and Northampton, USA: Edward Elgar.

28. See Jenny Stewart (1993), 'Rational choice theory, public policy, and the liberal state', *Policy Sciences*, **26**(4), 317–30.

Index